MR. BIG

A Sexy Rom-Com

SHOT

MR. BIG

A Sexy Rom-Com

SHOT

USA *TODAY* BESTSELLING AUTHOR

R.S. GREY

Entangled Publishing, LLC
644 Shrewsbury Commons Ave., STE 181
Shrewsbury, PA 17361
rights@entangledpublishing.com

Amara is an imprint of Entangled Publishing, LLC.

Visit our website at www.entangledpublishing.com.

Edited by C. Marie
Cover design by Elizabeth Turner Stokes
Cover images by autsawin uttisin/Shutterstock,
Zenzeta/Shutterstock, Honyojima/Shutterstock
Edge design by Elizabeth Turner Stokes
Interior design by Britt Marczak

ISBN 978-1-64937-841-5

Manufactured in the United States of America

First Edition July 2025

10 9 8 7 6 5 4 3 2 1

AMARA
an imprint of Entangled Publishing LLC

ALSO BY R.S. GREY

Arrogant Devil
Not So Nice Guy
Anything You Can Do
Three Strikes and You're Mine
His Royal Highness

Chapter One

Scarlett

Big law is a phrase used to describe the country's largest and most prestigious law firms.

Here's how to use it in a sentence:

- All the top graduates from law school accept offers from big law.

- Big law routinely dishes out the best salaries and bonuses across the industry.

Now, this is how you'll use it when talking to your therapist:

- I cried every day I worked in big law.

- Big law ruined my life.

- If not for big law, I'd be [married, happy, well-adjusted, sober].

And here's how *I'll* use it starting today:

- Oh, my first year at big law? It was a total breeze.

- I made big law my big bitch.

My alarm buzzes on my nightstand, blaring for the half-second it takes me to lean over and turn it off. The alarm wasn't necessary. I'm already awake; I have been for two hours. I'm standing beside my bed in an outfit chosen with care and deliberation. The sales associate at Barneys was popping Advil for a tension headache and rethinking her career path by the time I made it to the register.

I've gone with cool ankle-length slim-fitting black trousers paired with a belted cream blouse and the ever-popular Aquazzura bow suede pumps, though I'll stick with flats until I get to the office. For accessories, I have my hand-me-down Cartier watch; clean, manicured nails; and diamond studs in my ears—nothing else.

This must be what Batman felt like his first day on the job. I'll bet he took the time to run his Batmobile through a Mr. Suds the day before to get the wheels squeaky clean. Tearing the tags off those brand-new combat boots and stretchy nylon pants before clicking all those safety gadgets and gizmos into place must have been quite the rush.

I feel the same flutter of butterflies as I gather my work bag, already packed with everything I need *and more*. I walk outside, ready and raring to tackle the day...just in time for a bird to poop on me.

I freeze and look down, suspended in shock. It takes me a moment to register the white sludge dripping down the front of my blouse, headed straight toward my trousers. Panic sets in with a great big belated rush. *NO.* I was stalling at my apartment on purpose so I wouldn't feel silly about my extremely early arrival at the office, but now, *NOW,* I'm kicking myself for not camping out in front of Elwood Hoyt overnight. I should have slept under my desk. A little crick in my neck would have been nothing compared to this.

It's fine, I tell myself, trying to regain control of my heart rate; it's hovering somewhere near 190 bpm. I've careened right past cardiac arrest range and I'm creeping ever closer to spontaneous combustion. I walk-run my way back into the lobby of my apartment building and try not to cry as the elevator seems to have newly gone on strike.

Fortunately, I had my entire week's worth of outfits already chosen. A quick change of my top to a black silk version and then I'm skipping down the stairs, leaving the elevator for all the people who aren't about to start the first day *of the rest of their lives.*

This time when I exit my building, I have that bird locked in my line of sight. I swear it looks smug from its perch atop a spindly branch. No doubt it's stretching and flexing its sphincter muscles on the off chance I creep too close again.

I flip it off (secretly), hiding my finger behind my other hand so I don't look absolutely insane to everyone passing me by on the sidewalk. Then I turn in the direction I was originally headed and *begin.*

I've only lost ten minutes with my wardrobe change, but it feels like ten minutes too many. It's the first week of

October, and the everlasting heat of summer has finally gone. I'm grateful for the crisp autumn air as I race down the city blocks.

I'm in the heart of Chicago's downtown, the River North district, surrounded by luxe shops, quaint eateries, and sprawling skyscrapers. There's history on every corner, places I usually love strolling past at a leisurely pace rather than careening by at breakneck speeds. But alas, this morning, there's no time for a latte at my favorite coffee shop or a bagel from that place on the corner.

Thank god my apartment is within walking distance of Elwood Hoyt's office. I make the quarter-mile trek in no time, only stopping once when a delivery truck nearly sideswipes me as I dart across the street. The metal bumper comes within an inch of my thigh as the gruff man behind the wheel shouts at me through the open window. "You got a death wish, lady?!"

No! The exact opposite—I have a dream!

I turn the final corner and see it.

In a city like Chicago, every skyscraper is aiming to outcompete its neighbor. Corporations want to house themselves inside massive and formidable fortresses, and Elwood Hoyt is exactly that. Nestled along the Chicago River, it's one of the tallest buildings in the city. Its heavy stone-and-steel facade seems to stretch up into the sky forever, especially from where I stand, a speck at its feet.

Just outside the pristine glass entrance, I pause to swap my flats for my heels. I adjust my bag, smooth my hair, and make sure my name badge is hanging just *so* from the little clip at my hip. Then I confidently hold my head high as I walk through the sliding doors.

Barrett's there waiting for me, standing before the turnstiles and security checkpoint. His charming smile is a welcome surprise this morning. Of all my brothers (and I have *plenty* of them), Barrett and I look the most alike. We share the same slim face, high cheekbones, dark eyes, and olive skin. His chestnut brown hair is much, *much* shorter than mine, though I love that he's allowed the strands to retain some of their natural waves. I likely have Nyles to thank for that—he always protests when Barrett tries to go in for a trim.

Barrett is holding a coffee cup in his right hand, and when I reach him, I steal it away without a second thought. His wink tells me it was meant for me all along.

"Cutting it kind of close there, sis."

"I made it," I say, sounding affronted that he'd ever lose faith in me. He knows I'd never be late today of all days.

"You're sweating."

"I'm *not*." I aim a harsh glare at him before taking a sip of the drink. He did good; it's my usual cappuccino with an extra shot of espresso. In a few minutes, I'll be buzzing, especially considering I didn't have the stomach for my usual breakfast this morning.

"Slight sheen aside, you certainly look the part." He takes me in from head to toe, smiling with pride. "The outfit's great."

"You think? This wasn't my first option."

I decide it's best not to bring up the bird. I don't want to reignite my annoyance all over again.

"Yes. It's perfect."

"Grandma's watch," I say, lifting my wrist so he can see it. He smiles. "Nice."

If there's anyone I'd accept fashion critiques from, it's Barrett. Today, on a random Tuesday, he's wearing a dark blue pinstripe suit with a coordinating striped handkerchief folded neatly in his left breast pocket. His tie is the same shade as his suit jacket, and his shirt is a few shades lighter than everything, a bright hydrangea blue. He's an eye-popping splash of color in an otherwise neutral backdrop.

While most every other profession seems well on their way to embracing casual workplace attire with blue jeans and sneakers, law is not one of them. A firm like Elwood Hoyt is especially concerned with appearances. We offer comprehensive legal services in all corporate law areas. Our clients are large companies, investment vehicles, and family officers, and they appreciate the clout and reputation that comes with a firm like ours. They don't want a schmuck in flip-flops; they want a well-groomed lawyer in a fitted suit, someone who looks and acts like they have their shit together.

Hopefully, that's me.

Barrett nods toward the elevators. "Let's go. I'm going to escort you up."

I let him take the lead as he waves us past security with a flick of his hand as if he owns the place.

"Have you seen Dad this morning?"

"Oh yes. *He's here.*"

I swallow down my nerves. "And?"

"And I'm sure you'll see him before the day is through. Gird your loins."

I sigh and wait alongside him for one of the dozen elevators to reach the ground floor. A ping sounds behind us, and we turn just as the gleaming doors sweep open.

Once we step in, a young blond guy sporting a freshly minted Elwood Hoyt badge of his own is about to step on board after us when Barrett holds up his hand. "No. Take the next one."

The man is so stunned he blinks there at the threshold, stupefied as the doors slide shut in front of his face.

"Well *that* was rude," I say with a laugh once we're alone.

"It was necessary." Barrett turns to me with a determined brow. "I only have a few seconds to talk with you. I've been meaning to pull you aside for weeks, but I've been busy, per usual. Listen, you don't have to go through with this."

I frown. He pauses for a breath, and when he begins again, his words are more earnest than ever.

"No one will think less of you. I swear. You're the star of our family, the whip-smart baby sister we all love to bits, but *this*? Taking this role at Elwood Hoyt is completely unnecessary. I mean, look at Mom—where is she right now?"

I frown, unclear where this is going. "In the South of France on a buying trip…"

We spoke just yesterday. She gave me a speech eerily similar to the one Barrett is currently delivering. Have they teamed up on this?

"You could be there with her. You *should* be," he says, sounding desperate. Any moment now he'll start to shake me. "This place is going to eat you alive, Scarlett."

I fold my arms over my chest, growing angrier by the second. "Did you give this same speech to Wyatt and Conrad when they took *their* positions with the company?"

He sighs with impatience. "Of course not. Conrad is more cutthroat than any of us. He *had* to work in law; no other profession would have him. And Wyatt...well, you know Wyatt—there's no getting through to him once his mind is made up."

I lift my chin. "Right. So pretend I'm no different than them. *Drop it.* It's done. I've already signed my contract."

He rolls his eyes, less than convinced by this minor detail. "Oh, like Dad couldn't just rip that thing up right now."

I'm about ready to lose my temper. I shake my head, my brows furrowed, my free hand clenched into a tight fist. If he doesn't watch it, I'm about to clock him—for real. Not like when we were kids.

"Why are you *so* against this?"

"Because I love you. Because I want a better life for you." He says it so emphatically that I *almost* start to soften in response to the kindness in his tone, those big brown eyes pleading with me to see reason. I almost give in, but *no*.

I aim daggers at him then turn suddenly and face the front of the elevator. I'll tune him out if he keeps this up for much longer. His words really rankle me. He sounds so much like Mom and Dad, so much like Jasper. I swear they're all against me pursuing the profession I've dreamed about since I was a little girl and begged my mom to buy me a child-sized pantsuit. When we were really young and my dad would drag us up to this very office, my brothers would run around like absolute maniacs, tearing plants out of pots and writing on the walls, but not me. I'd sit behind his desk, pick up his phone, and mimic words I'd heard him say a million times.

"Judge, buyout, contract, bid. No! We won't compromise!" Then I'd slam the phone down and swivel around and around in his chair, all that fictitious power going straight to my head as my feet dangled two feet off the floor.

Sure, Wyatt, Conrad, and Barrett are good lawyers, some of the best, no doubt. But I feel like I have what it takes to surpass them all, and if not, then at least to stand beside them, carrying my own weight in the company our father helped found. I don't need to be coddled.

Barrett's speech doesn't dissuade me from my goal in the least. It was a waste of his breath.

"If that's all you wanted to tell me, we can just ride the rest of the way in silence."

He groans and shakes his head as our elevator flies ever higher toward our end goal: the 70th floor, aka mergers and acquisitions, aka my home away from home for the foreseeable future. A little ripple of excitement rolls through me.

"Fine. We'll pick up the discussion another time. For now, if you're really about to go through with this, I have some advice."

I turn toward him with a curious brow. Now *this* I want to know. I've been hounding my brothers for insight for weeks.

Barrett starts talking fast. "Find a buddy and stick with them. There's no way I would have survived my stub year—or my first year, for that matter—without a good team around me.

"Billable hours. Keep fucking track of them. Get in the habit of loading them into the system every night. If you let that get away from you, you'll regret it.

"Oh, and whatever goal they give you, add five hundred hours, easy."

"Five hundred *more*?"

He shrugs, unfazed by my shock. "And that's on the low end of what some of these associates will do."

"*Christ.*" I hiss the word under my breath.

The elevator comes to a sudden stop, and Barrett's eyes widen in alarm. Just as the doors sweep open, he comes closer, grabbing my arm, pulling me toward him as he lowers his voice. "Most importantly, whatever you do, avoid Hudson Rhodes at all costs. Do you hear me? He and I went to law school together, and the guy is heartless. There are four partners in mergers and acquisitions—any of them would be fine *except* for Hudson. Got it?"

Sheesh. "Got it."

Hudson Rhodes is the devil, pick anyone else—understood.

Now...time to kick some lawyer butt.

Chapter Two

Hudson

I know I'm the villain around here and I'm perfectly okay with it. I've got that kind of self-satisfied grumbly attitude the Grinch enjoyed at the beginning of his story, only I have the pleasure of knowing I'll never have to let my heart grow three sizes in the end. Projecting darkness has a lot of perks. Having people scatter like cockroaches when I walk into the break room means more donuts and a quicker queue at the coffee pot for me. Evading endless small talk in the halls makes my work day that much more efficient. I probably save hundreds of billable hours a year just by blowing right past people as they quake in their boots, trembling from my mere presence.

Not to brag, but I once made a first-year associate call his mommy from the bathroom like he was an eight-year-old off at sleepaway camp for the first time. "Hey, Mom, yeah, I hate it here. My boss sucks. Can you come pick me up?"

Now here's the part where I tell you that deep down, I'm looking to reform. My big bad ways have landed me in hot water, and it's high time I right my wrongs.

Cue smug grin.

The pleasure I got from pounding on that stall door and telling that first-year to "hurry it up" was a rush unlike any other.

I'm content with the way things are. I've been with Elwood Hoyt for nearly ten years. I've worked my way up from summer associate to partner at a lightning-quick pace, and now I'm looking to add a new title to my belt: *senior* partner.

It's absurd, really. Most of my peers would be happy to call it a day in my current position. A partner at Elwood Hoyt's principal offices in Chicago—that's it. *That's* the golden ticket.

But I want more. Like any good villain, I'd prefer world domination, but making senior partner would be a close second.

With this goal in mind, I accept an unprompted meeting from one of the head honchos. Anders Elwood is one of the two founding partners of our firm. Though well into his 60s, he's not going anywhere. So while I can blow past just about everyone else in this building, for him, I have to dig deep and pull out my last vestiges of humanity. My smile has to be genuine. For once.

"Hudson? I'm assuming you have a moment," he says when he strolls confidently into my office as I'm *in the process* of dialing my phone.

I mean, what power! He didn't even knock! Did Lucy even attempt to stop him? (Not that she could...)

I clap my phone back into place and stand up. "Of course. What do you need, sir?"

I expect him to bring up an issue with a contract, some amendment he wants me to glance over. Anders doesn't technically work in mergers and acquisitions, but when we have large-scale deals in the works with billions of dollars on the line (which we do, *most of the time*), he usually keeps a close watch on them, especially during preliminary review and closing.

"As you know, all my children followed in my footsteps to pursue a profession in law."

That's...not where I thought he was going.

He walks around my desk and takes a spot at the window, knocking over one of my achievement trophies positioned there. I wince when it cracks against the glass, but he doesn't even seem to register the sound.

"Barrett, Wyatt, Conrad—I'm proud they're all here at Elwood Hoyt."

I merely nod, choosing to keep my mouth shut considering I still don't have a good sense of where this discussion is headed. I can't think of a single other time Anders has strolled into my office to discuss his children. To discuss anything outside of work, really.

The Elwood brothers are infamous at our firm for obvious reasons. Thank god only one of them works at the Chicago office. The last thing I need is to be competing with three of the boss's kids instead of one. Though really, while Barrett is intelligent and capable, I don't exactly view him as my competition. Namely because he's not in this department, and last I checked, he was only projected to clock about 2,000 billable hours this year. Last year, I soared past 3,500. I was the firm's top earner, and that little trophy Anders is carelessly letting crash to the ground proves it.

"Unfortunately, my youngest has also decided to join the family business."

To call Elwood Hoyt a family business is laughable. It's like the Waltons calling Walmart a li'l general store. Elwood Hoyt employs thousands of lawyers worldwide, over 700 here in Chicago alone.

"I'm sure you're proud."

He turns to me with an annoyed scowl.

Okay, rewind, *not* proud.

"I'm furious." He spits the words. "Beyond. My Scarlett doesn't belong in this world, not among—" He looks me over with careless judgment before finishing his bold statement. "Men as cutthroat as you."

Good to know my reputation has pervaded every square inch of this office. If Anders Elwood considers me cutthroat, I must be doing something right. The man isn't exactly a gentle lamb himself.

"I'm sure your daughter will be able to hold her own." I have to bite my tongue before adding, *Now if that's all, would you mind…* while gesturing toward the door.

"Fortunately, I won't have to worry about that. *You* will ensure it's taken care of for me."

I blink, utterly baffled.

"She's taken a liking to mergers and acquisitions," he continues. "She'll start on this floor today. I just checked and she's meant to be under the wing of Amaya Chandra, and while Amaya is a capable lawyer, she hasn't been with our firm as long as you have. She doesn't have a vested interest in ensuring my daughter has an easy path ahead of her. Do you catch my meaning?"

My silence compels him to spell it out for me.

"Go easy on her. Lob her softballs. That's it." He has the audacity to smile at me before adding, "Have I made myself clear?"

"Crystal."

With a nod, he turns toward the door. "Good. I'm glad to hear it."

I pick up my phone the second he's out of my office and down the hall. My assistant, Lucy, picks up on the first ring.

"Whatcha need?" she asks, no formality necessary.

"Figure out when the first-years get in today. Are they already here? Have you seen them around the building?"

There's shuffling on her end. "Oh, they start today? Let me just..."

"Call me back," I say then hang up.

At a sprightly 79 years old, Lucy Sadler is likely the oldest person in this building, and she's been my trusty assistant since my first day as a senior associate. I inherited her from a partner who retired ten years ago. Lucy might have retired alongside him, considering she was *his great aunt*, but she chose to stay and now we're best friends, though neither of us would ever admit that.

My phone rings.

"Whatdoyougot?" One word, spoken fifty times a day.

"You said first-years?"

I rub my eye sockets. "Yeah, Luce. First-years."

"On it."

While I wait for her to get back to me, I reclaim my seat and open a fresh internet tab. I type Scarlett Elwood into Google. Like any good lawyer, I need to do my research.

I didn't know the Elwoods had spawned a fourth child. How many children does one couple need? Oh shit—who's to say there aren't *more* than four?

A shiver rolls down my spine.

Before the search results load, I picture Scarlett as a female version of Anders replete with white hair, sideburns, and whiskers sprouting from her nostrils. Then the first page of Google appears, and there, at the top of the screen, is a high-resolution headshot of the youngest Elwood. Huh, I was wrong. This girl—*girl*, because she can't be a day older than twenty-three—is a brunette bombshell. She takes after her mother, I suppose, same as Barrett. She has gorgeous hair, thick chestnut brown waves surrounding her demure face. Her eyes shine with hopeful youth, and her smile is seductive, though not in a come-hither way. She's chock-full of that dimpled charm you'd expect from your childhood crush.

When I realize my stomach has squeezed tight with *something*, I wince and scroll down until I land on what I'm really looking for: intel. There are a million law forums online. Even just searching "Reddit" and "Scarlett Elwood" pulls up plenty of results. Apparently, people really enjoy discussing her.

I read and scroll fast. There's no time to waste. I have a full day of work ahead of me that doesn't include stalking a stranger online.

Anonymous134_x: *This girl is so obnoxious. I was in her same year at Columbia Law and you should have seen the way the professors fawned all over her. I doubt she had to study for a single test because of who her *DaDdY* is…ugh. Barf.*

LawGirlXO: *I heard it's been like that her whole life. She grew up in this elite private school. A total pampered princess. It's just so annoying that people like her take spots away from lawyers who really deserve to practice.*

Anonymous134_x: *Exactly! She'd never have made it into Columbia without her family's legacy.*

Throwaway13339990: *@Anonymous134_x Proof or shut up.*

Anonymous134_x: *Uhh…I saw it with my own eyes. A professor gave her an extension on a paper because Scarlett wanted to go on vacation in San Trope with her family or something. That would have never flown for the rest of us. There was other stuff too…but trust me when I say, we were all aware of her privilege. There was an understanding among the staff that she was untouchable, like her dad was pulling the strings or something. Meanwhile, the rest of us were actually working our asses off…*

I scroll a few more pages then decide I've seen enough. While the idea of people anonymously spewing hate online reeks of cowardice, the sentiment behind all these posts still stands. It's not hard to parse out the pertinent information from the mean-spirited vitriol. Furthermore, I don't need to wonder if there's truth behind any of these stories; I just had it confirmed for me by her own father. He waltzed into my office and made himself very clear: go easy on Scarlett. Smooth out the path before her...*or else.*

This isn't daycare. This is the top law firm in the nation. People fight tooth and nail to be here, sacrificing everything, putting themselves into debt up to their ears—all so they can watch someone like Scarlett breeze through, no problem? Infuriating.

I'm actually glad Anders has asked me to bring her onto my service. I'd love nothing more than to take Scarlett Elwood along for a day in my life. I bet she doesn't even survive the morning. I'll give her until 10:00 a.m., then she'll go running for the hills. Sure, maybe her dad will want my head on a platter for going against his wishes, but something tells me he understands the score here. If his daughter isn't capable of being a real lawyer, that's going to become apparent sooner rather than later, no matter her team placement.

And if he's intent on pushing this, on letting her play lawyer while the rest of us do real work, he'll have to find some other dummy to do his bidding 'cause it ain't gonna be me.

Chapter Three

Scarlett

WELCOME, says the banner over the top of the conference room door.

You're doomed, says the glare of the nine new hires looking my way as I scoot into the room and try to assess my seating options. Oh yes, I was hoping for the creaky chair way in the back, the one that looks like it was pulled out of storage for today only. Every seat in the front—where I would usually sit on my first day at a new job—is filled, save for one, and when I take a step toward it, the blonde girl claiming the spot to its left says, "*It's taken*," with enough snark that I don't feel up to challenging her.

Okay then.

Footsteps sound behind me, and I feel a little bit smug that even with my bird poop incident, I'm not the last one to arrive this morning. There is *one* guy who comes in after me; it's the guy Barrett just pissed off at the elevators. He sends me a death glare as he walks in to claim the last seat next to all his friends...the seat the girl was saving for him.

Dammit, Barrett!

I'm left with the chair in the back. When I sit down, it *squeeeeeeaaallls* like it's two hundred years old.

"Sheesh. Anyone got some WD40 handy?" I ask with a little self-deprecating laugh.

No one turns around.

All right, so *that's* how it's going to be. I figured today could go one of two ways: the best and least likely outcome is that I immediately make friends and find my place among my peers. The worst and most likely outcome is that everyone already realizes who I am, hates me for it, and decides they're better off banding together in their mutual hatred of me.

Just to confirm which option I'm dealing with, I lean toward the rail-thin boy a few feet in front of me. He's far enough away that no one would mistakenly think we're sitting together but close enough that I don't have to raise my voice much to ask him if he knows who I am.

He shoots me an incredulous look. "Of course. Don't talk to me." He looks up quickly to check if the blonde girl in the front row has heard him. Fortunately for him, she's engrossed in an animated conversation with the people around her.

I'm not surprised everyone already seems to know each other. No doubt every single person here—besides me—

worked as summer associates together. It's a really big deal to land one of the coveted summer spots at big law firms in between 2L and 3L (aka year two and year three of law school) because nine times out of ten, the firms look to their summer associates when considering offers for full-time positions come graduation time.

Just because I wasn't here last summer doesn't mean I was slacking off, mind you. I just decided that instead of slogging through another Chicago summer, I'd go abroad. I was a summer associate at Elwood Hoyt's London office in an effort to spend some time with my brother, Wyatt. Also, it was convenient and fun to backpack around Europe on my free weekends (what few I had). As much as I enjoyed my time in London Town, I knew the choice might come back to bite me in the ass.

It looks like alliances have already been formed.

Barrett's first piece of advice was to make friends, wasn't it? Well, sorry, bro...that's not going to happen today, it seems.

High heels clap in quick succession and then a woman enters wearing a steely-eyed glare. Harsh expression aside, the lady's in one hell of an outfit. I immediately take note of her understated diamond necklace and the sleek way she's knotted her black hair at the nape of her neck. Her dark skin is complemented nicely by her camel-colored dress. I peer over and—yes, her shoes coordinate perfectly as well. Ten out of ten.

She walks to the front of the conference room and looks out at us with a lazy perusal. A few people actually squirm in their chairs in the uncomfortable silence. I sit stock-still until her gaze scans around the conference table, finally landing on me. Her eyes narrow. No doubt, she's placing me. Barrett and I look too similar for her not to put two and two together right away. Word has likely spread around the firm that yet *another* Elwood is joining the ranks.

Jesus, how many of you are there? she's probably wondering.

Without giving anything away, her gaze cuts sideways and she begins in a clipped, crisp tone. "I'm Bethany Quinn, a senior associate in mergers and acquisitions. I'll help each of you get placed with your team today. HR will meet with you at some point as well, so most questions should be directed at them, not me. After this meeting, if you bother me, I'll send you a bill for my hours. Understood?"

Everyone nods with slack-jawed expressions.

I'm the only one smiling.

I love her. I want to *be* her. No nonsense, just boatloads of attitude and confidence.

"Most of you were summer associates here, so welcome back and, more importantly, *congratulations*. In your current position, you're no longer on the lowest rung of the ladder. However, you haven't proved yourself yet. There are four partners in mergers and acquisitions, so you'll be broken up into small groups and absorbed by each of the four teams. The junior and senior associates you'll be working alongside will have very little patience and very little time for hand-holding. You were not accidentally chosen for this job. Each of you is capable of learning fast and thinking on your feet. You're getting paid gobs of money to perform as an asset to this company. *That being said*, we don't want mistakes. Triple-check your work. Ask for guidance if it's absolutely necessary."

She scans over us. "I want to be perfectly clear about the reality of a firm like Elwood Hoyt. None of you are ignorant about this world. Take a good look at the peers around you because by this time next year, a quarter of you will be gone. In two years, only half will be left standing. Likely less."

Oh god. What is this, *The Hunger Games*? Are we about to have to kill each other off? Because if push came to shove, I do think I could take the scrawny guy near me in hand-to-hand combat. I've been kickboxing like crazy this last year.

"Now I know you're all weighted down with the guidelines and handbooks from HR concerning Elwood Hoyt's training policies. Pertaining to the mergers and acquisitions side of things, we have a different hourly requirement than most other departments. We want you all to aim for at least 2,500 billable hours a year. How you decide to break that up is your concern."

2,500 billable hours...and Barrett said to add 500 to their base requirement, meaning he wants me shooting for 3,000 billable hours. Taking into account two weeks of vacation and holidays, that leaves me with sixty-hour work weeks on the low end. More than likely, I'll be pulling ten to twelve-hour days and working some on the weekends too.

I peer around the group, though there are no wide eyes, no bleak expressions. It's all furrowed brows and fierce determination. Everyone knows the score, apparently.

It's hard to believe though. A quarter of us won't make it through the year? When do people start dropping? Right now, it doesn't seem like anyone's even remotely interested in walking away.

Bethany pulls out a memo on the firm's letterhead from the padfolio she brought in with her.

"I'm going to read out the teams. Find who you're grouped with, exchange numbers, get close. These people will be your support system for the next few months. It's impossible to survive here alone."

One by one, she starts listing the partners followed by the associates assigned to their team.

"Mr. Beltran—Makayla Hammon, Dilan Phan, Ramona Dalton."

A guy in the center of the room turns to two girls sitting beside him and they give each other surreptitious high fives.

Thaddeus Welch, Vihaan Robles, and Andy Pace land on Mr. Pruitt's team.

My name is called next, first up for Amaya Chandra's team. After me, she calls the names of two other girls. One of them sits over near the window by herself. She looks back at me and shrugs as if she doesn't really care that we've been placed on the same team.

I'll take it! Open apathy is better than blatant loathing.

Also, I've managed to evade landing on Hudson Rhodes' team. Of all of Barrett's advice, at least I lucked out in that regard.

She finishes assigning everyone else. The blonde girl up front—Kendra Crane, I learn—doesn't get her name called until the very end, and I smile (internally) with glee over her assignment for two reasons. One, she's been placed with Hudson. Two, rather than being placed with *two* other new associates, she only gets *one* other team member: the boy near me.

Makes sense. There're only eleven new hires in this room; one team had to be one short. Oh well. Poor Kendra will have her work cut out for her, that's for sure. I do hope Barrett wasn't exaggerating about Hudson. It'd be such lovely karmic retribution if he was an absolute monster.

When Kendra realizes her lackluster placement, she immediately raises her hand in protest. Bold. I expected her to sit quietly and take it on the chin.

"Excuse me?"

"What is it?" Bethany asks, not even bothering to look up. She's reviewing her memo, likely confirming she's done everything she's supposed to do so she can release us into the wild. We've already taken up too much of her time.

"I was hoping to be placed with Ms. Chandra rather than Mr. Rhodes," Kendra says kindly. "I was on her team while I worked as a summer associate, and when interviewing for this position, I was told I would likely be working alongside her again."

Bethany finally deigns to look up, and now she does so with a shrewd sneer. I get the impression she's not all that impressed with Ms. Seat's Taken. "I think the operative word in that sentence was 'likely'. Was it stated in your contract that you would be in her service?"

Kendra rears back. "N-no—"

"And did you speak with Amaya personally beforehand about this special assignment? Surely, if you had, she would have confirmed your placement with HR."

Kendra stays silent, only offering up a slow shake of her head.

"Right. Then there will be no switching, under any circumstances." She looks out over us all now, likely wanting us to learn this lesson once so she won't have to repeat herself again when the next person starts grumbling with complaints. "The team I placed you on will be your team for your entire first year here at Elwood Hoyt, if not longer. We don't play favorites—"

For a split second her eyes cut to me, and I all but cringe down into my seat. *Hey!* I wasn't the one asking for a swap. I took my assignment in stride, thank you very much.

"Assignments are at random. End of discussion," Bethany states quickly. "Now, in a moment a member of your team will arrive to escort you and your peers to your new desks. Beyond that, HR wants each of you to go down to the fiftieth floor sometime today so they can confirm your ID badges are in working order. There were a few issues this morning, as I understand it. Also, while you're down there, it would be an opportune time to pick up your parking badge for those of you who are—"

Powerful knuckles suddenly pound on the door, breaking through her words. She huffs under her breath at the interruption.

When she pulls the door open and looks at the person on the other side, she stands just *that* much taller, shifting her weight and lifting her chin, affecting an entirely new countenance on behalf of our guest. *Intriguing.* I can't help my curiosity. I lean over in my chair to try to get a better look at the person.

The man's handsomeness takes absolutely no time to register. The moment I lay eyes on him, I realize he's a male in rare form. A gift to us all. And I'm allowed to say that even if I'm in a relationship with Jasper. It can't be wrong to appreciate beauty like this!

And so what if this *beauty* happens to be 6'3" and suited to perfection? Rich brown hair, of course. Alluring brown eyes, *check-check*. A side profile that's chiseled and cut... well it's no wonder I haven't shifted back into my seat even though my side is starting to ache. I can't move *or blink* to save my life.

"Mr. Rhodes. Hi."

His name registers impossibly slowly, as if it had to travel around the entire world before it landed in my ears.

Mr. Rhodes.

What?

That's him?! Talk about delivering the devil in a pretty package. Not fair. He's handsome in the same way a venomous snake is beautiful, alluring...*deadly.*

Don't you worry, Barrett. I have my wits about me. I shift back into my seat having fully come to my senses. Then, to add another barrier between us, I look down and mind my business. Whatever he's doing here has nothing to do with me. I might as well be whistling and twiddling my thumbs.

"Are you here for your associates? I just finished announcing the assignments, actually."

"Good then I'll collect them," he says with a sexy voice. It's not too burly, not too high. That perfect cocky in-between. "I need Kendra Crane and Scarlett Elwood."

My name on his lips is so shocking I go rigid in my chair. Surely he didn't just list me. *Scarlett.* I heard wrong.

I'm even shaking my head, no. Bethany is too.

"I hesitate to contradict you..." She looks back down at her memo. "I have it here that you have Kendra Crane and Eli Little. Scarlett Elwood is part of Amaya's team."

Hudson's gaze shifts past Bethany for the first time and his eyes rove over the room, searching impatiently until he spots me and stills. Laser beams would be less intense than his unwavering gaze. I'm melting into my seat. Soon, my trousers will be fused with the metal.

"Actually, she's with me."

Ugh, that voice. I'd shiver if I weren't so damn focused on my impending doom!

I'm with *him*? Hudson Rhodes?

No, no, no. My brother gave me three directives, and this one seemed like the most important. I can't screw it up.

"I think you're wrong," I say meekly.

Perfectly done; when talking to the devil, it's best to seem scared shitless, that way he knows he can easily walk all over you. Follow me for more brilliant advice.

He looks me over—top to bottom—like he's determining if I have all my body parts and a working brain, because why else would I have made such an absurd comment? Then his eyes crinkle at the edges as he narrows them, smiles a sadistic little smile, and shakes his head. "I'm not wrong. *You're with me.*"

Chapter four
Scarlett

Kendra shoots up out of her chair with a smile already in place. I'm shocked to realize she's a pipsqueak. I'm 5'6"—not exactly a giant—but still, I'll bet Kendra barely comes up to my shoulder.

"Mr. Rhodes, it's an absolute honor," she says, rushing toward him with her hand outstretched.

Oh really? Tell the truth, Kendra. Not two minutes ago you were begging to be free of him.

I roll my eyes, and Hudson catches it. Great.

"Are you coming, Ms. Elwood, or would you like me to write out a formal invitation?"

Smug jerk. I shove out of my chair and grab my bag, aware of everyone's eyes on me as I shimmy around the conference table and make my way toward the front of the room. My cheeks burn red hot. My anger and indignation brew right under the surface. My mom has always had a bit of a temper, and unfortunately, the apple doesn't fall far from the tree.

"*Asshole.*"

I don't miss the sharp intake of breath from every person in the room. Bethany actually groans.

My new boss stares at me like he's never been more bored in his life.

"Are you done?"

I stay absolutely silent, immediately regretting my impulsive outburst.

Without another word, he turns and walks away. We're clearly meant to follow.

Kendra shoots me a lethal glare the moment he's not looking our way. "Are you *insane*?!" she whisper-hisses. "He's a partner!"

Dammit.

I should have held my tongue. I know that. I'm just...I've never been good at thinking first and speaking second. Why do you think I'm here working in mergers and acquisitions rather than in criminal law?! I could never cut it in a courtroom. I'd lose my cool the moment the judge sided with the opposing counsel.

No, this is where I belong, in a nice, orderly specialty, one where you cross a lot of t's and dot a lot of i's—all from the confines of a quiet desk. I just...have to make it to that desk first.

Hudson storms down the hall up ahead like it's his goal to lose us. I keep up, no problem—I'm still angry, after all, so there's a lot of energy to burn—but poor Kendra is basically having to all-out sprint.

She curses as her bag slips off her shoulder and a few of her things tumble to the carpet. I turn back to help her, grabbing a tube of lipstick before it can continue rolling away, but she wrenches it out of my hand before I can offer it to her.

"I don't need your help," she bites out snidely.

It's on the tip of my tongue to respond with something equally rude, but then where would we be?

Instead, I push to stand and leave her there to collect her belongings on her own. Hudson hasn't slowed his pace up ahead. I watch as a young associate walks out of a door to the right just in time to cut directly into Hudson's path. The associate's eyes go wide as he halts, pivots, then darts right back into the room he came from. It'd be funny if not for the fact that I'm in no position to laugh at the moment.

Finally, Hudson reaches a glass door through which I can see a formal reception area. This is Hudson's corner of the 70th floor, where he and his team all work together. There's a neat row of gold plaques bolted into the wall beside the door.

Hudson Rhodes, Partner
Sophie Smith, Senior Associate
Bethany Quinn, Senior Associate

There are more names, but I don't have time to read them before Hudson yanks the door open for us. I'm right behind him, but Kendra hasn't fully caught up since her mishap with her bag.

It gives him and me an awkward few seconds to stand there, beside one another, absolutely painfully quiet while we wait for her.

How would I normally act when meeting a partner for the first time? That's easy; I'd be deferential and polite, so...I dig deep for those emotions as I peer over at Hudson out of the corners of my eyes.

He's not looking my way. To him, I don't exist. He's skewering Kendra as she scurries the last few feet toward us.

That's fine. I take the opportunity to size him up while his annoyance is focused elsewhere. He's wearing a black suit and a pale blue tie. Everything looks to be designer. *Ho-hum.* Can't fault him there. I look down at his watch tucked partway beneath his crisp white cuff. The pronounced veins in his hands. Rather large hands...though of course they would be. He's tall, much taller than me, which makes him hilariously huge compared to Kendra. I'm smiling at the mental image when his eyes slowly slice to me as if he's been aware of my attention this whole time.

I almost stumble back from the intensity of his gaze.

"I'm Scarlett El—"

His brusque voice cuts me off. "I know who you are."

My brows furrow. "We've never met," I clarify. I'm sure of it.

"You look just like your brother," he explains.

He takes me in for another moment—assessing, no doubt—and then Kendra finally reaches us.

"I'm sorry! My bag spilled."

Ignoring her apology, Hudson waves us through, and we enter his domain. I'll be honest, it's less hostile than I was expecting. No burning hellfire. No extreme blast of heat. Not even a single stray black cat. On the contrary, there's a light floral scent in the air and beautiful furnishings artfully arranged in the sitting area, but I doubt Hudson had anything to do with the hospitable environment.

Past a series of offices, he knocks on an open door, drawing the attention of a tall black-haired woman sitting at her desk.

"Sophie, they're yours, though I'd like a quick word with Scarlett before you start."

The woman—Sophie Smith, I assume, from her plaque on the wall—nods and invites Kendra to come into her office.

Hudson looks at me and says with all the enthusiasm of a funeral director that we can go to his office down the hall. On the way, we pass more offices before we dead-end at another smaller sitting area, this one circular. His own personal space. There's a coffee station on one side and a desk on the other. We walk past Hudson's receptionist, a tiny older woman wearing a pink wool blazer and matching skirt. She looks up as we pass, her pale blue eyes assessing me over the top rim of her glasses. She smiles then goes back to sipping her tea.

Interesting.

At the threshold of his office, Hudson allows me to enter first. I catch the subtle scent of his cologne, and then he shuts the door behind us and I get sidetracked. I survey the space quickly because I'm nosey and god knows when I'll get another chance to be in here. I fully plan on rectifying this wrong the first chance I get. By the end of the day, I'll be on Amaya's service and Hudson will be somewhere, I don't know...weeping, probably.

His walls are paneled and lacquered in blue-gray paint
that I *love*. His desk is made of deep brown wood—an antique
from the looks of it. There's a wall of built-ins housing what
looks to be an *entire* law library. Across from that there's a
door that likely leads to a personal bathroom. Ah, the perks
of being a partner.

Two large landscape paintings are hung beneath gallery
lights on opposite walls, similar in style to a few I saw out in
the hallway and sitting area. They're abstract and full of my
favorite colors, sage green chief among them. In another life,
I'd enjoy asking him about them, maybe even inquiring about
the artist, but that's definitely not happening here and now.
I've been summoned for unclear reasons, but I am sure they
don't have anything to do with idle chitchat.

Hudson's gone behind his desk and taken a seat. Failing
to offer me one is yet another thing to add to my growing list
of grievances.

Worse still, he doesn't immediately get on with it. He leans
forward, drops his elbows onto his desk, and looks me over. I
manage about three seconds of his undivided attention before
I transform—*yet again*—into a firecracker. I have a short fuse
this morning. Blame it on the bird.

With my bag hiked up on my shoulder, it's easy enough to
cross my arms. "If you're hoping for an apology concerning
what just happened in that conference room, you'll be sorely
disappointed."

For even more dramatic effect, I cock my chin in a show of
resolute stubbornness and defiance.

I wish I could say I never behave like this, but truth be
told, you don't survive growing up with three arrogant older

brothers without finding *some* way to defend yourself. On top of that, I also spent my youth at an intensely exclusive private school filled with kids practically *salivating* at the chance to take advantage of my every weakness. My mouth has *always* gotten me into trouble, but when dealing with authority figures, I can mostly rein it in. It's been years since it's landed me in hot water like this.

I guess Hudson is just special.

"Not good at delivering apologies?" he asks mildly. "I'm not surprised."

Well there it goes, the last ounce of decorum left between us.

"Right. Let's just cut to the chase then, shall we?"

His lip quirks before it flattens into a harsh line. "I brought you into my office to let you know that on top of doing any and everything requested of you by Sophie Smith and the other senior associates, you will also take ownership of any tasks I give you. Consider it a sort of favoritism in reverse."

Favoritism.

Ah.

I now understand clearly what this is. No doubt, he thinks this turn of events will cause me to erupt with protest, but at this point in my life, I'm utterly resigned to my fate. Here's the funny thing about nepotism: everyone always assumes having influential parents opens every door for you, but for every door it opens, it also slams one directly in your face.

I am fully aware of the privileges I've been afforded and, let me be crystal clear, I'm not complaining. I know I'm only here in my position at Elwood Hoyt because of my last name. Even though I got the grades, did the work, hustled hard just like my fellow peers…it doesn't matter. No amount of dedication will ever wipe away my legacy status. Because of it, I carry a big target on my back, an invitation to take me down just because of who I am.

But that's okay. Living like that for so long has forced me to toughen up. Sorry, Hudson, you don't scare me. You're no different than everyone else.

"Fine. These extra duties…what should I expect?"

This is the first time I've surprised him all morning. I like the little spark of curiosity in his eyes, love catching him off guard with my nonchalant response to his curt behavior. I consider it a win even as he starts to lay it all out there, confirming my fate with a smugness that grates on my every nerve.

"We'll figure it out as we go along. I'll email a list of admin tasks for you to take care of—"

"I thought you had an assistant." I point toward his closed door. "Wasn't that her outside?"

"Lucy, yes. Don't bother her."

My hand drops. "Right. And to be clear, am I reporting to you or Sophie?"

"Both of us."

Great.

"Do the tasks you give me supersede those given to me by Sophie?"

I want to be sure I understand the chain of command.

"They're exactly equal. Meaning, you don't leave here each day until *all* the work is done. Understood?"

I'm about to shoot him a sarcastic salute, but I grind my molars together and muster up just enough patience to bite out a "Yes, sir."

This is utterly ridiculous.

"And I suppose if you're unhappy with this arrangement, you could phone your dad and he'd steal you away to some other partner." He reclines back in his chair, cool as a cucumber. "It's your choice. I really don't care."

Well isn't that just great. He already knew what I was going to do the second I walked out of his office, and he's calling my bluff. *Stick it out or run and tell Daddy.*

I'll be damned if I call my dad now. Whether or not it was by mistake, I'm on Hudson's team, and I'm not giving him the satisfaction of calling mercy.

This situation is nothing I haven't dealt with before. He's just another bully, no more menacing than all the rest I've had to contend with my whole life. It's only hard to stand confidently before him today because I'm still getting used to his presence, I suppose. He's intimidating, I'll give him that—what with the broad shoulders and sculpted jawline—but I'll get used to those cut cheekbones in no time. Those piercing brown eyes won't even affect me by next week, just watch.

When I smile, it's so genuine and real I feel a little flutter of satisfaction in the pit of my stomach.

"It's an honor and a privilege to work with you, sir. I'm happy to do any extra tasks you require of me, and I promise, *I won't let you down.*"

There it is—the saccharine words he never thought he'd hear from my lips during this meeting. Even better, they end up sounding like a big *Eff you.*

His gaze hardens as I turn for the door, dismissing myself. I'm about to reach for the handle when he speaks, stalling me for a moment.

"Why are you here, Scarlett?"

I wasn't expecting his question, which means, for a moment, I'm almost caught off guard enough to give him the truth: to work hard and take my rightful place in this company, just like my brothers.

But under these circumstances, he doesn't deserve to know the truth. So instead I look back at him over my shoulder, dropping the nice act completely.

"That's none of your business."

And then I wrench that door open and leave because some of us have *extra* work to do.

Chapter Five
Scarlett

It's nearing lunchtime and I'm still jittery from my encounter with Hudson. Though to be fair, it could just be general first-day nerves. It might not even have anything to do with Mr. Tall Dark and Deadly.

I've had a busy morning. Once I joined Sophie and Kendra, Sophie introduced us around the floor so we could meet the other junior and senior associates, people we'll be working with on a daily basis. Our tour culminated at our office. Yes...*OUR* office.

Kendra asked about it before I could.

"Surely there's enough space in this huge building for everyone to get their own office? When I was here last summer, new associates didn't have to share."

Sophie smiled grimly. "It's intentional. It's not about the space, actually. I think there's a memo about it waiting for you all in your inbox."

There was. I read it.

Basically, they're trying to foster a more collaborative work environment, especially among new hires who are just getting their feet wet in a professional setting. They feel like this will cut down on depression and anxiety in first-year associates, which like, okay thank you for taking my mental health into consideration, but could we possibly go back to the drawing board because this is my literal nightmare!

In the office, there are two desks facing each other. Kendra took the larger one—the one that was obviously here before they converted the space to accommodate two attorneys. My desk is made from flimsy particle board (at best) and shoved in the corner as an afterthought.

There was no discussion about who would go where. After Sophie left, Kendra plopped her bag on the larger desk and immediately went around to open her brand-new work-issued laptop. We each got one.

"This is ridiculous that they have us both in here," she bit out in anger.

"I agree."

But no more conversation came from that little bonding experience. We've been sitting in ominous silence ever since while we configure our computers and get through a few HR modules. We've left the door open intentionally. Our office is right by the break room, which seems to get a lot of foot traffic. Closing the door would reduce the noise, but then...

we'd really be stuck in here together, and I definitely don't want that. Kendra almost scares me more than Hudson if I'm being honest.

I'm just completing one of my HR modules, eager to cross it off my to-do list, when I hear a familiar booming laugh out in the hall and my heart simultaneously soars and sinks.

My dad—God love him—is about to make my life ten times worse. His timing is impeccably bad. Though Kendra and I have been mostly silent for the last few hours, it seemed like here within the last few minutes, things were starting to thaw between us as evidenced by the fact that when I sneezed a moment ago, we exchanged your classic "Bless you" and "Thanks"—which seemed really promising.

I was wondering when this was going to happen. I imagined a million different scenarios in which my dad could simultaneously celebrate, humiliate, and torture me all in the name of familial love. Examples include but are not limited to this set of things he's already proven capable of doing in the past:

On my first date to the movies as a fourteen-year-old, when the boy (and his mom) came to pick me up, my dad made us pose for a fifteen-minute photoshoot for a commemorative scrapbook he'd completed by the time I got home at 9:00 p.m.

On my sixteenth birthday, he came to my school and sang "Happy Birthday" to me over the PA system. Accompanied by my gym teacher Mr. Rollins.

When I got accepted into undergrad at Cornell, he came to my afterschool job at the ice cream shop dressed up as "Touchdown" aka Big Red Bear, holding up a "Go Scarlett Go" banner.

I'm his youngest child and his only daughter. He was never going to be hands-off with me the way he was with my older brothers. I'm honestly surprised he's lasted this long before coming to surprise me. Almost 1:00 p.m.? For him, that's showing real restraint.

I barely have time to brace myself, and unfortunately, I don't get the chance to pre-apologize to Kendra for whatever is about to go down before my dad turns the corner with his phone held out right in front of his face, and oh, look at that— he's already taking pictures of me.

How do I know? The flash is on and blinking about every half second. He's going to have seven hundred versions of me wearing a dumb expression as I try to yank his phone out of his hands.

"*Dad!*"

He's roped his two assistants into this too—Janice and Linda. Janice holds up a multi-tiered cake that might have been stolen from someone's wedding it's so insanely huge. Linda is holding enough balloons that a) I can't see her face and b) I'm genuinely concerned she's having a hard time keeping her feet on the ground. We're about to have to call maintenance for a ladder to get her down from the ceiling.

"This is a lot, even for you," I say drolly.

He laughs before obtusely asking Janice to snap a photo of us.

"Dad, her hands are full. So are Linda's."

Unperturbed, he turns to Kendra. "Right. Okay, here. Would you mind taking a picture?"

Kendra has to really battle with herself over her reply to this question. She doesn't want to have to give in and be nice to my father and, by extension, *me*, but she certainly can't be rude to the owner of the company. There's really only one choice. I watch her force that smile and give her best enthusiastic nod. "Sure thing! This is *so* sweet of you!"

The moment—and I mean down to the millisecond—she finishes taking our picture and hands my dad's phone back, her smile drops and she returns to her resting bitch face.

I don't let it bother me. I turn to my father and give him a side hug. Honestly, I'm just glad to see a friendly face after my long morning.

"Balloons *and* cake, Dad?" I rib him.

"What?" He drops a kiss to my head. "Can't I celebrate my one and only daughter on her first day at her new fancy job?" Then his eyes widen like he's remembered something, and he looks behind him. "Janice, come on, show her the cake."

Though it seemed over the top from a distance, up close... I'm actually speechless. There's a little miniature version of me planted into the icing on the top tier. Did he get it custom-made? He must have. The figurine has a leather briefcase, brown hair, and brown eyes. She's also holding a little pennant flag that says: I ♥ ELWOOD HOYT.

Despite how much this is going to hurt me in the long run, I can't help but feel grateful for his support. I know he doesn't approve of my position here. There were many, *many* late-night discussions over rounds of Scrabble where I convinced him this was what I truly wanted. I appreciate him putting his feelings aside today and making me feel loved.

Unfortunately, Janice takes the cake to the break room, and when I go in to get a piece after lunch, most of it's already gone, and my figurine, well...someone stuck her headfirst into the cake so all that's sticking out are her feet and that pennant flag. Which now reads: "LOSER."

Later that night, I try to tell Jasper about it all, laughing while I do it.

"Like sure, they could have come up with something slightly more creative than *loser*, but the overall effect was still pretty funny."

My boyfriend sets down his silverware and eyes me with tenacious concern from across his dinner table. "That's not funny, Scarlett. You need to tell your father, or at the very least, Barrett. They'll be able to do something about it."

Panic has me leaning over to touch his arm, to reassure him that it was really nothing. "No. Come on, lighten up. So they wrecked my cake? Big deal! I still got a big ol' slice for myself. I just happened to also accidentally decapitate my figurine in the process. They really stuck that sucker down in there."

I laugh, but I'm alone in it, so I let it trickle away as he shakes his head at me. It's like I'm in as much trouble as they are. I didn't destroy my cake!

I should have known not to tell Jasper. He's completely by the book. Everything is right and wrong, black and white. With him, there's no nuance to life. It makes sense, I suppose. He works for the district attorney's office. Those guys all fit a certain kind of mold, and I don't mind it, truly. Jasper is wonderful! A perfect boyfriend! We're about to celebrate our first anniversary. He was a year ahead of me at Columbia Law, and we were introduced through mutual friends. We didn't jump into things right away. Jasper courted me like we were in the Victorian era. First, we'd see each other in group settings, then we slowly developed a steady friendship. From there, we moved infinitesimal step by infinitesimal step toward a relationship that was mostly long-distance as he took a position in Chicago and I stayed back in New York to finish my final year of law school.

When I asked him a few weeks ago what he saw for our future, he said it was already mapped out. At our two-year mark, he'd ask me to marry him, and an appropriate amount of time after that, we'd have the ceremony.

"And what if I propose to you first? The day *before* our two-year anniversary?" I teased.

I meant it as a joke, but Jasper looked at me like he was horrified.

"That would make no sense, Scarlett."

He's looking at me much the same way now as we discuss the silly cake situation.

"The point is, it's disturbing. I'm going to call your dad if you don't."

I try not to be overly annoyed by his threat. "*Relax*, Jasper. You're taking it way too seriously. There was always going to be a little bit of light hazing. What job doesn't have some of that? Think back to the way they treated you when you started at the DA's office last year!"

"That was nothing. The guys made me wear a T-shirt at work that had my middle school graduation picture on it, big whoop."

I wrinkle my nose. "I've seen that picture. It's *pretty* bad."

Jasper has neatly combed blond hair and a cute spray of freckles across his cheeks. Though a little dorky in middle school, he's attractive now, but that's not really why I'm with him. He's kind and respectful, dependable and honest. He's a good man, and I'm lucky to have him.

He tilts his head and frowns at me like I'm not quite getting his point. "I understand you don't think it's a big deal, but with everything else you've told me, I'm worried about you. I didn't want you taking that position in the first place, Scar. If you're not comfortable telling your father or Barrett about what happened today, at least tell your department head. Who is it? Which partner did you land with?"

I haven't been hungry for the last few minutes, but now I suddenly go back to picking at my food. "You don't know him."

"Not Barry Pruitt? I told you I played soccer with his son when I was younger, didn't I? Great guy."

I shake my head. "No, not Barry. Another guy. Hudson something. Sorry...it's been a long day and I met a lot of people."

I stand and reach for my plate to carry it over to the sink. I hate that I'm doing this. Why am I even bothering to lie to Jasper about Hudson?

Like I don't know Hudson's last name. LAUGHABLE. I know his first, last, *and* middle name. I looked him up on my walk home—sue me. Wait, don't sue me; I've only just passed the bar.

Hudson Samuel Rhodes.

I know his entire educational track and can recite all his accolades and honors; chief among them is being the youngest person to make partner at Elwood Hoyt. I have no doubt he stepped on a lot of people to get there too. You can't be that successful *and* well-liked by everyone. It's one or the other.

He's clearly chosen his path, and I doubt he regrets it.

After our encounter this morning, I didn't hear anything from him for the rest of the day. I expected him to really pile it on me on my first day on the job, but I didn't receive a single email from him, no phone calls, nothing. I even went by his office around 4:00 to check in with his receptionist, Lucy.

Her phone rang just as I was walking up to talk to her. She apologized to me before answering it quickly and chatted briefly with the person on the other end of the line before finishing with, "Yes. Absolutely. Let me transfer you."

Only when she went to do just that, she accidentally hung up. The heavy dial tone rang out crystal clear in the quiet space. She looked up at me. "Well crap."

I smiled. "Don't worry, I won't tell him."

"I should have jotted down the man's name. I always forget something. Darn it. Anyway..." She shook her head and composed herself, refocusing her attention on me. "What did you need, sweetie?"

I stepped up and gave her a little wave. "Right. *Hi.* I'm Scarlett El—"

She cut me off with a cheeky wink. "I know who you are. Gosh, let me get a better look at you, all grown up." She shooed me with her hand so I'd take a few steps back, and then she grinned. "Cute as a button. All fancy in your work clothes. You look just like your mom. You know way back in the day, when you'd come up to the office with your dad, I'd sneak you and your brothers lollipops."

My mouth dropped. "I remember those lollipops!"

Lucy grinned. "That was me."

I felt an overwhelming urge to hug her. Instead, I just smiled as she opened her desk drawer. "In fact, I still have some in here. I probably have the same bag from when you were little. Want one?"

"Er...I'm okay for now."

"Right. Busy busy today, I'm sure."

I capitalized on her momentum and squared my shoulders, getting back to the point of why I'd come in the first place. "Yes, well, I was just coming by to ask if you know if Hudson sent any tasks for me to complete? He said he would, but I haven't received any by email or by phone. I wasn't sure if the company sometimes sends paper memos? I just really want to be sure I didn't miss any correspondences."

I tried to stay glued to my desk all day, but I did use the restroom a few times. Also...there were those few minutes when I was getting cake in the break room. If Hudson had called my desk then, I wouldn't have known, and it's not like Kendra would have reported it to me either.

Lucy was already reaching for her phone. "Here, let me ask him."

"It's okay!" My voice was screechy high as I held out my hands to stop her. "Don't do that."

She frowned and tipped her head down so she could get a better look at me. "You don't want me to?"

"No."

I didn't want to wake the beast for no good reason.

She clicked her phone back into place. "All right then... how about I see if I can get you booked into his schedule tomorrow for a meeting? It'll be tight, but—"

"*No!* No. I don't want to take up any of his time. I know he's a busy man."

I was already starting to back away, realizing I made a mistake coming here.

"Oh, sure sure, but not too busy for you." She waved away my words like they were nonsense. "I'm sure he would want to see you considering you're a part of his team now."

Believe me, he *wouldn't*.

"Don't worry about it! Nice meeting you again! *Bye!*"

Then I took off like a bolt of lightning, scared that at any moment Hudson would walk out of his office and see me there talking to Lucy and accuse me of...I don't know, wasting company time.

I think it's wise not to bring Jasper up to speed about Hudson. If he was offended about the cake, the rest of my day would really set him off. There's no sense in worrying him.

I'm a tough girl; I can survive all of this and more on my own.

Probably.

Chapter Six

Hudson

It's Wednesday, my favorite day. Well, any day I'm in the office is my favorite day. I'd sleep here if I could. Or better yet, not sleep at all. At the moment, we have a few different deals in the works, and the tides could easily turn with any of them. I love the excitement and the drama—don't let anyone tell you law is boring. Elwood Hoyt isn't your uncle's dwindling tax law practice.

On my current rotation, I have a major pharmaceutical merger (worth $63 billion), I'm representing Zion Oil as they attempt to purchase a renewable energies company (for $148 million), and I'm helping a British luxury fashion brand who's anxious to scoop up a few smaller brands (collectively worth $597 million).

I'm in such a good mood I almost give in when a senior associate attempts to strike up a conversation with me in the elevator.

Almost.

On the 70th floor, I head straight for my office. Lucy's in there, laying out documents on my desk like she usually does in the mornings. I zero in on the steaming mug of coffee sitting right in front of my computer.

My eyebrows nearly touch my hairline. "You brought me coffee?"

This is an absolute first.

Lucy snorts. "Over my dead body. If you think I'm about to start waiting on you hand and foot, you've got another think coming. It's from Scarlett. She brought it to me to give to you a little while ago, but I told her to just set it down herself. I still needed to go to the printer anyway."

I scowl at her in a way that would cause anyone else to worry about losing bladder control. Doesn't even faze Lucy though.

"You let her in here on her own?" My voice booms.

She rolls her eyes. "What was she going to do, steal company secrets?"

I look around my desk for anything damning, but it's neat and tidy, completely free of personal effects—just the way I like it. "You have a point. Were you able to print the latest 409A valuation for SolarCo?"

"The appraisers haven't sent it to us yet."

That was supposed to be done *yesterday*. "How long does a damn appraisal take?"

"Well…"

"That was a rhetorical question. Did she spit in it, you think?" I'm pointing down at the mug now. It's tempting to take a sip. She filled it all the way to the top, no cream.

"The coffee? I would have."

"No way to tell if it's been poisoned…" I hold it over toward Lucy. "Here, you taste it first."

"That's above my pay grade, I'm afraid. How about I get by my phone in case I need to call 9-1-1 real quick?"

"Real quick? You've never been quick in your whole damn life."

"Right, well, good luck with your poisoned coffee. Oh and by the way, Scarlett came by yesterday afternoon too. Seemed kind of rattled. She wanted to be sure you hadn't tried to contact her about anything. I asked if she wanted to schedule a time to meet with you and she nearly jumped out of her skin telling me no."

"I can see from your accusing stare you think I've done something to her."

"You better not have."

"*Relax*." Then I harden my features. "Though I'm not sure why you'd care."

She props her hand on her hip. "I knew that girl when she was still in diapers. Cute as can be—still is." She smiles. "Ah, so you noticed that too."

I immediately relax my face just in case I was giving something away. "What the hell are you on about?"

She waggles her finger toward me. "I saw that little spark in your eyes when I mentioned her."

I roll my non-sparking eyes. "You've really lost it. They

say your mind can go"—I snap—"just like that at your age."

She barks out a laugh and shakes her head, turning to leave my office. "I left your mail for you on your desk. Now I don't want you bothering me for *at least* an hour. I'm going to drink my tea and do some of my crossword in peace before the phones start ringing off the hook."

"Whatever you say." I'm already reaching down to rifle through my mail. Invitations, marketing materials, letters—I get all my correspondence sent here, rather than my house. Near the middle of today's stack, I spot a cream envelope that feels luxuriously heavy in my hand. Boy do rich people love thick cardstock, let me tell you.

I slice through the top of it with my letter opener to see it's a save the date for Conrad Elwood's wedding. The first weekend in March, he'll marry a woman named Hannah Kline here in Chicago. I'm not surprised I've been invited. Though Conrad practices in the Los Angeles office now, he was assigned to my team as a summer associate at the Chicago office years and years ago. On top of that, this will likely be a massive wedding. I wouldn't be surprised if every partner at the firm has received the save-the-date.

I set it aside so Lucy can add it to my calendar. Then, quickly, I pick it back up to read how they've addressed the envelope: *Hudson Rhodes and guest.*

Oh goodie.

I'm mulling over my date options—all zero of them—when Lucy shouts a belated, "Mr. Elwood wants to see you!"

I gotta get a new assistant, man.

Scarlett's brother is already walking through my door, not bothering with a knock. That's what I get for leaving my door open. When he leaves, I'll deadbolt it shut.

"Barrett, a pleasure. Wish I had time for whatever you're about to say, but I don't, so if you could—"

"Humor me, Rhodes. You can spare two seconds, I'm sure."

Wanting to get this over with quickly, I wave for him to get on with it. At least I can continue opening my mail while he talks. Multitasking is a particular joy of mine. I can do two, three things at once at any given moment.

"Word spread about the new-hire assignments. Scarlett shouldn't be on your team."

Here we go. I'm not surprised he's here to discuss this. I figured he'd come find me eventually.

"Your dad put her there, so take your issue up with him." I say this while glancing over a junk mail flyer for a car detailing service. Fifty bucks for interior *and* exterior detailing—that's not bad.

"You didn't move her yourself?"

I flip the flyer over to review the front. "Why would I have done that?"

He shakes his head, frowning, thinking... Obviously, this isn't how he thought this conversation would go.

"Take your sister off my service. I don't care, but this whole charade is getting a little tiring. I'd rather not have a rotating door of Elwoods coming in and out of my office every day."

He's frowning at me, giving me the macho act. "If he wants her on your service, that's fine. But *I'm warning you*, if you—"

I suddenly groan like I'm being choked to death. "Oh god. *Save it.* Your dad already beat you to it. You know you two are really doing her no favors. Enough with the cavemen bullshit.

Is she an attorney or is she not?"

He scowls, but at least he shuts up. That's progress.

"Your sister is going to be fine." I reach for my mug. "She actually brought me coffee this morning."

I go for the first sip, taking a gamble on the whole poisoning thing. I'd hate to give Barrett the pleasure of watching me die an agonizing death, but I figure it's worth the risk to see his shocked expression.

Mmm. Freshly brewed pecan blend, my favorite.

"You have her bringing you coffee?"

Oh, he's pissed.

My smug smile nearly sends him over the edge. These Elwoods are so easy to toy with. Scarlett has the same temper as her brother, as evidenced by her little outburst yesterday. I've never had an associate—a *first*-year associate at that—call me an asshole. *To my face.*

I almost smiled when I heard her say it. I had to bite down on the inside of my cheek to keep my amusement from showing in that conference room.

"Getting a partner a cup of coffee is hardly outside the realm of possibilities for a new hire," I tell him.

Barrett clenches his jaw before wisely turning to leave so things don't escalate further. "Do us all a favor and, for once, be a decent human."

A decent human!? Now that's asking too much...

Sure, I could have cleared the issue up with him, told him his little sister *voluntarily* brought me coffee this morning rather than me demanding it of her, but eh, too late.

"Hey, Luce!" I shout. "Come get this flyer and schedule my car to get detailed, will you?"

To which Lucy replies, loud and clear, "No!"

Fucking crossword book—that's the last time I get her a Christmas present.

I work tirelessly through the morning and, occasionally, I think of Scarlett. I'm not totally sure what tasks I should send her way. I mean, I know I could do all the usual fun things: laundry pick-up, a little shoeshine, send her across town to get one single cookie. All of that is great, don't get me wrong, but where's the inspiration? Where's the real wickedness?

Truth be told, when I told her I'd have extra work for her yesterday, I was talking out of my ass. I don't have extra work. I do my work—with pleasure. I'm a control freak, and the last thing I'm going to do is let some first-year associate come anywhere near one of my contracts.

I'm still at the drawing board concerning the Scarlett situation when, around lunchtime, I head down to our building's food court. Usually, Lucy will come down to get us both something to eat. Today, I volunteered to do it. I've been at my desk all morning and needed a little break. No, it has nothing to do with Lucy complaining about a headache.

I enjoy the quick walk. Later, I'll use the building's gym to work out, but for now, browsing the restaurant options in the food court will have to suffice for physical activity. Lucy requested Chinese food, which is just plain insane. Chinese food in the middle of the day? I opt for a sandwich and salad combo from a deli instead, knowing full well I'll put away half of Lucy's Chinese food when she inevitably doesn't finish it. This way, though, I get the added health benefits of eating two lunches instead of one.

I'm waiting for the deli to finish making my turkey club when I scan the crowded seating area. I'm not consciously looking for Scarlett until I spot her left of center at a table by herself. She's eating a salad topped with—I narrow my eyes trying to make out her plate from way over here—grilled chicken. Huh, so she's health-conscious like me.

"Wait, did you want double cheese on this?" the teenager behind the counter asks me.

"Yeah, load 'er up."

Scarlett's reading a book while she eats, stuffing bite after bite into her mouth in quick succession like she's in a hurry to get out of here. Maybe she's in a rush to get back to work, or maybe she wants to avoid the other first-years from our department who are sitting only a few tables away from her. All ten of them are together, everyone sitting and goofing off while they eat—everyone except her.

Why?

Is it by choice? Did the group invite her to join and she declined? That doesn't seem right. Why alienate yourself from your peers this early on? I mean, *I* didn't make friends when I was her age, but that's different.

I'm still watching when a guy walks up to her table and bends down to talk to her. Scarlett's face lights up. The guy points down at the unoccupied chair right beside Scarlett, and I expect him to tug it out and sit down to join her. Instead, he pulls the chair away and plops it down at a new table, leaving Scarlett there, still all alone.

She looks up and around, her cheeks red. When our eyes meet, her gaze widens, and then she looks down quickly, brushing her hair behind her ear and acting as if it never happened.

"Here's your turkey club."

I take my sandwich and am about to curve around the edge of the food court and head toward the elevators. That's the plan, at least until I somehow get lost on the way and end up right in front of Scarlett.

She's looking down. She hasn't seen me. From this angle, she seems so small and fragile.

Christ, when's the last time I thought that about someone?

"What are you doing?" I ask the question brusquely, but that's just how I talk. Ask Lucy; she'll confirm my factory settings are gruff or gruffer.

Scarlett's head shoots up in surprise, and I love watching the flurry of emotions race across her face. First is shock, but that quickly gives way to suspicion. I see it all in her inquisitive brow. Then, oh yes, anger. Her red lips thin into an annoyed line.

"I'm eating," she says pointedly. She doesn't like that I've come over here and interrupted her, I guess. Or who knows—I can't possibly begin to understand this girl. All I know is she's looking up at me with a scowl like she'd like me to excuse myself as efficiently as possible. I bet she's wishing she had an evacuation button she could employ.

"Why not with them?" I tilt my head in the direction of the other first-years.

She looks their way and then turns back quickly, her cheeks turning red again. "Who cares? Does it matter? I'm just finishing up my salad while I read."

She flips a page to prove her point. I'll just bet she wasn't done reading it yet. She'll have to turn back when I walk away. The thought almost makes me laugh.

"Is it the last-name thing? Like you can't deign to lower your standards and befriend a group of regular people?"

Her jaw drops. "Are you *kidding*?"

Okay good, so she's not a snob.

"So then they're being assholes."

That's what I assumed, and I'm glad my intuition was right.

"Your brother came to my office this morning. That marks two visits from family members warning me to go easy on you. Should I expect your mother this afternoon?"

She rears back, surprised, and I wonder if she knew about either visit. Her tone lightens a little with her reply. "My mother's in Europe, so no. But...don't be shocked if you get a call from Wyatt or Conrad." She sounds resigned as she continues, "They're just as protective as Barrett."

Then she looks back down at her book, turning yet another page. Dismissing me *again*. At this rate she'll have to turn back a few chapters once I leave.

"I want you to sit in on a call with me this afternoon and take notes."

She looks up and blinks fast, trying to compute this new task in her head. "Okay, I'm supposed to finish up a draft of a contract for Sophie, but I can push that and—"

"I don't need your entire life story. Find a way to be in my office for a 4:00 p.m. phone call."

Then I walk away before I do something stupid, like ask her if she wants to come and eat lunch with Lucy and me.

Chapter Seven

Scarlett

'm in the lobby outside Hudson's office by 3:50 p.m. and not a minute later.

Lucy's at her desk, watching a little TV that's set up on the built-in counter behind her desk. It's barely a foot wide in any direction with a grainy screen and a slot for a VHS tape.

"How *old* is that thing?" I can't help the question from tumbling out.

"Shhh! It's just getting good. She's about to tell him the baby isn't his."

She's watching a soap opera. While at work.

I have so many questions…

"Get in here," Hudson says from his open door before he turns and storms back into his office.

I roll my eyes and call out to him as I follow. "Have you ever heard the expression you catch more flies with honey than vinegar?"

Lucy bursts out laughing. "You tell him!"

"Don't listen to her," he retorts dryly, referring to Lucy. "She's senile."

"Look at that! Another vacation day added to my schedule!" Lucy shouts back tauntingly.

Hudson totally ignores her as he reclaims his seat behind his desk.

I look around the room. "Where should I…"

He frowns at the question. "Anywhere. Have you never been inside an office before? Where there's a chair, yeah, that's where you're allowed to put your butt."

A sassy response is begging to be set free. Truly, this is the hardest I've had to work at holding my tongue in…forever.

But yesterday, I let my whims get away from me with that "asshole" comment. Today, we're repenting. I'm going to zip my lips and take my chair and pretend I'm sitting across from the nicest man in the world. A real saint.

"Not that one," Hudson says with an exasperated sigh when I choose a chair halfway across the room from him. I was trying to put a bit of distance between us. For safety. "You won't even be able to hear the damn call if you're way over there."

"Then tell me where you want me!"

Ope, look at that. Back at square one.

I squeeze my eyes closed and do a deep breathing exercise I make up right now on the spot. *Picture Hudson as a balloon floating far, far away, never to be seen or heard from ever again.*

Oh, an even better one! *Picture Hudson as a balloon stuck up on the tallest branch of the tallest tree for the rest of eternity.*

"Here."

My eyes fly open as he curves around his desk to grab a heavy upholstered chair. He drags it around the corner so it's not exactly behind his desk where his chair is, but it's not where guests normally sit either. It's in a weird in-between spot, and it puts me only a few feet away from him. In the danger zone, so to speak. I can smell his cologne from here. If I go any closer? Who knows what could happen.

He points to it until I walk around and take my seat, dutifully.

"Now just listen and take notes."

"Will this be for a grade?"

His eyes narrow, but underneath the stern exterior, I swear he's enjoying this. "Are you trying to test my patience?"

"Quite frankly, I'm not sure. My original plan was to be nice to you today."

"And how's that going for you?"

I arch my brow just as the phone on his desk rings. He's still looking at me as he answers it.

"Rhodes," he says by way of greeting. Then, "Yeah, listen, TJ, let me put you on speaker. I've got a junior associate here with me and she's promised not to interrupt."

I made no such promise, but I do know when to pick my battles and this is not one of them. I mime closing a zipper over my lips, and Hudson swaps the call over to speakerphone so I can hear both sides.

There is no explanation or context given, no attempt to get me up to speed from either party. Hudson and TJ both act like I'm not there as they launch into their meeting. Unsurprisingly, there's no small talk or polite conversation. I can't even imagine Hudson asking someone how their day is going. It's laughable. Though to be fair, with attorneys, time is valuable, and there's no sense in squandering it for no good reason.

I gather most of the pertinent information quickly enough, because, thank you, I'm not completely useless even though everyone in my life seems to think I am. TJ is a partner at our Los Angeles office. Apparently, he's helping Hudson on a pharmaceutical merger.

After only a few minutes of them chatting on the phone, I clue in to their pending problem. They're both concerned about how the regulatory requirements set by the HSR Act will affect the merger and the closing timeline. I know both parties in a merger have to file an HSR review with the Federal Trade Commission and the Department of Justice. This was already done, I gather from their conversation. Unfortunately, that preliminary review proved that further investigation is needed.

This is bad news for everyone.

"I've never had a clearance process take this long. A few days, sure. A week or two, *okay*. But it's been over two months now," TJ complains. "Why doesn't the FTC just take it over and get the ball rolling?"

"Because I think they're drawing this out so they can put together a task force with a group of FTC and DOJ staff. I mean who knows how far they'll take it. They could pull in the attorney general, academics, other experts—the sky's the limit."

TJ groans. "You're kidding me."

Hudson's apparently not one to sit during phone calls. He's been pacing behind his desk, walking a few short feet and then abruptly turning back, all the while fidgeting with a stress ball. Now, he sets the ball down and starts clicking and un-clicking a pen. "I had it happen to me two years ago. It was hell to slog through, let me just say that. Our client was extremely unhappy about how long the process took, and I had to hear about it *daily*. Both companies threatened to walk away a few times before closing."

Hudson stops behind his desk and leans over on his hands, letting his head hang suspended. I'm in a relationship and also not looking and also this is my boss's boss or something like that, so this doesn't count—but say I were *any* other person in *any* other setting...let's just get one thing straight: Hudson is so, *so* sexy it's almost unbearable to be in this office alone with him right now.

First of all: the suit. We need a moment of silence to honor the tailor who poured this man into *this* particular cut and style. And navy wool...chef's kiss.

Beyond that: it's the body. Formidable height, wide shoulders, tapered waist. Every last thing about him is noteworthy from his tanned hands splayed powerfully against his desk to that thick dark hair—short on the sides, longer up top. It's just begging to be tousled by a set of hands *THAT AREN'T MINE.*

I realize I'm completely and shamelessly ogling him, and I chastise myself.

"So how do we smooth things over?" TJ asks.

"We don't."

"We could fail to comply."

I balk, and Hudson shoots me a death glare. Oh right, I'm meant to be an invisible fly on the wall.

"I'm going to assume you were kidding just now."

"What?" TJ adds incredulously. "There are certain loopholes. We could take the naive approach, say we were unaware this merger met the HSR Act thresholds and beg for forgiveness afterward. They'll slap us with civil penalties—"

"You're talking about two of the biggest pharmaceutical companies in the country playing dumb about an antitrust act put in place to prevent a market monopoly? Tell me that's not your bright idea."

Hudson is absolutely in the right here. TJ's suggestion was just plain stupid. There's no begging for forgiveness from the FTC.

"Since 2009, the FTC has challenged nine consummated mergers," I say, to myself, but Hudson still hears it.

"And I refuse to be number ten." He turns back to the phone. "Think of something else."

Then he picks up the receiver and sets it down, ending the call.

God, that was...exhilarating.

My entire body is buzzing.

I feel like I just had really great sex.

Hudson looks over and studies me, likely aware of how much I just enjoyed that phone call. I have no doubt there's an excited sheen in my eyes, a rosy color on my cheeks. Oh god, am I breathing hard?

"What are the current HSR thresholds?" he asks, obviously wanting the answers quickly.

"They change annually."

His dark taunting brow says, *Humor me.* "What are the *current* thresholds?"

"There's the size-of-traction test that's met if the value of the equity or assets to be acquired exceeds $90 million."

"*And...*"

"Size-of-person test, which only applies if the transaction is valued between $90 million and $359.9 million."

He nods like he's proud.

"However, there are variations to these tests," I go on. "Depending on whether the parties are engaged in manufacturing. Also, at least one party must be operating in the United States for either test to apply."

He nods. "Good, now go."

I deflate in my chair.

Go? We were just getting started!

"Surely there's more. We could brainstorm ways to work around the HSR filing delay. Maybe call the FTC or DOJ and—"

"Get back to your own work now, Scarlett."

He's already refocused his attention on a document on his desk.

"Will you tell me what you two figure out?"

"*Go.*"

"That's not fair. You can't bring me in on this and not let me see it through. That's painful."

He chuckles under his breath and shakes his head, still not looking at me.

"Should I have Lucy come escort you out? She might not look tough, but she has a little muscle on her."

I scowl at him, wishing I could do more.

"So what was the point of this then?"

He flips a paper over. "To learn. That's all. I would have begged to sit in on a phone call with two partners when I was in your position."

"So you want me to beg?"

His head snaps up and he flays me with those brown eyes. "So help me, Scarlett...get out of my office."

Even now, even as worked up as he is, I just can't seem to fear him the way I ought to. Maybe I should see a therapist. Maybe there's a screw loose in my head. This is Hudson Rhodes! The worst of the worst, and I can't seem to feel truly threatened by him, only slightly annoyed. It's like he's an itch I can't scratch.

I gather my things and start to head toward the door. I'm in no rush to get back to that office with Kendra. She hasn't said a single word to me all day.

Hudson has gone back to reviewing that document, but he still has a few departing words for me. "You could try to change their opinion about you."

I pause, but I don't turn back toward him. I know he's referring to my fellow first-year associates. He saw me sitting alone at lunch. What he doesn't know is that all of them came by my office to pick up Kendra on their way down to the food court, and every last one of them ignored me sitting there at my desk.

I even looked up and tried. I smiled and waved to see if we couldn't get something going, but they must all have been under strict orders to pay me no attention because there were no returned smiles or waves, no acknowledgment of any kind.

"Did you *see* her cake yesterday?" Ramona asked on the way out.

"Daddy's little girl!" Makayla replied with the same bitchy tone.

My stomach squeezes tight with the painful memory, but I shake myself free of it as quickly as I can. There will always be difficult people. I don't have to let them hurt me, or worse, stoop to their level.

"I don't really care what they think about me."

"Right. Well if it becomes a real problem, you could always tell your dad, or HR."

I don't respond right away. Hudson is suggesting I go talk to my dad in a totally different way than Jasper suggested last night. This feels more like a test, like Hudson wants to know where my head is at, wants to figure out what kind of person I really am. Am I the type to fold or the type to fight?

"No," I finally say with tenacious resolve, turning to look back at him.

He's the embodiment of power, standing there behind his desk with the cityscape framed at his back. He's the fiercest enemy you could ever meet. I hope I seem even a *quarter* as capable as he does. Maybe I should ask where he gets his suits, if there's a lady's version of that silver watch on his wrist. Maybe I could ask him to teach me how to furrow my eyebrows in that subtle way that's both handsome and terrifying.

"Well that leaves your third and final option," he says with resolute determination. "The one I would choose myself. You can ignore them and get to work. You can define yourself on your own terms rather than by the opinions of others. Outwork them all, Scarlett."

I lift my chin and leave his office.

Don't worry. *I plan to.*

It's after 8:00 p.m. by the time I leave. Kendra left at 6:45 to get drinks with Ramona and Makayla. I wasn't invited, obviously, so I stayed behind and I worked. I had to cancel my usual post-dinner workout with my kickboxing trainer, and I suppose I could drag myself down to my apartment's state-of-the-art gym after I scrounge together something to eat, but I just don't have it in me today.

When I get home, I push open my apartment door with an armful of packages I just picked up from the mail room downstairs. Don't ask me what any of it is. Late at night, I have no self-control. When those targeted ads reveal to me some revolutionary water bottle or a never-before-invented bra, I'm such a sucker.

My cat Moira (aka Moira Rose) sits on the windowsill in the living room with her long white tail dangling off the edge, waving back and forth with fluid, lazy motions. She makes no move to greet me, not that I expect her to. On any given day, I'm barely allowed within a few feet of her. If she had it her way, I wouldn't enter the apartment at all. I'd shove a can of extremely expensive, putrid-smelling cat food through a slot in the door and leave her the hell alone.

My dad gave her to me as a law school graduation present. "She's a British Shorthair. I read all about the breed. They're friendly and smart, supposed to make great family pets."

I'm not sure if he read the wrong Wikipedia page or if my British Shorthair is just defective, but if I had to list adjectives to describe Moira, "family friendly" wouldn't make the cut. She's sassy, arrogant, and mean. Smart, yes—too smart for her own good. More than once, she's figured out how to slide the deadbolt on the front door so I couldn't get into my apartment until the building's super could come down and disassemble my lock.

She's the queen of this dwelling, and she'd like me to never forget it.

"Did you miss me today?" I ask cheekily.

I swear she rolls her eyes. Her bored expression tells me she was hoping I was flattened by a trash truck on my way home, but alas, since I'm here, I might as well feed her.

I set down my packages, wincing when I see the one from La Perla. I remember the lacy black lingerie set I ordered last week on a whim. Now, in the light of day, it just seems cheesy as hell. Who am I going to wear that for? *Jasper?*

He'd choke.

We don't do any of that. I mean, I don't think he's against it or anything, but he's never been open in that way. He's a traditional guy when it comes to most things. Even discussing sex makes him blush, like it's some weird shameful thing. The lingerie will get sent back or, more likely, because I have zero extra time for running errands at the moment, stuffed into the farthest recesses of my panty drawer.

Moira jumps off her window perch and screeches like, *Open your crap on your own time. I'm hungry.* Inside the cupboard beside my refrigerator, I grab her food—all seventy-five different things I have to mix together twice a day to prolong her crabby little life according to the fancy vet I take her to.

"You know some cats live in the streets and eat garbage."

She's not listening; she's licking her butt.

Once I set down her bowl on the hardwood, she nudges it over to where she prefers it: smack dab in the center of the kitchen runner I splurged on when I moved into my apartment a few months back.

"No, please, try to get as much of that smelly fish ground down into the rug. Thank you."

I sigh and look at the mountain of packages and junk mail on the counter. Then I decide to forgo opening any of it in lieu of opening the freezer. Dinner tonight will be the finest Ben & Jerry's ice cream purchased from the finest dingy corner store down the block. I crack the lid to find I have less than half a pint left, which is disappointing, but I'm certainly not hauling my ass back out into the world to get more, and ordering it on a delivery app is out of the question. With all their weird fees and tips, another pint would cost more than that ridiculously priced La Perla set.

I work my bra off through the sleeve of my shirt and grab my laptop and phone from my work bag before finding the section of the couch that allows me to burrow deepest between the center cushions. Once my fuzzy throw blanket is covering my legs and my favorite candle is lit—oh baby, *it's on*. Short of nuclear war, I will not be getting up from this spot for the remainder of the night.

I'm a little reluctant to check my phone. I've been ignoring Jasper's text messages all day. We don't talk all that often during the week; we're both busy. He's in and out of court, and I never know when I'll be able to reach him. I don't want to accidentally call him if he's in the middle of something important, so we usually reserve communication for the end of the day, or really, every other day. Or on the weekends, actually. My friends from law school think our entire setup is weird, but it's not weird. We're adults. We don't need to send each other cutesy text messages and memes every five seconds.

I think their argument is that we don't spend enough time together in general. When I graduated from Columbia and moved back to Chicago, everyone expected me to move in with Jasper, but I was not interested in that at all. I made some excuse like, "Oh *ha ha*, not until there's a ring!"

But in truth, I just...am in no rush to shack up with him. I like my mean cat and my girly scented candles and my all-white bedding. Why would I want to have to accommodate a stinky man?

Not that Jasper is stinky. Just...I don't want to live with him yet.

Hudson suddenly comes to mind, completely unbidden. The thought of him here in my apartment. His scent masking my floral candle. His suit jacket slung over a dining room chair.

My tummy flips and I refocus my attention on excavating a morsel of fudge from the bottom of my ice cream pint like I'm a highly trained archaeologist. Once it's melting on my tongue, I check my phone. I have 29 unread text messages. Most are from my group text with my law school friends, a group of four girls I lived with in the city last year. Since graduation, we've all moved on to our big girl jobs and big girl lives, though not everyone has started work yet. Big law firms have varying start dates through September and into October. Two of my friends don't start in their positions for another two weeks, so they're living it up in Mexico, happily spending their advances at an all-inclusive resort. They've sent photos of the beach and the sunset, and I don't want to rain on their parade with details of my last two days, so I respond to their lives instead, asking about the resort and demanding a running tally of their poolside piña coladas.

Then I reluctantly open the texts from Jasper that I've been ignoring all day.

Jasper: *Have things cooled off at all at the office? If not...talk to your dad. You shouldn't have to work in a hostile environment.*

Jasper: *I just called Barrett to talk to him about it, but he didn't answer.*

Then, a few hours later:

Jasper: *My parents want to have us over for dinner on Friday.*

Oh great. The last thing I want to do after my first week of work is spend my Friday night with Jasper's parents. Don't get me wrong, the Beringers are nice, but they're completely overbearing. Their house is extremely formal, and their idea of a casual dinner at home includes a hired chef and multiple uniformed staff. It's all for show. They're no more well off than my own family and yet you'd think they were British aristocracy or something with the way they flaunt their fancy lifestyle.

A casual dinner at my house consists of my mom making appetizers while my dad whips something up on the grill. He loves making steak or hamburgers, and sometimes he'll grill salmon—my favorite. Barrett and Nyles usually volunteer for dessert duty, and when the weather's nice, we eat outside on the back patio, barefoot and happy with a few uncorked bottles of wine.

I obviously can't refuse Jasper, though. We don't see his parents all that often, and I don't want to make it difficult for him.

Scarlett: *Friday sounds good.*

Then I toss my phone aside and open my laptop. I check my email first to confirm if anything has come in from work since I left the office. There's a new meeting request from Sophie that I add to my calendar, but otherwise, I'm still caught up with everything I wanted to complete today.

With nothing else to do and because I've been desperately wanting to do it since I left his office this afternoon, I spend the rest of my night educating myself on Hudson's pharmaceutical merger. I happened to know the answers to his questions today, but if he invites me in on another phone call tomorrow, I want to be sure I know my stuff.

Chapter Eight

Scarlett

I think, though I can't be certain, that Kendra has shifted my desk so it's pressed farther into the corner of the office. I don't remember hitting my head on this plant yesterday, but now every time I swivel in my chair, the fronds tickle my hair.

After an hour of dealing with it, I groan and shoot to my feet. My first attempt to move my desk is an utter failure. On the second try, I put some real muscle behind it and manage to shift it a few inches, creating a screech so loud every person across the city just winced and covered their ears.

"You mind?" Kendra snaps.

She has her headphones on while she works. She's not on a call or anything though, so…I ignore her and push my desk another few inches. Better. I'll no longer have to sit beneath a leafy canopy, at least.

"God you're insufferable."

"*Me?*" I snap, whirling around to face her.

She rolls her eyes.

I cross my arms and stand up tall; suddenly I'm over it. "Did you move my desk?"

"No. I didn't move your desk." Her mocking tone makes it clear she thinks I'm nuts.

God, have I lost it? With a heavy sigh, I try a different tactic. "You know we don't have to keep doing this. It's day three—surely you're starting to get tired."

"Tired? Of what?" she asks, pretending to be stupid now that I'm actually calling her out on her rude behavior.

I don't even keep the sarcasm out of my tone when I reply, "What's your goal exactly? To make me suffer?"

She looks at her computer. "I have no idea what you're talking about."

"I'm not that different than you. We could be friends, you know."

Her mouth thins with disgust at the idea. "I'm all tapped out on friends at the moment."

Fine.

I go around my desk and take my seat. I'm about to refocus my attention on a contract when she speaks up again. Her tone isn't nasty, but it's still harsh. "For the record, you are different from me and my friends. Most of us don't have daddy dearest as a safety net. We have hundreds of thousands in student loans to pay back, a career on the line. We've *worked* to get here."

My jaw tightens in annoyance. "I earned my place here. Same as you."

She rolls her eyes. "Sure."

"I scored a 169 on my LSAT."

She laughs. "Like I care? I'll bet you had every single tutor imaginable, someone to guide you through step by step. I'm actually surprised you didn't get a *perfect* score to be quite honest. Meanwhile, I took the LSAT while I was working part-time at a law library *and* putting myself through college *and* taking eighteen hours of upper-division courses."

"That's incredibly impressive. You should be proud."

She rolls her eyes.

Suddenly, I know, no matter what, I'll never win with her. I could tell her I finished second in my class at Columbia Law and she'd find some way to twist it around on me. No amount of hard work will amount to much in her eyes.

At the end of the day, she's right. Out of the two of us, she had the harder road getting here. I won't argue that. I just don't understand what she wants from me now.

I steady my voice, trying my hardest to smooth things over once and for all. "I understand that I had a leg up in this industry, and I'm not trying to lord that over anyone. In fact, I'd like to separate myself from my last name as much as possible. I want to work and prove myself here, same as you."

"Okay, Kendall Jenner..."

Her snide remark is the last straw. Is she kidding?! I'm not using my long legs to strut down a catwalk. I'm using my brain to practice law. I want to explode in a myriad of ways, to argue my point until the cows come home, but Hudson's advice from yesterday comes through just when I need it the most.

Ignore them and get to work.

He's right.

I grab the contract I need to review and work straight through lunch. Sophie wanted me to edit a letter of intent and get it back to her by 3:00 p.m., so I do one better and get it to her *with* additional notes by 1:00. Then, I also draw up an exclusivity agreement for her to review.

A lot of my work as a lower-level associate involves constant communication with clients. Even though it's only my first week on the job, I'm already sending and receiving over a hundred emails a day, *easy*. A large portion of that communication results from being part of a team. Since I'm working beneath Sophie, most emails she gets, I'm CC'd on as well. Compared to Hudson's workload, Sophie's deals are small potatoes, but it's still a lot of responsibility.

There's a closing scheduled for next week and another scheduled for the week after that. Both deals require a lot of documentation, and it's my job to confirm we're getting everything delivered to our clients to review in a timely manner, signed, and filed away appropriately. Staying on top of paperwork in mergers like this is half the battle, and though it takes time (*unpaid* time) for me to do it, I'm trying to stay as organized as possible.

I don't leave my office until 7:32 p.m., and Elwood Hoyt is far from empty. Half of the office is still going strong, which makes me think maybe I should still be working too. Kendra's gone. In fact, none of the first-year associates are still here. It's Hudson's corner of the office that's abuzz with life. Upon closer inspection, I see Lucy's at her desk, but other attorneys file in and out of Hudson's office. Some are even splayed out on the floor or the couches in his reception area. Whatever is going on must be big if it requires all hands on deck.

I'm slightly envious of everyone involved, which is hilarious given the circumstances. *I wish I were getting the privilege of staying late, getting orders barked at me by Hudson Rhodes?*

Well…kinda.

I almost emailed him last night and again this afternoon, just to check in and confirm there wasn't anything else he needed from me. He hasn't reached out once since I left his office yesterday afternoon, and I refused to bring him another cup of coffee this morning. There have been no further tasks, none of the "favoritism in reverse" he promised me. I should be happy about that, I suppose.

I'm about to pivot toward the elevators and be on my merry way when I suddenly stop.

Be assertive. Go after what you want.

Hudson's office draws me in like a moth to a flame.

Associates are everywhere. Papers. Memos. Highlighters. Pens. Laptops. Empty soda cans. Venti coffee cups with ice cubes swimming in pale dregs. Bethany and Sophie are sharing Lucy's desk. Bethany has two pens tucked behind her right ear and another behind her left. She's furiously flipping through pages when she looks up and sees me standing in the threshold between the hallway and the sitting area.

"Do you need help?" I ask with a lopsided smile.

It's a dumb question. It's like I'm watching a person drown in a pool, and instead of jumping in to help, I call out to them, *Hey! Everything good?*

She's probably about to tell me to fuck off. Instead, she points to a thick stack of papers bound with black plastic rings.

"Sit down, read through that. Highlight anything pertinent. We're examining KinBio's numbers, comparing them over time and benchmarking them against competitors."

My ears perk up. KinBio is the pharmaceutical company Hudson discussed on the phone yesterday. Did the FTC get back to him today? Is the merger moving forward?

I drop my things immediately and am about to pick up the bound pages when Bethany's stomach audibly growls. Sophie laughs, and I look around the room, registering that most everyone is in the same boat: tired, overworked, hungry.

"Have any of you eaten?"

An attorney across the room jerks his head up with wide eyes. "Shit. *Dinner.* I knew I forgot something."

The concept of an evening meal hadn't even occurred to him, or anyone else in the room for that matter.

"Why don't I—"

Bethany's already waving her hand for me to get on with it. "*Order*, yes! Whatever. Just get something here ASAP."

I go with pizza and salads from my favorite place down the street, and I charge it to the company card Bethany hands me. Firms like Elwood Hoyt are happy to pay for a $12 slice of pepperoni pizza while you continue working overtime helping to make them millions upon millions of dollars, so I go overboard. I make sure everyone has a fresh drink, and I tack on a bunch of appetizers and a few dessert options because who doesn't want an ooey-gooey brownie fresh out of the oven after having ingested enough grease to require a truckload of Tums?

I add a rush delivery fee, and when my phone chimes, I run down with an empty supply cart and meet the delivery guy at the entrance.

"Did you uh…order all this?" The stoned teenager can't comprehend how little ol' me could need this much pizza. Now that I'm seeing it, it's a lot. Oh well.

I sign the bill and help him load everything up on the cart.

"Please tell me you brought the plates and silverware I requested."

If not, I'll have a mutiny on my hands.

"Yeah, it's all in there."

Perfect. I tip him generously then cart the food to the 70th floor, trying not to salivate from all the delicious smells surrounding me during my trip up in the elevator.

My reappearance is met with what could only be described as the reaction Jesus might expect to get on his homecoming.

"OH MY GOD."

"FUCKING HELL YES."

"*MOVE!*"

They can't get to me—or my pizza—fast enough.

I start opening boxes, explaining the options. "That one is meat lovers, this one's margherita."

I pass out plates and drinks, toss the salads, and get everyone in the sitting area taken care of before I start loading up plates and bringing them into Hudson's office.

There are four attorneys inside. Two work from his couch, using the coffee table as a desk. Another one is spread out at a side table that was covered in achievement awards yesterday. Now those sit on the ground. Hudson sits behind his desk on a call, tilted back in his chair, tossing his stress ball up into the air over and over again in quick succession so he can catch it and continue. He clocks my arrival with predatorial precision. His brown eyes lock onto me and then narrow slightly.

My stomach flips. He's sans suit jacket and tie. The sleeves on his white button-down are rolled up on his toned forearms. It looks like maybe he hasn't shaved since yesterday because he's sporting a sexy amount of scruff. He looks meaner with it, too tough for this setting. Truth be told, that face is wasted in this job. He should be working security for some mafia boss, interrogating moles. Those thick expressive eyebrows say everything he can't while he's on the phone.

I hold up the food in question.

He nods toward the other attorneys while continuing his conversation.

"*Thank you!*" the guys each say quietly, quickly accepting the plates.

I rush out to get drinks, sweeping my gaze around to make sure everyone out here is still good to go. Then I start to make Hudson a plate. I'm not sure what kind of pizza he likes and I can't ask him while he's on the phone, so I just give him my favorites: plain pepperoni and a slice of supreme. I add a little salad on the side and, on a hunch, grab him a Coke too.

Back in his office, I find him leaning over his desk, still on the phone, his stress ball forgotten near an empty coffee cup. He watches me as I walk in with his plate and drink. It feels like miles between his door and his desk. I manage to get there without stumbling and spilling his soda everywhere, but only because I take small, measured steps and hold my breath the whole time, thus pleasing the karma gods.

Because I'm not about to accidentally get grease stains on anything important, I set his plate down on the farthest corner of his desk. I straighten and am about to flee as quickly as possible, but I realize he's still watching me with careful reverence.

I look to him, mouthing, "Greek salad," so he'll know what to expect. Then, "Pepperoni. Supreme," pointing at each of the pizzas. Uh, *duh*. It's a little unnecessary to explain to someone living in *Chicago* what pepperoni pizza looks like, but too late to backtrack now.

He shakes his head and mouths, "Have you eaten?"

I shake my head right back, and even though no sound leaves his lips, I'm still absolutely certain from his furrowed brow that he's not pleased with me or my answer.

He's the one actually wheeling and dealing here. He needs the sustenance.

"Eat," he mouths.

I shake my head, and his eyes narrow. I roll my eyes, and before I know it, he's reached out his leg to hook the side of a chair positioned behind me. With his foot, he drags it closer until it bumps the back of my legs. He points, and I sit. Then he waves for me to take a slice. I go for the pepperoni, and he takes the supreme.

"Did you already meet with Nicholson?" he asks the person on the phone.

God.

His voice.

It's...toe-curling. That's what it is. My damn toes are trying to curl in my pumps, and I should be focusing on this pizza and minding my own business. I'd stand and leave if not for the fact that I'm curious about the crisis situation and the person he's on the phone with. Is it TJ? Did the FTC get back to us? The DOJ? Is that why everyone's in a tizzy tonight?

I peer over at Hudson from beneath my lashes and find his attention has strayed to my legs—specifically the stretch of thigh exposed by my skirt riding up a little.

I go rigid and he looks away, but truthfully, it might have been a coincidence. His expression was sort of far-off, like maybe he didn't even realize where he was looking. He didn't flinch or show any other outward signs of guilt, so I write it off and listen as their phone call concludes and Hudson hangs up.

"The pizza's good. Are you going to eat that salad?"

"No, here. It's yours. The Coke too."

I give him a minute to eat before I bombard him, though apparently that was everyone else's plan too. He's immediately flooded with questions and demands for an update. I just sit like a deer caught in headlights, absorbing every second.

Everyone else seems to be wide-eyed and nervous, but Hudson isn't fazed by the intensity of the situation, which actually has nothing to do with the FTC clearance process. Or it does, but not in the way I initially suspected.

The big news of the day is this: our big pharmaceutical merger is headed south and fast. KinBio and Chapman International are suddenly at odds because Chapman's bankers claim (as of today!) that their evaluation of our client, KinBio, shows a rapidly eroding financial profile.

Hudson thinks this is "complete and utter bullshit."

The fact is, Chapman International first approached KinBio with an unsolicited buyout offer three years ago. KinBio turned down that deal and a subsequent one that came a year later before they were finally persuaded to play ball when Chapman agreed to pay KinBio a $570 million breakup fee contingent upon the DOJ and FTC's antitrust ruling. Meaning, if the two companies were prohibited from merging, Chapman International would owe KinBio a lot of money as a consolation prize for all that wasted time and effort.

And guess what decision is looming on the horizon!?

Dum dum DUM...

"Someone talked," Bethany says emphatically. "An informant. Either that or Chapman is just getting spooked about the DOJ's decision and they don't want to have to pay that fee."

Every head in the room swivels in Hudson's direction, waiting for his response. He's the least pissed person in the room. Even *I* feel enraged over this issue, and I've barely dipped my toe into this merger.

He shrugs. "Either way, it's irrelevant. Chapman knew KinBio's financial profile well before today, and we'll be able to prove that. They've had three years to perform their due diligence. If they try to renege on the deal now, they'll have to pay that breakup fee."

He sounds so absolute, so sure of every word that comes out of his mouth. I realize I'm still staring at him, mouth agape, long after he's finished talking, but it's only because I'm slightly amazed by him. He's horrible or whatever, but he's also...brilliant.

I want to be just like him. I want him to teach me his ways step by step.

"You put the breakup fee in the contract."

It's not a question.

His brown gaze slides over to me. "I did."

Even with us all on the same page about what's going on, the fact remains: we have a lot of work ahead of us if KinBio has to go up against Chapman International in court.

I won't be going anywhere anytime soon. Good thing Moira is already taken care of. Two months ago, on one of my late-night shopping sprees, I bought an automatic cat feeder for her. It's just a little food dispenser I can use on days when I get home really late. She hates it, of course. She's tried to dismantle it on multiple occasions. I can sense her fury even from a distance.

Out in the sitting area, Bethany sets me on a task, and I'm about to make myself comfortable on the floor when Hudson barks my name from his office door on his way to get more pizza.

"What are you doing?"

I look up and blink in confusion. Everyone is staring at me accusatorially, like, *Good going! You pissed him off!*

Have I missed something? Did he not realize I was here the whole time? The one feeding him pizza?

"You don't have to sit on the floor," he clarifies, flipping open pizza boxes, trying to decide between his options. "There's room in there."

He means in his office.

"*Oh.*"

There's an audible sigh of relief from the senior associates as if they're glad he's not going to totally annihilate me. It's not that they care about my well-being; it's that they've got enough on their plate without having to worry about skirting around blood on the ground.

I scoop up my things and re-enter the devil's lair. It's weird how much easier it gets each time I do it. Eventually, I'll be stepping into the underworld without so much as a blink.

"Please don't be annoying, just sit down" is Hudson's advice to me as he reclaims his seat and motions for me to take the one he already got for me.

He's...offering to share his desk. He even shoves aside some papers to clear more room for my stuff.

He's a partner. He could quite literally order me to work from a grubby toilet seat in a tiny bathroom stall down the hall and I would be like, *Yes, of course. Let me get right on that.*

Well...with any *other* partner, that's what I'd say. With Hudson, I'd probably argue. A little.

The point is, this is nice of him, and I don't know how I feel about that. Maybe we're both a bit weirded out about the arrangement because we work in silence for a good long while. I start to get a slight crick in my back, and I stretch my arms overhead, trying in vain to work out the kink that won't go away.

I feel Hudson's attention on me and look over to see two deep wrinkles between his brows.

"You can go home, you know."

I smile like, *Yeah, duh.* "I know."

"But you're going to stay." He says it like I exasperate him.

I shrug. "Looks like it."

A few minutes later, I make a point of toeing off my heels and crossing my legs up under me. Formality can go to hell for all I care because it's later than late, my little toesies have been stuck in these high heels for the better part of fourteen hours, and I'm not enduring it for one more patriarchal second. Hudson notices, of course. His brown eyes drift over my legs, but he manages to keep any biting-slash-witty-slash-devastating remarks to himself before he turns back to his work.

And I have to say, I'm kind of disappointed.

I continue my task, reviewing and highlighting, reading and reading and *reading*. My eyes are about to go permanently crossed. I rub them, probably smearing my mascara beyond repair. Then—

"*Scarlett.*"

My eyes freeze on a line of text. The familiar voice doesn't belong here, in this office.

My heart plummets when I look up to see Jasper standing at Hudson's door wearing sweats and a look of fierce determination. My eyes widen in panic. *Oh god. What is he doing here?! How did he even get through security?*

Surely he's not about to take matters into his own hands regarding my not-so-nice coworkers. It's just like him to draw up to my office like a valiant knight in defense of my honor. Never mind that I've made it perfectly clear I'm not in need of any knights! My honor is just fine!

Jasper's worried eyes scan the room, stalling a beat too long on Hudson before he looks at me with relief. He looks suddenly unsure. The tops of his cheeks redden.

"I was worried about you," Jasper tells me. "You weren't answering your cell. I tried your work phone too and nothing. Your doorman said you hadn't come home yet tonight…"

So…*he came to my office?*

On some level, it's considerate, but it almost makes me feel like a child. Especially as all the senior associates in the room *and* the ones out in the sitting area listen in on this conversation.

I feel everyone's attention, the weight of Hudson's gaze heavier than all the rest. Oddly enough, he's the one who speaks first, before I can even muster the right words or gather the courage to figure out what to say in this awkward situation.

"Go home, Scarlett. Work will be here tomorrow."

Either because Hudson is right or because I don't want to argue with him, I quickly collect my things, slip on my heels, and hurry to join Jasper at the door. My cheeks are hotter than hot. The flush is spreading all the way down my neck. With my gaze locked on Jasper's, I shake my head just once to make it perfectly clear I don't want to discuss any more of this while we're still in earshot of my coworkers.

Bethany and Sophie wave bye to me, and I throw them quick nods before walking toward the bank of elevators.

"Did we have plans tonight that I forgot about?" I ask once the doors slide shut behind us and we're alone.

"No."

"Okay..." Already my slight annoyance is starting to dissolve. Jasper isn't a bad guy. This isn't his fault, not really. "Listen, I apologize for not texting you to let you know I'd be at the office late, but that's just going to happen sometimes, Jasper. Probably a lot. You know how bad I am with texting."

"Right." He turns to me. "Texting issue aside...I don't get why you were up here working late. You just started *this* week, Scarlett. That's ridiculous if they're already expecting this much of you."

"They aren't!" I say with a forced laugh, trying to defuse the situation. "No one made me stay—I did it voluntarily."

And though I'm still bitter about getting pulled away from Hudson's desk, I don't want to take it out on Jasper. I wanted to stay as long as Hudson did, burning the midnight oil with him. It was incredibly satisfying to be a part of that team tonight, and I worry Jasper might have just imploded any future opportunities for me.

He reaches out for my hand and squeezes it. "I understand it was a slight overreaction on my part, but I know you walk home from work and I just worry about you."

"You don't have to worry about me."

I say it though I know it's completely futile. Jasper is Jasper—he's not going to change. It's funny considering I'm exasperated by a part of him other women would probably *love*. He took the time to come down to my office and hunt me down, to confirm that I was all right and not in harm's way. I get it. I don't need to be mad anymore.

Still...

"How'd you even get up there?"

"Barrett helped. I called him from the security desk."

I cringe and decide maybe I don't want to know any more details. He contacted my doorman, called my brother, snuck his way up to the 70th floor—is that sweet? Or slightly overbearing?

"Let me walk you home and then I'll leave you in peace, okay?"

I suppress a sigh, tuck away the last of my anger, and nod. "Sure. That'd be great."

Chapter Nine

Scarlett

It's 7:30 p.m. on Friday night when my phone buzzes in my pocket. I wouldn't normally check it at the dining table, but the Beringers have been telling a meandering story about their experience at a cheese shop and how "you just can't find good help anymore," and I can only listen with a pseudo-sympathetic ear for so long before my face starts to melt. I couldn't care less about their make-believe customer service problems.

"He couldn't even tell me what region of Scotland the brie came from."

Cue rich people laugh.

Buzz.

My phone vibrates again and I surreptitiously retrieve it from my purse, using my napkin to conceal it as I angle the screen so I can read the text. It's from Sophie Smith.

> *Hey, I know it's Friday night, but we're up at the office and could use some backup. No pressure. I've asked a few other first-years too.*

YES.

I look over at Jasper to see he's already looking at me, his mouth turned down in a disapproving frown. "Everything okay?"

"It's work."

"On a Friday night?" Jasper's mom, Annette, asks. "*Goodness.*"

Annette has never worked. She met Jasper's dad while they were in college and they were struttin' down the aisle before graduation. I'm not judging her for her way of life. I just wish she wouldn't judge me for mine.

"There's a fire we're trying to put out at the moment," I explain. "A merger that's gone south."

She smiles tightly and raises her eyebrows as a way to suppress her true thoughts on the subject. I wouldn't think much of her reaction except for the fact that Annette has pulled me aside twice in the last six months to discuss my relationship with Jasper and our future plans together, namely when shc can expect me to focus my attention "where it matters".

The first time went something like this: "I just don't know how I could have managed to raise Jasper right *and* go off to a job all day long." Worse than that one was a snide remark she made right in the middle of a group conversation, so seamlessly it felt like I was the only one to hear her say it. "Oh, Scarlett doesn't think being a mom is work *enough*."

When I brought it to Jasper's attention later that night, he laughed it off. "So she's prickly about her life choices compared to yours—big deal. Don't let it bother you."

Now, she just can't help herself. "Aren't there *always* going to be fires to put out at a law firm of that size?" she asks her husband with a condescending tone.

I look to Jasper, hoping he heard the comment and witnessed the way she delivered it, but he's too busy waving down the hired waiter to ask for a refill on his wine. Never mind that the wine is sitting on a side table *right* there within reach. He could just get up and get it himself, but instead he's playing into this silly game of *Downton Abbey*.

All at once, it's too much.

I jerk my chair back and dart up. "I...have to leave." I look at Annette and Charlie. "I'm sorry. I know you both went to so much trouble to put together this dinner"—i.e. you paid people a lot of money to cook in your kitchen while you observed and critiqued them from afar—"and I feel bad rushing off, but this is really important."

Charlie—nice, aloof man that he is—nods. "Of course, Scarlett. Don't worry about it."

Annette doesn't look up, and she doesn't address me. I know I'll be paying for this quick exit for weeks, if not months, to come.

Jasper stands and follows me out of the dining room like a heavy black cloud. I know he's upset with me.

"Two late nights in a row, Scarlett?"

I ignore him and pull up the Uber app.

"My parents really wanted to spend time with us," he continues.

"I'm sorry, Jasper."

He sighs and grabs his keys from his pocket. "Let me drive you."

"I already called an Uber. Stay with your parents. I know they want to see you. It's so hard finding time to get together."

"Are you sure?"

Positive.

I lie and tell him the Uber's already there just so I can go outside. It's colder than I expected, but I don't mind the October chill. The fresh air feels like it's cleansing me of the last hour and a half. I stand on the curb, looking down the road for a black Nissan SUV.

Voices carry from the catering team standing in Annette and Charlie's driveway. They're just shooting the shit while they smoke and take a break. One of them catches my eye and nods, and I nod back. Given the choice between going back into the sprawling two-story red brick mansion to continue dinner with Annette or bumming a smoke from those guys, I'd pick the latter. And I don't even smoke.

It's a twenty-minute ride from Jasper's parents' house to the Elwood Hoyt offices. The Uber driver talks on the phone the whole time, and I don't mind one bit. Twenty minutes of sitting in the back seat, not saying a word? It's like a mini spa trip. And he offers me free water and a cord to charge my iPhone! Thank you, Mr. Uber Man. You will be getting a good tip from me.

I'm buzzing when I hurry through the ground-floor foyer, flashing my ID at security since I don't have my badge on me. I assess my clothes when I'm in the elevator. I didn't go home to change, and I'm slightly regretting it. The long white slim-fitting dress I wore to dinner is nice, though not exactly work attire. The halter neck has wide straps that twist around and tie beneath my hair, paired with a sculpted bodice. There's no cleavage, thank god, but it's still more skin than I'd prefer to show in the office. Good thing HR's not making the rounds at 8:00 p.m. on a Friday night...

I head down Hudson's way after making a pit stop in the break room for two coffees in two matching Snoopy mugs. I expect the same frenzy as last night, but it's suspiciously quiet near his office. There's an older man hunched over at Lucy's desk, but he doesn't even glance up when I walk by him—his focus remains down on the document he's redlining.

At Hudson's office door, I peer in to find he's alone inside, working at his computer. I give myself the briefest moment to take him in: his ruggedly handsome features highlighted by the warm glow of his computer screen, those perpetually furrowed brows. I wonder if he's realized how dark his office has become since the sun went down. Probably not.

"Where is everyone?"

He peers up. If he's surprised to see me, he gives nothing away with his expression.

"I gave them thirty minutes for dinner." He checks his watch as he sits back in his chair. "They'll be back soon."

I nod as I walk in to give him his coffee. It pleases me to no end to see his large hand wrapped around the handle of the cutesy Snoopy mug. He studies my smile but doesn't ask about it. Of course not. He doesn't care.

After I take a sip of my own coffee, I set about adding some light to the room. He's practically Count Dracula in here. I start with the floor lamp in the corner near his desk. Then I cross the room to turn on another lamp perched on the side table. My spine tingles from Hudson's gaze. He's watching me while he drinks his coffee. Maybe the dress is worse than I previously thought... I'm suddenly very aware of every square inch of skin on display. Even the skin *beneath* the light fabric doesn't seem protected enough.

I try the final lamp, but when I twist the switch, it doesn't turn on. When I glance down, I see it's been unplugged by accident. Of course the damn outlet's shoved halfway behind the couch. I hike up my dress and bend down to stretch my arm back there—praying there aren't like 456 dormant spiders waiting for a tasty finger to eat—and once I plug it in, the lamp turns on. Now the room is much more inviting.

I turn to see Hudson is still watching me, curiosity sparking his brown eyes.

"There. Better. Have you had dinner?"

He nods. "Yes, Mommy. Leftover pizza."

I roll my eyes when what I really want to do is let loose a belly laugh.

"Have you?" he asks, lazily taking in my getup.

I just nod, not wanting to get into it. I don't want him to ask me where I've been. But I shouldn't worry; Hudson's in no hurry to ask me probing questions. He doesn't care about trivial things like my social life.

Out in the sitting area, I hear the man stand up at Lucy's desk. He walks to the open office door and holds up the document he was working on. "Finished with edits. I gotta head out. My wife's gonna kill me if I don't make it home before she puts the kids to bed."

Hudson waves him off. "Thanks, Jansen. Hand that over to Scarlett before you go. She'll input the changes."

Jansen gives me the bound document, and I nod in confirmation.

Well, there's my task. Time to get to it.

I decide it's best if I work in my office tonight. There's no reason to linger near Hudson, especially while we're the only two people on the floor. It just feels dangerous—not because he'd ever do anything inappropriate. Last I checked he was minding his business, whipping through papers on his desk, a red pen wedged between his teeth. It's more like *I'm* the inappropriate one. It's becoming increasingly difficult to keep Hudson contained in the tidy box in my head labeled: BORING MALE COWORKERS I OTHERWISE DON'T CARE ABOUT. He's inching ever so slowly toward a new box titled: MEN I FIND SO ATTRACTIVE I CAN BARELY STAND IT. So far, that box is filled with Brad Pitt (specifically *Legends of the Fall* Brad Pitt) and George Clooney (in his current silver fox era).

Putting myself down the hall, in my office, is the smart thing to do.

Except that five minutes later, Hudson calls me back down to *his* office because his printer isn't working.

"Did you do something when you turned that lamp on?" he accuses.

"Yes," I say drolly. "I broke your printer by turning on your lamp."

His gaze eats me alive.

I gulp and look away. "Maybe it needs more paper?"

"It has paper."

"What about ink?"

He drags his hands through his thick hair. "Dammit. Where's IT when you need them?"

"I'm pretty handy," I tell him, kicking off my heels so I can bend down and see what the issue is. Really, I'm not *that* handy, but if there's an opportunity to fix something and impress Hudson in the process, I'm going to take it.

Of course his printer is shoved in the bottom of a large built-in cabinet, so I have to bend down to confirm that yes, unlike the lamp, the printer *is* plugged in. That's a good start.

"What's the issue?" I ask, turning just in time for Hudson to bend down next to me. He's so big and looming and that scent—my god, it's good. Citrusy, clean, invigorating, that fresh-out-of-the-shower aroma I *love*.

"Shove aside, will you?" he says suddenly.

"*I'm trying to fix it*," I argue, not budging an inch. "*You're* the one who called me down here."

"Yes, well, you're not exactly doing a bang-up job."

"You haven't given me a chance to do anything yet!" I snap and then groan when my head hits the bottom of the cabinet. "I was just checking to see if it's plugged in."

"Of course it's plugged in. Let me see if I can figure out the error code."

He presses his shoulder into mine and, like a petulant child, I shove right back against him. "I can—"

Before I know it, he has me by the waist and he's lifting me up and plopping me down away from the printer like I'm a sack of potatoes he'd like to dispose of elsewhere.

"You know what? Fix your own damn printer," I huff, reaching down to pick up my heels.

"Watch your damn mouth."

"*You* watch your mouth. God, you're insufferable."

I start to storm back down the hall, barefoot with my heels in my hands, when he calls out after me. "And next time don't come to work in a dress like that!"

"What's that supposed to mean!? The dress is fine. *You're the problem!*"

I swear I hear him mutter something before I turn the corner back into my office and plop right back down at my desk. I'm breathing hard—worked up, as per usual in Hudson's presence—when the elevator dings and everyone trickles back in from dinner. It's much the same crew from last night, plus a few additional first-year associates, Kendra included.

"Oh god," she says with an exaggerated eye roll when she sees me at my desk.

"Fuck off, Kendra."

She rears back, obviously surprised by my outburst. But guess what? You can only *poke and poke and poke* a bear so many times before the bear bites your freakin' hand off.

And while I'm not exactly impressed with my behavior—I mean, I won't be doling out advice on how to conduct yourself in a corporate setting anytime soon—it *does* succeed in shutting her up. She doesn't let out another peep while the two of us get to work.

Later, she asks me rather politely (for her, at least) if I have a certain file I can email to her, and after I do it, she mutters a quick, "Thank you."

A half-hour later, when I go into the break room to scrounge around for a snack (aka candy), I pick up two mini bags of Skittles and toss one on her desk when I walk back into our office.

She doesn't say anything, but she does tear into the bag straight away.

So there you go. Progress, I guess.

From down the hall, I hear, "Someone come fix my fucking printer!"

And I sit at my desk, smiling my little smile and working my butt off. It's the happiest I've felt all day.

Chapter Ten

Hudson

I've been summoned to speak with God this morning.

Anders' office is ten floors above mine, so high that when I stand at the windows overlooking downtown Chicago, I feel a rush of adrenaline. He has quite the setup, expansive floor-to-ceiling windows covering two of the four walls, more space than he knows what to do with. There are four segregated seating areas inside his office. Why would four different groups of people need to meet in one place together? I don't care. I love it.

I look down at the pedestrians crossing over the river, caught in the sunshine and going about their day, when Anders begins. "I'm incredibly satisfied with how you've handled this KinBio issue."

I'll bet he is. I've clocked 236 hours in the last three weeks. I've had associates working around the clock too. The issue is out of my hands now. As we expected, the FTC ruled against the merger, and KinBio will be seeking the breakup fee Chapman International agreed to in our original contract. Though now, of course, they're refusing to pay it. I won't be going to court over it. That's for our litigators to handle, but I've given them everything they should need, and we'll continue to work closely with them over the coming months. There's no doubt we'll get KinBio those millions, and I will be rewarded handsomely as well.

"I understand my daughter helped your team."

"She did."

She's been at the office more than any other first-year associate. I've had to kick her out of the building more than once while she grumbled under her breath. God, I love her mouth. I love her feistiness. I shouldn't be stoking the flames with her. I should be keeping us on the straight and narrow, leading her with dignity—but that's not my style.

Besides, Anders must know what his daughter is like at this point. I doubt she's a perfect angel outside the office...

"My daughter seems extremely happy here. I take it you're going easy on her like I requested?"

Good thing I'm facing the windows so he can't see my smile. The question should be: is *she* going easy on *me*?

"I asked her about work last night at dinner," he adds. "She said she likes her team and credits a good deal of that to your leadership."

I turn back. "What about her fellow first-years?"

His forehead wrinkles in confusion. "She didn't mention them much."

Interesting. So she really is handling the animosity all on her own. I have to hand it to her, it hasn't been easy these last few weeks. Though I suspect the bullying instances are lessening, Scarlett hasn't been let into their tight-knit group yet. She still eats lunch by herself, still arrives and leaves the office on her own. I suspect there's more. There's no telling the ways they're antagonizing her, but she takes it in stride. Keeps her head down. Focuses on work.

I check her billable hours at the end of every day, comparing them against her peers. She's leading the charge, and knowing that makes something like pride unfurl in my chest. "What does her direct supervisor say? Sophie Smith?"

"Nothing but compliments, though of course no one's going to give it to me straight for fear of offending me. But with you—" He chuckles. "I don't have to worry about that."

Right.

"Scarlett is fine," I answer curtly.

His eyebrows rise. "Just fine?"

"What do you want me to say?"

He smiles. "Something more than that."

"I don't get paid to wax poetic about your daughter."

I've done plenty of that in my head, on my own time.

He laughs, nodding now. "All right. Fair."

I'm tempted to dismiss myself, but I get the sense that there's something more. He walks over toward the windows, mirroring my posture from a few moments ago. He sighs and suddenly, his age shows. I wonder how many more years of law he has left in him. There will be a power vacuum after he leaves. David Hoyt retired five years ago, and we've only just regained stability here in the Chicago office.

"Truthfully, I don't want her here. Maybe I never will," Anders admits quietly. "I wish she had chosen to work with her mother. Katherine is an antiques dealer. She's had a shop over in West Town for thirty years. She tries not to let on about it, but I know she hoped Scarlett would join her in the business one day, the way the boys have joined me."

"It'd be a waste," I say, truthfully. "She's a better lawyer than Barrett."

Anders barks out a laugh. "Jesus, you don't mince words."

He knows it's true.

Barrett is fine, don't get me wrong, but he doesn't have the commitment level you need to really succeed in a firm like this. He travels a lot and has no qualms about leaving the office every day at 5:00. It's obvious his passion isn't law, at least not the way I suspect it is for Scarlett.

"Why did you ask me to take her on?" I ask, studying his profile. The question has been plaguing me ever since Scarlett's first day at the firm.

"I respect you."

I hum in disapproval. "Well...truthfully, I haven't gone easy on her, and I don't plan to." I'm taking a real gamble here. There's nothing and no one Anders Elwood cares about more than his kids, and I get the sense he has a special soft spot for Scarlett. "If you want someone to baby her, pull her off my team."

He turns and assesses me with those sharp gray eyes for so long it becomes uncomfortable. I'm about to say something—

to call attention to the awkward moment—but then he nods, only once. "Understood."

And just like that, I'm dismissed.

Outside the 70th floor and the food court, I've seen Scarlett twice over the last few weeks, working with a boxing trainer in the building's gym. The first time, I didn't believe it was really her. She had swapped her work clothes for tight leggings and a hot pink sports bra. Her long brown hair was pulled up into a high wavy ponytail and she was lobbing hard punches *one after another after another* against her trainer's cushion-covered hands.

I stood, dumbstruck—just like every other fucking guy in there—until she finished the round and turned to walk to the corner of the ring to get some water. She was bent over, closing the lid, when her eyes flicked up and she caught me staring.

I was going to make some joke about her picturing my head for every punch, but my words failed me. Heat coursed through me.

God she was sexy. In her work clothes, yes. In that sports bra and leggings? *Criminal.*

She frowned at me then turned back to rejoin her trainer, and that was that. I relegated myself to the other side of the gym where, for the better part of an hour, I tried to do exercises that made it easy for me to see Scarlett in the mirror. Crunches, curl-ups, jumping jacks—there was no rhyme or reason to my workout. I was breaking a sweat, sure, but I was also completely unsure of how many reps I'd done of what exercises, and by the end of it, I'd accidentally overdone it with the leg workouts. When Scarlett saw me limping into the break room the next day, she laughed.

"Pulled a muscle, old man?"

"Ha ha, yes. Now move so I can get an ice pack for my ass."

She tossed her head back and laughed, and I stood there looking at her like I was under a siren's spell.

I'd like to note that I've been working in law for a decade, and I've never—not a single time—developed a crush on a coworker. In fact, I've never even come close. I'm usually so focused on the task at hand that I'm more liable to forget the name, face, employment status, etc. of the person I'm dealing with than to develop a real human connection with them. When I first started working with Lucy, I'd call her "Hey lady out there" until one day she got so fed up she threw her rolled up newspaper at my head and told me I'd "better get some manners" and I'd "better get them real quick."

So to have this reaction to a coworker, a junior associate, an *Elwood* no less...

It's laughably bad.

The same day I needed the ice pack, Scarlett had a care package delivered to my desk around lunchtime. Inside of your aunt's chunky wicker basket from the '60s was a jumbo-sized bottle of Aspirin, a pill organizer labeled with each day of the week, a pair of reading glasses, a crossword puzzle book, and some caramel candies. A corresponding note said, "Take it easy, old timer!" which just...goddammit it made me smile, okay?

I ended up giving the basket to Lucy. She absolutely loved it.

Well...she loved it once I convinced her I was only giving it to her out of the goodness of my heart and no she didn't have to work late and no she didn't have to come in on Saturday and just take it already!

My one real saving grace in all of this—other than my surly attitude perpetually turning Scarlett away from me at every instance—is the fact that Scarlett is spoken for. Scarlett Elwood is not single, and I'd do well to remember that when I'm jerking off like a horny teenager in my shower every morning thinking about her.

I need a fucking hobby.

Chapter Eleven

Scarlett

"Moira, it's just a pretend pumpkin! Leave it alone!"

Moira doesn't listen before she swipes my little festive pumpkin from Target's dollar bin right off my TV stand. It's the third Halloween decoration she's tried to sabotage. The small hanging ghosts I attempted to put up over the weekend were so personally offensive to her she had them ripped out of the ceiling in a matter of minutes. The black papier-mâché bats? Reduced to dust.

Maybe Halloween just isn't her thing. Maybe in another life she was one of those moms who didn't let her kids read *Harry Potter* and thought Halloween was just a way for the devil to access your soul through slightly melted snack-sized Snickers bars.

Or you know what? Maybe Moira is just more of a Christmas girlie. Either way, she will not let me get into the spooky holiday vibes!

I yank the wooden pumpkin off the floor, and she hisses like she wants me to know there'll be a round two if I'm not careful.

"I'll put the pumpkin away, okay! You did it! You beat Halloween, you asshole."

There's a knock on my door. It's Jasper, here with our dinner, and not a minute too soon because I was about to rip into my pantry and eat another few fistfuls of pre-dinner chips.

"Come in, come in!" I say in a rush. Then I help him unload the brown paper bags from our favorite Thai restaurant onto the kitchen counter. *Yellow curry, yellow curry, yellow curry.* I'm just repeating it like that in my head, doing a little happy dance while I get plates and forks.

I haven't seen Jasper in almost a week because of our hectic work schedules, and it doesn't even occur to me until he stares at me with two arched brows that I forgot to greet him in a proper girlfriend way.

I laugh. "Sorry! *Hi!* Thanks for bringing dinner!"

I arch up on my toes and plant a kiss on his cheek. It feels weird, but then again, everything with us feels weird lately. Ever since I started working full-time, we've fallen out of sync somehow. He moves left, I move right. He's free, I'm busy. He wants to go out and meet friends, I want to chill after a long day. I feel like I'm getting on his nerves and vice versa. Worse, we haven't slept together in weeks.

But it doesn't feel like I can just snap my fingers and make it better. In fact, there's this niggling feeling in my gut that I'm purposely pushing him away and I don't know how to stop, or if I even *want* to stop at this point…

He's already launched into talking about his day at work, and I nod along, having a hard time keeping up with all the key players. It changes so much week to week! Like I thought Helen was an attorney in *your* office, but she's the opposing counsel? Oh, you *do* work with a Helen, but this is a *different* Helen. Okay, but can you just please pass me the pad thai before I dart across this table and yank it out of your hands because how long could it possibly take you to scoop a little mound of it onto your plate and keep it moving? Why do you keep stopping to emphasize your point? I will listen to whatever story you want me to hear *while I'm eating.*

"I feel like you aren't listening," he says with an exhausted sigh.

I blanch and look away from the to-go carton in his hand. "I'm sorry. I am."

My stomach gnaws on itself, and he sets the pad thai down a mile away from my outstretched hand. Like did you not think I would maybe want some of that right after you? I'm the one who requested it. *ARGH.*

"You're distracted, I get it," he continues. "It's hard to wind down after a long work day and I know you have it harder than most working with a difficult team like yours…"

I frown, not sure how I've given him that impression. Short of the first week I started, I've been extremely mindful about what I share with Jasper concerning my relationships at work. I know he'll take every tiny situation and blow it out of proportion. *No*, things have not really improved with Kendra and the gang, but it sort of feels like it's been put on ice for now. In the last week, there's been a decline in snide remarks. No one's inviting me to lunch, but I'm not holding out for that. I'll just take a neutral work environment. That's all I want.

"My team is fine," I insist.

He snorts. "Barrett told me who you're working for. Hudson sounds like a total prick."

"You don't even know him."

My tone takes us both aback. Moira too, apparently, because she latches onto Jasper's leg under the table.

There's a feline shriek and then Jasper flies back off his chair. "Shit. Get off me!" Then, under his breath, "*God* I hate your cat."

"She was just trying to protect me," I fire back, fiercely protective of the wild beast I let live in my apartment rent-free.

I mean, I think that's why she attacked him. You never know with Moira. She might have just seen Jasper as the weakest link standing between her and the shrimp in our takeout.

When he's not looking, I reach for a shrimp and call for Moira so she'll follow me into my bedroom. Usually, I don't let her in here without me because she enjoys nothing more than cleaning her anus on top of my pillow, but right now I think it's best if I separate the two of them.

She comes, but her begrudging attitude says, *Why me?*

Kick Mr. Blondie out instead. He sucks.

She kind of has a point.

"Here, have a shrimp."

I shut the door and sit back down at the table, trying for polite peace. "Sorry about that."

"You really should have her trained," he mumbles.

"Can you train cats?" I ask with levity in my tone as I reach for more food. "I thought *they* trained *us...*"

"Scarlett..."

This conversation isn't going anywhere good, and he must sense it too because he shifts topics. "My parents want us to meet them downtown for dinner on Saturday."

"Oh."

I thought I did a good job of masking my initial annoyance, but it seems Jasper still catches it because he frowns across the table, making me feel like I need to tack on, "We just saw them. That's all."

"Three weeks ago," he admonishes. "And you cut out early from dinner, remember? My mom brings it up every time we talk."

I'm sure she does. I can only imagine how much shit they talk about me during their daily phone calls.

"Saturday won't work though. My company is hosting a Halloween party. Did you see the evite I forwarded to you?"

He wrinkles his nose. "I sort of thought we'd skip out on that."

My jaw drops. "No way. Are you kidding? It sounds awesome."

"A party full of corporate lawyers?" He winces like just the thought alone gives him heartburn.

"It's my dad's company, Jasper."

It's important for me to show my face at things like this, but more than that, I really want to go! I have the best costume. I rented it from a legitimate costume shop rather than buying something generic online. I'm going as Dorothy from *The Wizard of Oz*. Moira was supposed to be the Wicked Witch of the West (hello, perfect casting), but she peed on her black hat. I have the trademark sparkly red shoes and a little basket with a stuffed Toto poking his head out. A professional is coming over to do my hair and makeup in the afternoon so I'll have those signature ribboned pigtails as well.

"I put your costume on hold at the shop. The lion one."

He reaches for more noodles. "The cowardly lion?"

"I mostly picked it because of your hair color, not your personality," I say with a light laugh, trying, trying, *trying* to get us back to our old place. Why does it just seem so hard with us lately? "If it's not your jam, you can go down and look for something else, but with it being so close to Halloween, I wouldn't be surprised if everything's been picked over already."

He shrugs. "Yeah, I'll just figure something out."

We eat the rest of our dinner in terse silence. Every scrape of our forks is louder than the last. When I load my dish into the dishwasher, it sounds like a bomb detonating.

I invite him to stay the night while, in my head, I actively hope he declines the offer. Maybe he can sense my true feelings because he shakes his head and claims he has an early morning anyway, just like I do. He kisses my cheek at the door, and he leaves.

After I put away the leftovers and wipe up the kitchen, I open my bedroom door to find Moira completely splayed out on my pillow like the Queen of Sheba, the tip of the shrimp's tail dangling out of her closed mouth. She doesn't even have the decency to look embarrassed that her lady parts are on full display.

"Don't worry," I tell her. "He's gone."

Chapter Twelve

Scarlett

I love costume parties, but I *especially* love costume parties planned by my mother. All the passion I channel into law, she channels into entertaining. She's been throwing Elwood Hoyt parties since before I was born—hell, I was probably born *because* of an Elwood Hoyt party. She has such a knack for turning a forgettable event into something spectacular and noteworthy. It helps that she has a team of party planners on the company payroll, of course, though the vision is all her.

She's been sending me pictures of the event setup all day. The party coordinators rented out the rooftop deck of the St. Regis and had a crew in here first thing, creating the most over-the-top magical menagerie, replete with circus tents housing each of the four bars, sweeping floral arrangements that arch into the sky, and antique circus stalls filled not with animals, but with Cirque du Soleil performers painted and decked out to *become* animals. It's sexy and fun and when I walk inside, I'm greeted by a fire breather blowing a plume of flame *just* over my head. I know it's going to be a great night.

"You've seriously outdone yourself," I tell my mom, leaning in to kiss her cheek.

She only returned from Europe a week and a half ago, and she's managed to get everything just right for the party. I have no idea how she does it.

"Looks great, Katherine," my dad says lovingly while holding onto her shoulder, delicately enough that his hand drapes partly against her neck.

They've dressed for the theme, of course. My dad is a ringmaster. My mom sourced the suit from France. She said she found it at one of the markets and it sparked the inspiration for this year's party. He looks the part, as if I snapped my fingers and drew him here from the 1930s.

A clown walks past us, pauses, and returns to entertain us with a wicked gleam in his eyes. He slips the eccentric yellow top hat off his head and digs his hand inside. I think he's about to draw out some never-ending rainbow scarf when instead, he presents each of us with the evening's signature cocktail.

My mother's is yellow, my dad's is blue, and mine is pink. There's a color-coordinated ball of cotton candy my mom tells us we have to eat fast or it'll dissolve into the drink. A laugh of delight spills out of me as I hurry to eat the sugary pink treat, which I was expecting to be bubblegum flavor but instead tastes like champagne heaven.

"Mom!"

She laughs and shrugs one shoulder like it's nothing.

She's dressed up like Lillian Leitzel, the German-born acrobat who famously performed for the Ringling Brothers and Barnum & Bailey Circus. She's wearing a tight dress that flares out at her hips like a demure tutu. Her legs are wrapped in tights, and her shoes are pale pink ballet flats that tie up around her ankles. I hope I'm half as stunning as she is when I'm older.

No one else is dressed to theme, of course. None of us knew what we were about to walk into, so there are all the usual suspects floating around: a vampire beside a cat, a bloody Jason in his telltale white mask chatting up a Barbie and Ken duo.

"Did Jasper say he was going to meet you here?" my mom asks coolly.

"He said he was going to try," I reply with a smile. "He's having dinner with his parents first."

Before they can prod any further about the Jasper situation, a photographer dressed like a mime motions for us to get close for a picture. Just as he snaps it and my eyes adjust to the flash, I see Hudson over near one of the bars. He's wearing a super realistic-looking flight suit with aviators tucked into his collar. It's silly that he looks so handsome considering it's just a costume, but quite frankly he looks like he just walked off the set of *Top Gun* and it's fulfilling some kind of weird fantasy I didn't even realize I had until this very instant.

Barrett and Nyles haven't arrived yet, but they swore they'd be here. I could really use them right about now because my mom and dad are immediately swept up into conversation, leaving me on my own just as I spot the other first-year associates clustered together in a group nearby.

Kendra is dressed as a cat—she's the fourth one I've seen so far—and Makayla is a Handmaid, but I can't really tell what everyone else is supposed to be. The guys aren't in costumes at all, which I'm sure they're regretting now because this is not a party where you show restraint. All the senior associates and partners have gone all out. It just makes it seem like the first-years take themselves *way* too seriously.

"Is that *Dorothy*?"

I spin around just as Barrett and Nyles walk into the party beneath the floral arch dressed as the Tin Man and Scarecrow. I gasp, totally in shock. I mentioned to Barrett the other day that it seemed like Jasper was going to skip the party. Maybe he could tell I was a little hurt by it, but I never thought they'd go to the trouble to do *this*!

The photographer hurries back to take our picture just as they join me. He captures a picture of Nyles wrapping me up in a tight hug, and I already know I'll want a copy to frame. I mean, they really went all out. The costumes look homemade. While the photographer snaps away, I try to figure out the logistics of Barrett's Scarecrow costume.

"Did you stuff your overalls with real hay?"

"Yes! That's what a scarecrow is, *city girl*!"

Nyles didn't half-ass it either. He's painted his face and neck and hands so his deep olive skin is covered with silver paint.

"You know the real actor was hospitalized from the aluminum makeup they used on set," I tell him, peering closer to try to discern what he used. Whatever it is, it's completely covered his skin. He's applied it so well it blends into the little tin hat he's pinned to his hair. Usually, it's jet black, but tonight he's sprayed it silver.

Nyles laughs. "Don't worry, I skipped the aluminum, sis. Now where can I get one of those fancy drinks you're holding?"

"Find a clown."

His eyes cut to me with suspicion. "What?"

I smile. "I'm serious. One of them pulled it out of his hat, though I'm sure you can do it the traditional way and just order one from the bar."

Nyles takes me on his arm, and we follow behind Barrett. The two of them save me. For the next hour, we mix and mingle. Barrett introduces me around to the senior associates and partners from other departments I haven't had a chance to meet yet. For the most part, everyone is kind. There was one guy who was slurring his words and made a point to tell me I was the "hottest Dorothy he'd ever seen" before Barrett intervened and pulled me away. Apparently the guy is already on his last leg with the firm anyway. I doubt we'll bump into each other again, tonight or ever.

"For the record," Nyles says quietly, "you *are* the hottest Dorothy, and don't you forget it."

I laugh and scrunch my nose at him, realizing just then that Barrett and Nyles have unintentionally pulled me into a group of attorneys that happens to include Hudson.

I notice him right away, but he doesn't notice me. He's across the circle, holding the neck of a beer, chatting with the man on his right. Well, chatting is a strong word. The man is talking at Hudson, and Hudson is pretending to listen. I notice now that his flight suit is unzipped *just* enough to reveal a glimpse of his tan chest. I realize I'm chewing on my bottom lip, and suddenly, I release it, appreciative of the long-wear red lipstick the makeup artist used on me.

I'm not surprised he hasn't spotted me. We're not in a perfect circle; that's not the way it works at parties. I'm stuck a little behind Barrett's shoulder, sandwiched behind him and Nyles. The party has really picked up in the last hour; the rooftop is packed with Elwood Hoyt employees, invited guests, and all the performers. They're the best part. At any moment you might cross paths with a knife-eating enchantress or a juggler on stilts or a magician ready to steal the diamond right off your ring finger.

"Jansen, have you had the chance to meet my sister? She's a first-year in your department."

Jansen—the guy I saw in Hudson's office a few weeks ago, the one who had to hurry home to help his wife put his children to sleep—turns in my direction with a nod. "Scarlett, yes. We've seen each other around but I haven't been formally introduced. You're on Hudson's team, right?"

We shake hands as I nod and smile. "I work primarily with Sophie, but yes, technically, I'm under Hudson's umbrella."

It's like every time we say his name, we're casting a spell. I check to see if he's aware we're talking about him, but he's still caught up in conversation with the man on his right.

"Whoa!" someone shouts from behind me. "How'd you do that?! Babe, he took my watch right off my wrist!"

The commotion draws Hudson's gaze. He looks up, only instead of finding the person who shouted, that piercing brown gaze lands on *me*. I go rigid as my stomach squeezes tight. There are a dozen people separating us, and yet the heated friction feels like it's eating away at me. He doesn't look away. He should...and he doesn't.

"Excuse me," I say to the men around me. "I'm going to use the restroom. I'll be right back."

I turn and run like I'm actually running from something when really what I'm fleeing from at top speed is that feeling in the pit of my stomach, that curling need I've never felt before, not from my current boyfriend, not from any ex-boyfriend. I feel shamed by it and yet I can't make it stop. Every day, it grows worse.

I misjudge my route and end up curving near the group of other first-years by mistake. Ugh. A few of them catch sight of me and laugh. I feel their judgment like a bad sunburn, but honestly, what's funny, Danny? *I'm* in costume and you're wearing a wrinkled button-down with jeans you bought in high school, so who's really winning?

"*Dorothy?*" One of them barks out a loud laugh.

But Kendra, noticeably, stays quiet for once. She's in costume too—*barely*. The cat ears and whiskers are a total copout. She watches me pass the group, and I duck my head and keep it moving.

When I leave the bathroom—after I've touched up my makeup and stalled (literally *in* the stall) as long as possible—I know I can't go back to Nyles and Barrett if they're still in that group with Hudson, which leaves me to wander aimlessly in search of my parents. I should have known they'd be the center of attention. A magician is performing a trick for my dad while everyone huddles close.

"A cocktail?" a passing waiter asks me, but I smile and shake my head. If I have another, I'll be teetering haphazardly on these heels, making a fool of myself. As it is, I'm just slightly buzzed, tingly, happy.

I walk around the edge of the party, behind one of the big top circus tents so I'm mostly shielded from the other partygoers. I don't want my coworkers to see me standing over here by myself.

I reach for my phone and check to see if Jasper has called or texted. The last we talked about it—two days ago—he begrudgingly said he'd try to be here, but now that it's past 10:00 p.m., I highly doubt he's going to show. He went to dinner with his parents at 6:00; there's no way they're still at the restaurant. He's had plenty of time to change into his costume and head over, *if* he even has a costume. I called the shop yesterday to ask if the lion costume had been picked up.

"It's still here, and unfortunately, your hold expires after lunch. Sorry, store policy around Halloween."

I couldn't argue with the clerk, and I wasn't about to pay the outrageous rental fee for a costume Jasper probably wasn't even going to wear anyway. I thanked them for putting it on hold in the first place and hung up.

Now, I call Jasper, holding the phone up to my ear as I look out over the railing. This rooftop has one of the best views of anywhere in the city, almost better than our office, especially with how close we are to the harbor and riverwalk. People are boozin' and cruisin' out on the blue water. All the big yachts are out along the river.

Jasper's phone rings and rings, and I feel silly hanging on to hope until the last moment, when it cuts to voicemail.

"You've reached Jasper Beringer. Leave a message."

I don't. I hang up and slip my phone back into my Toto purse just as someone comes to join me at the balcony railing. I want it to be Hudson so bad that when I look and find it really is him, I almost don't believe it at first.

His scent lingers between us. I hate that I know it's *his* scent. Subtle, citrusy, it binds me like an ever-tightening rope.

I could talk first, but this feels like a challenge. He came to me, but he didn't strike up a conversation. It's confusing. He's close enough that it doesn't feel totally accidental, but at the same time...I'm not absolutely certain he realizes I'm standing here.

We've been circling each other all night. At certain moments I've felt his gaze on me, though every time I turn to find him, he's focused on his own conversation, circulating through guests, surprisingly social for a man who seems to want nothing to do with people most of the time.

I take on his same posture, leaning on the railing. I get the impression he could hold out all night, could stand here for hours without saying a single word. The thought alone drives me insane.

I break first.

"You dressed up."

That's when I realize something. My head whips around quickly, finding Lucy talking to my mom. I didn't realize it before, but they're matching! Lucy's also in a *Top Gun* flight suit.

"Was it Lucy's idea?"

His gaze cuts to me, almost regretfully, as he nods. "She ordered them."

I smile. "Cute. I love it."

He shrugs, indifferent. "I swear I catch her watching that beach scene from *Top Gun: Maverick* at least once a week on YouTube."

Can't say I blame her...though why she's bothering with Miles Teller when Hudson is right there, flesh and blood is beyond me. He's much sexier.

I flush like my thoughts were just shouted out loud, and then I busy myself looking for another waiter. I was planning to cut myself off, but...

"Dorothy, huh?" Hudson asks.

I tap my heels together in reply, eliciting a dimpled smile from him.

He takes in my legs, and I feel compelled to explain, "The dress was longer when I tried it on in the shop."

"Hmm." He doesn't sound bothered. "People are wearing less."

His gaze rises to the circus performers behind me, the ones who are all but naked in their cages.

"That's not comforting."

He looks back at me, and a sort of relief settles over his expression. I get the sense that he's been dying to do this all night—just stand here with me, having a simple conversation. "You have long legs. That's the problem."

I look down at my legs. They're covered in white stockings up to my knees. He's assessing those too.

"Should we be talking about my legs?" I ask, working up the courage to peer up at him.

He looks away and narrows his eyes out on the river. "Probably not." Then he takes another sip of his beer.

"Maybe we shouldn't be talking at all."

"Okay." The suggestion doesn't bother him in the least.

He really is the worst opponent to go up against because he isn't bluffing; he truly doesn't care about any of this. I wonder what makes him tick, if there's anything for him outside of work.

This isn't the first time I've wondered these same things. I'm inexhaustibly curious about this man, and the more silent he is, the more indifferent he acts—the more I want to peel him apart layer by layer. Where does he live? What does he do when he gets home from work? Does he watch TV? Does he even *own* a TV?

Am I as mysterious as he is?

The thought makes me choke back a laugh.

Dorothy, you already know the answer to that.

"Looks like you're missing your lion... You've only managed to wrangle the Scarecrow and the Tin Man."

Ha. If only he knew the full story.

"The lion canceled last minute."

He shakes his head sympathetically. "How very *cowardly.*"

I try to hide my smile by looking down. He turns his body so his hip leans against the rail, and his full attention rests on me in an unnerving way. Everything about him is so intense, from the sharp angles of his jaw to the smolder in his gaze.

I'm left trying to keep things light between us, bringing up subjects that feel safe—though I'm not sure why. We're not alone; we're at a party surrounded by hundreds of people.

"It's sweet that you dressed up with Lucy."

He balks. "I didn't really have a choice."

"So she wears the pants in your relationship?" I tease.

"One hundred percent."

He watches the smile spread across my lips, staring a beat too long.

"Where's Jasper?"

I rear back at his question. "Jasper?"

"Your boyfriend," he says with a pointed flare of annoyance.

I'm sorry, but I find it hard to believe he a) knows I have a boyfriend and b) happens to know his name. I suppose he gleaned all of this a few weeks back when Jasper came to collect me from his office, but I didn't think it'd stick with him or anything.

Also, on top of all of that, *why does he care?*

"He went to dinner with his parents." My brows furrow disapprovingly. "But you...you shouldn't even be asking about him."

I hate that my voice shakes with nerves. I'd love nothing more than to match his boldness step for step. Usually, I can, but not tonight.

He relents with an easygoing shrug. "You're right. I shouldn't. Enjoy the rest of the party."

He's already backing away and my mouth opens like I'm about to plead with him to stay or maybe even apologize about cutting off his line of questions, but it feels necessary to keep the wall up between us. Safer that way.

But damn...I wish I'd picked the reckless option instead.

I wish I'd told him the truth: Jasper and I are almost certainly done as of ten minutes ago.

Now why do you care?

Chapter Thirteen

Scarlett

I give Jasper the benefit of the doubt about the party, but when I open up Instagram the next morning and see that he's been tagged in a bunch of photos with friends from last night, I realize how done we *really* are.

It's one thing to skip out on the Halloween party to meet his parents for dinner. It's a completely different situation to ignore my calls and ditch me to hang out with other people, most of whom I don't even recognize.

I know he's been going out without me the last few weeks, and I haven't been concerned about it. Just because I've been working around the clock doesn't mean his life had to stop, but we let it go too far. We missed the chance to repair what's damaged, and now, the thought of trying to slog through all this mess just doesn't seem worth it. I don't care about him enough to try, and that's damning in and of itself.

He finally returns my call later that morning, and I suggest we meet somewhere for brunch. He's hungover when he arrives at the diner. I'm already in a corner booth working through my second cup of coffee, and before he apologizes to me for being late, he waves down a passing waitress and orders a cup for himself. His usually soft features are held in tight tension, like there's a headache brewing just beneath the surface.

When she's gone, he sheepishly turns to me. "Hey."

He barely holds eye contact before he grabs the menu, and I'm kind of taken aback by his demeanor. I mean, *I* know I'm about to break up with him, but as far as *he* knows, everything is hunky-dory between us.

"How was your night?"

He nods, looking anywhere but at me. "Good, yeah. You?"

His blond hair is a little disheveled, like he just rolled out of bed a few minutes ago.

"It was fun. My parents asked about you…"

"Yeah, same," he says defensively.

Right.

"Didn't you tell them I had my company party?"

The waitress comes back with his coffee, and he thanks her before topping it off with enough cream and sugar that it's about to spill over the rim.

"Jasper?"

"Yeah, I told them." He has no patience for me this morning. "It just doesn't really matter, Scarlett. They were disappointed you couldn't make the time to see them, especially after what happened a few weeks ago."

This is getting a little ridiculous. "I think you're being unreasonable."

"I don't feel like arguing about this."

I swallow my retort as he rubs his temples.

"Okay, I'm sorry."

"Whatever."

He still hasn't looked at me.

"What'd you end up doing last night?"

He shrugs. "Just hung with the guys. We went to a bar in Uptown."

"Cool."

He doesn't ask about the Elwood Hoyt party and I don't feel like continuing to ask him questions about his night, so we revert to browsing the menu in silence. Once the waitress leaves with our breakfast orders, Jasper finally glances over at me, and I see the end is there for him too.

It's obvious to me now that everything I've been feeling in the last few weeks, he's also been struggling with. In a way, I'm glad. Jasper isn't a terrible guy. I'd prefer if our breakup was amicable rather than one-sided. It's better for everyone.

"Jasper…"

He shakes his head. "Yeah, I know."

"I really needed you at that party last night."

"And I really need to feel like a priority for you."

I sigh.

"It's not just the work stuff. I feel like we could figure it out if that was the only issue…" He winces and shakes his head like he doesn't want to go down that road.

"I mean, I agree it doesn't feel like we've been on the same page lately."

I'm trying to help him out, but he doesn't look relieved. "It's not really that. I mean, I guess it is...*in a way*."

I'm so lost.

"Is this about last night? About your parents?"

His eyes widen with horror. "*No*."

"Okay..."

He sighs and rubs the back of his neck, mumbling, "Forget it."

That's impossible. The more he doesn't want me to know, the more I have to press. It's human instinct.

"I'm just trying to understand your side of it," I say, trying to be helpful.

He toys with the handle on his coffee mug. "It doesn't matter."

"Is it the time thing? Like I said, I understand how you might have felt like you weren't—"

"No, Scarlett. Jesus, just...I don't feel like we mesh well together."

"What?"

I resist the urge to add, *Speak up.* He's talking so meekly. His shoulders are slumped and he's leaned forward so that his mouth is aimed at his legs, not at me.

"Yeah. I mean, it's—"

"It's what?" I prod impatiently. "*Just say it*."

"I feel like we're not compatible." He looks up, resigned now. "*That* way, you know? I mean god, I hate to say it like this. I feel like a complete ass, but sometimes it just felt a little—"

"What?"

"Boring. In bed."

I freeze. Blink. Process. My anger drew the words from his lips, and I can tell he regrets them the second they're out there, plunked down between us like a living, breathing thing.

I feel the color drain from my face.

Sex with me is boring.

He's been bored.

I'm baffled enough that I don't immediately do anything. I sit and I stare at him, trying to sort through this new font of insecurity he's just dumped on my head. I'm boring in bed. Boring. BOREDOM.

"I..."

Nothing comes after the first word. I just let it dangle there before I start to scoot out of the booth in a trance-like state. I'm walking away before I realize I forgot my purse. I turn back and grab it, toss down a few dollars for my coffee and wasted breakfast, all while Jasper fumbles over his words, trying to reach out and take my hand. I won't let him. He thinks I want him touching me?

"I didn't want to hurt your feelings, Scarlett. That's not what this is about. I just, I'd want someone to tell me."

Oh my god. He thinks he's a hero! He thinks he's doing a great act of service or something! *"Someone had to tell her."*

I close my eyes to try to push my anger deep down inside me. If he keeps talking, if he keeps digging himself deeper into this hole, I truly *will* lose it.

"I get it, Jasper. Seriously. Say no more."

"You can just be a little uptight."

"Oh my god. SHUT UP."

He could have just let me break up with him over a short stack. We could have cut into our hash browns and plowed through some crispy bacon like civilized adults, but now I have about thirty years of therapy I need to be getting to, so if you'll excuse me...

"Scarlett," he pleads as I walk away. He's delusional if he thinks I'm turning back.

God, all the things I could have offloaded onto him but didn't. Every little annoying thing I buried for the sake of our relationship comes pouring in now that I've opened the floodgates. It's all there, at the forefront of my mind.

He never made me laugh. In fact, his personality kind of sucked. I was willing to dress him up with words like "kind" and "nice" and "respectful", but in reality, he was barely any of those things. He was just quiet, which can sometimes be confused for other, better qualities.

His relationship with his mom is weird. They talk *multiple* times a day. About what?! *Why do you need to chat with your mommy that much, you adult man-child?!*

And his fucking hair. Guess what? It's receding. Yeah. He's going full-on Prince William, and I would have *never ever* made him feel bad about that or even CARED, but *Mr. BALDING MAN, you don't get to call me BORING IN THE BEDROOM while you have a literal crop circle on the top of your skull that I had to look at the ONE time you went down on me in our entire relationship.*

Oh my god. He and I were never going to work long-term. He wants to marry Annette Jr, a dutiful wife whose life goal is to wait on him hand and foot, who's ready to pop out children and roll through the carpool line and play tennis at the club and Mahjong her day away. He masked it well, of course. He made it seem like he was worried about me surviving at Elwood Hoyt every time he suggested I rethink my career decisions, but really, it was always about him and his needs.

I hate that I wasted a year on him, but then, that's how it goes.

Live and learn.

Barrett is the first person I call on my way home, and he puts me on speakerphone with Nyles. I'm in a fog. Deep down I'm seething, but on the surface I'm oddly calm.

"I broke up with Jasper," I tell them, wanting to rip the Band-Aid off as fast as possible.

Nyles' response absolutely slays me. "Oh, sweetie, of course you did. You were never going to marry him. *He's blond.*"

I play dumb. "I'm confused."

"No you aren't."

I burst out laughing.

"Also...can I just say, I saw you speaking with that man in the flight suit at the party last night, and I'm surprised you didn't swallow your tongue. God, he was good-looking."

"Are you talking about Hudson?" Barrett asks incredulously.

"Oh is that his name?" Nyles says. "He's your rebound man, Scarlett. Mark my words!"

I hang up on them.

Chapter Fourteen
Scarlett

In the two weeks since my breakup with Jasper, I've been kickboxing and working out more than ever. It's my favorite form of self-care, and it's convenient that the Elwood Hoyt building has a world-class gym that takes up the entire second floor. If my body allowed, I'd be there every day after work. As it is, I manage to sneak in a session with my trainer every other day during the week.

Jasper never loved my preferred form of exercise, though of course he'd never outright say it like that. He always masked it with concern. The last time he brought it up was the night he brought Thai food over to my apartment, the night Moira attacked his leg.

Apparently, I had a little bruise on my right arm.

"Scarlett, I think you've taken the kickboxing thing too far. Have you tried Orange Theory? I just took my third class and I really enjoyed it. Also, my mom raves about her Pilates studio. You could look into that?"

I have nothing against Orange Theory or Pilates or any other form of exercise people choose to do. I couldn't care less. It's just the fact that he couldn't get behind what *I* love. A bruise on my arm is hardly a reason to cut back.

I've never felt as strong or as lean as I do on my current workout regimen, and I love feeling this way, like I have complete control over my body, like it's powerful and fierce. Jasper never could understand that, but then again, Jasper is no longer my problem.

He came and picked up what few things were left at my apartment, and we did that awkward second-breakup-after-the-first-breakup thing where he tried to apologize (and justify) why he said what he said at the diner and I had to pretend I wasn't seconds away from unloading every angry thought onto him. Fortunately, I succeeded.

Now, I run on the treadmill in the Elwood Hoyt gym, finishing up my two-mile cardio warm-up while I wait for my trainer to get here. We used to work out together at his gym before I started at Elwood Hoyt, but since it's hard for me to make it over there with my current workload, he's agreed to train me here instead. Unfortunately, I don't think today is going to pan out. I check my phone to see he sent me a text while I was running.

Jake: *Had a trainer no-show for work today. I can't leave the gym. Sorry. Let me know if you want to reschedule. This week will be hard, but I could maybe get over to you later next week.*

It's a bummer, but I understand it's hard for him to drive the thirty minutes just to train me when he has an entire gym to run. There's probably someone else I could bring on, maybe another trainer he works with—though from the sound of it, he doesn't exactly have people to spare at the moment.

I step into the locker room to tuck my phone away with my purse and clothes, and then I head back out into the gym. Hudson is here, by the weights.

He comes as often as I do, though our days don't always sync up. (Not for lack of me trying, by the way.) I'm not ashamed to say I would rework my entire schedule for the pleasure of seeing that man work out. He's not a gym rat. Picture: overly buff dude mainlining testosterone while wearing a two-sizes-too-small tank top that for some inexplicable reason has huge gaping arm holes??? No, no. Hudson usually pulls from a variety of old college T-shirts or concert shirts. So far I've seen Dave Matthews, the Grateful Dead, and Foo Fighters. We love a man with taste! Along with these, he usually wears Lululemon shorts and, if the gym gods decide to bless me that day, a backward hat (*sob*).

The gym rules as of late are as follows:

    - We do not acknowledge each other.

    - If we do accidentally get in each other's way,
      Hudson pretends I don't exist.

Once, I was coming out of the hallway that leads toward the locker room while he was coming in, and I almost ran smack into him. He grabbed my shoulders and brushed past me, saving me the embarrassment (and pleasure) of squashing my cheek directly into his hard chest. I know his chest is hard because while his T-shirts aren't *tight*, they're tight, you know?

I don't know why these rules exist for us, but they've been especially in play since the Halloween party. In fact, I rarely see him in the office. Sophie's kept me plenty busy, and Hudson hasn't gone out of his way to pull me in on any spicy deals or mergers. It's a bummer considering how much I'd love the distraction right now.

I only really have work to keep me occupied at the moment. My social life has dwindled down to nothing. I've had dinner with my parents a few times. Last weekend, Nyles and Barrett dragged me out with their friends and it was a lot of fun, but I'm still just adjusting to this new life and the title I now have to endure: BORING IN BED.

There is no getting over that comment, by the way. It'll be with me until the end of time.

I head straight for the punching bags hanging in the corner near the boxing ring and work through a circuit my trainer usually puts me through that incorporates strikes and kicks alongside jumping jacks and crunches. After, I pull three-pound weights off the rack.

It's fine. I mean my heart rate is up and I'm sweating down the front of my black sports bra, but when I'm done, I still head for the punching bag.

My dad bought me pink boxing gloves for Christmas last

year, and my mom had them monogrammed with my name in curly script. I love them and use them every chance I can get.

I rear back and punch the bag, right-left-right, trying to remember to use the proper form Jake is always drilling into my head, then I freeze when I sense someone behind me.

"Want to get in the ring?"

I turn back to find Hudson standing there, sweaty and hot in his black T-shirt. No backward hat today. His hair is a shade darker near his temples, damp and slightly unkempt. There are pronounced veins in his arms. He's clearly been working hard over there with the weights.

With my AirPods in, I'm not sure I heard him properly. I take them out and ask, "Pardon?"

He nods toward the empty ring. "Want to join me?"

I laugh. "Hilarious."

His face gives nothing away. "I'm serious. Come on."

"Isn't it against company policy?"

He tilts his head like he's not quite getting it. "To work out together?"

"For me to kick your ass on the premises..."

Now *this* makes him smile.

"That's cute."

"I'm pretty good, you know."

"Yeah, I've seen you with your trainer."

Nothing fazes him, does it? "But you think you're better?"

He doesn't answer that. He walks over to the empty ring and holds the elastic rope down so it's easy for me to crawl up and onto the mat. Then he follows after me.

I go to one corner and adjust the Velcro around my wrist. "I'm serious, I don't want to hurt you."

He looks at me with unabashed amusement. "How about I promise to tap out if you're hurting me?"

"Fine..." I arch a brow. "What are you proposing?"

"A little light boxing. You attack, I'll parry. I don't have my gloves with me so we can't get too carried away."

Is that warning for him or for me?

This sort of game is nothing I haven't done with Jake. It's usually the last thing we do at the end of our sessions, mostly just to goof around. It's really fun though, and not only is it good exercise, it's also a good lesson in self-defense.

I'm no expert when it comes to actual boxing strategy. I'm not like a secret black belt, but I've memorized the key areas my trainer has drilled into me, so I go for those places. The thing is, though, for such a big guy, Hudson's faster than I thought he would be.

He blocks my first punch *and* my second, and on my third, he grabs my wrist and twists me around so my back is flat against his broad chest. My arm is wedged between us, and if I try to finagle my way out of the hold, my shoulder screams at me. Worse, he doesn't let me go right away. "*Okay!* You've made your point."

He lets go and I shake out my arm as I turn around. My eyes are narrowed suspiciously now.

"You've clearly trained in the ring before."

He shrugs. "I've done a bit of boxing over the years."

'A bit', my ass.

I would love nothing more than to sweep his legs out from under him and take him down to his back. Oh my god,

I'd be so satisfied I doubt I'd be able to wipe the smile off my lips for *months*.

"You going to just stand there?" he taunts with a lift of his chin.

"I'm trying to decide if I want to go for your face. It'd be a shame to wreck your pretty boy image."

He frowns like he's seriously worried I'm about to deliver on that promise. "No faces, Elwood. We don't have mouth guards in."

"So you *are* worried about your face…trying to impress someone?"

I strike while he's distracted, going for a jab to his lower stomach, but he swipes it away easily. The odds are not in my favor.

"You aren't using your size to your advantage," he tells me gruffly, like he's annoyed I'm not beating him up harder.

"I'm trying!" I groan.

"Stop circling around me. You're wasting your energy."

Fine. I reach out to try for a one-two punch to his chest, but it's no use. In the process, Hudson leg-sweeps me. In a flash, I end up flat on my back, the air whooshing out of my lungs in a painful gasp.

Like the arrogant ass he is, he leans over me so his handsome, sweaty face blocks out the bright fluorescent lights. I stare at his full lips, those sharp cheekbones, those perpetually angry brows, and I feel lit up like a live wire. It's the adrenaline.

"Is that all you've got?" he asks deviously.

He reaches his hand down so he can help me back to my feet.

Before he can blink, I hike my legs up and bring them around the back of his, taking him out at the knees so he crumbles to the ground beside me. We lie flat on the mat together, breathing hard. My right leg is pressed against his.

"Is that all *you've* got?" I tease right back before rolling over and purposefully grinding my elbow into his stomach as I push to stand up.

Now *that* was a satisfying workout.

Chapter Fifteen

Hudson

I'm a man in my thirties *with a crush.*

It's embarrassing. I'm obsessed. And I don't get obsessed with anything outside of maxing out my billable hours. Ever.

I've been looking into how to get rid of these inconvenient feelings, but apparently, there's no over-the-counter pill or cream for that. Maybe I need a shaman? I'm so desperate to go back to the way I was before Scarlett Elwood walked into this office, and if that means paying a back-alley priest $200 to spritz me with "holy water" out of a Gatorade bottle, so be it.

Slightly less worrying than my developing feelings for very-young, very-off-limits Scarlett but still annoying is the fact that winter has descended on us. It snowed over the weekend. The city is currently blanketed with white fluff. So far, ten people have said the words "I just love the first snow of the season," so now I'm playing a game with myself: if I hear it fifteen times before lunch, I'm allowed to take a shot from the For Emergencies Only tequila bottle I keep in a side cupboard in my office.

The last emergency was Lucy's birthday. She got me so drunk I slept on the floor under my desk, but it's been months since then, and I've mostly forgiven her.

I'll have to relegate it to a single shot today though. I'm supposed to meet Scarlett in the gym later this afternoon.

At least I *think* that's the plan. We're not in fucking elementary school comparing our Lisa Frank planners in art class. Just...we met last week on Monday, Wednesday, and Friday, so I figure we'll do the same this week. I mean, it would be convenient if we had a time set so I didn't have to pace around that boxing ring for an hour waiting on her, but I refuse to look like a simpering fool. If I have to wait for her, I'll just work later to make up for the wasted time. It's fine.

During last week's sessions, Scarlett tried to take me on in the ring, and I tried to mostly keep my gaze above her collarbone while dodging her surprisingly well-timed blows. For someone so small, she's feisty. She landed a solid punch to my stomach on Friday. I had to double over and breathe deep. She immediately gasped with horror and ran over to check on me, her hand rubbing soothing circles on my back (inappropriate), her face down near mine (tempting).

"Did I really hurt you?" she asked, sounding concerned.

"Yeah."

"Are you crying?"

"A little."

She laughed and pushed me away playfully. God, I love making her laugh.

Fortunately for me, I have a big closing in two days for the Zion Oil and SolarCo merger. It's scheduled for the day before Thanksgiving, and it's given me a lot to focus on outside of Scarlett. I work straight through lunch with my team, but by 2:00 p.m., everyone's cranky and we're starting to make stupid mistakes. I dismiss them down to the food court, and I'm about to figure out food for myself when Lucy's phone rings. A few minutes later, she shouts out.

"It's your mom! Line two."

"Why does she call you first? She has my direct line."

"She likes me!"

I pick up the phone. "Why do you call Lucy first?"

"I like her!" my mom says as if they corroborated their story beforehand.

Of course.

I wedge the phone between my ear and shoulder and keep working. "What's up?"

"I'm calling to see if you're joining us for Thanksgiving dinner."

I wouldn't miss it, but still, I string her along. It's the Rhodes way.

"What's on the menu?"

"Turkey. Now are you comin' or what?"

"What kind of sides are we working with? I noticed last year you tried to experiment with a new sweet potato dish, and I didn't care for it."

"You know what? You can get your butt in the kitchen and help make *any* side dish you want. How about that?"

I think if people at work were to meet my mom (something I've avoided at all costs because I do not like to integrate my separate worlds), they'd understand my personality a little better. She's a single mom who raised my sister and me while working full-time. She also put herself through night school to get her social work degree after my dad left us. For the last twenty years, she's worked in the foster care system, but don't let that fool you. She's not soft. She's like an old southern grandma fused with a calloused New Yorker, *from Chicago*, a combo that should make you shiver and avert your eyes. She will say everything that's wrong with you straight to your face, and she has done so to me plenty of times.

"I'll be there and I'll bring pie," I tell her.

"Chocolate mousse or pumpkin. Don't get cutesy and bring cherry."

"I like cherry."

"Eat it on your own time. You'll be in my house and I want chocolate mousse or pumpkin."

I laugh. "Understood."

"Should I expect a plus-one?"

"When's the last time I brought a woman home to meet you?"

She doesn't even have to think before she replies, "2004."

"Right."

I've been in relationships since then, but none I felt were worth bringing in front of a family audience.

"Well I just thought I'd ask. Here, connect me to Lucy and I'll get the real answer."

"Don't interrogate Lucy about my love life."

"*What love life?!*" Lucy shouts back.

I really need to get better at closing my door.

"Just me," I confirm to my mom.

"All good." Her voice softens. "I can't wait to see you, kid."

"Same here. Love you."

"You too."

I was going to rely on fate to bring Scarlett and me together in the gym, but with this closing, I end up emailing to let her know I won't make it down to work out until close to 9. I figure she'll beg off. Just because it's a hard week for me doesn't mean she has to be in the office that late. The snow has picked up again; everyone wants to be home, cozy in front of their fire.

Her email comes back right away.

See you then.

I stare at those three words, trying to quell the pure elation. Then my phone rings. Someone with questions about the closing, no doubt. I click away from the email and answer it before the second ring.

As I expected, the gym's a little less crowded than usual when I arrive. Scarlett and I will have the back corner to ourselves while we train. She's already on the treadmill doing her warm-up; she sees me in the mirror but doesn't smile or nod. We play chicken with each other, seeing who's going to be the one to cave first.

Fifteen minutes later, I'm working through a series of bench presses when she leans up against the railing nearby to watch me.

"Don't...interrupt me," I say, focusing on pushing the weights up. I went heavy tonight because I've got energy to burn. I've been stuck at my desk all day.

"I was just saying hi," she remarks, all innocence.

"See? I lost count."

"You were on twelve."

"How do you know?"

"It's too embarrassing to admit."

I laugh and then holster the heavy weights before I accidentally send myself to the hospital because I'm too distracted by Scarlett. I sit up and wipe my hands on a towel, taking my sweet time before I give in to the urge to look at her. I'm sure I look cranky, but she doesn't even balk.

She's wearing an electric blue workout set tonight: skintight leggings that *thank the lord* are high-waisted and a scoop-neck sports bra that doesn't do enough to conceal her cleavage. I haven't seen the outfit before, and I know that for a fact because I catalog everything she wears to the gym in my mind for future reference. If HR had access to my thoughts... *oof.* I'd be fired ten times over.

"Almost done?" she asks, propping her hands on her hips. For a second, I imagine her hands are my hands. I wonder what she'd feel like, how smooth...

"No," I bite out brusquely.

She frowns. "Well too bad. I'm ready for you."

Then she turns and walks off.

Ten minutes later, we're in the ring together. Her fists pound against my padded hands. She's completely focused on her quick-fire punches. She has good form, good concentration. She puts her whole heart into it when we're in the ring, though

I'm not surprised. It's clear she bleeds passion for the things she cares about.

"Pick it up a little," I challenge.

Her eyes spark with excitement. Sweat trickles down her neck, running over her collarbone, pooling in the cleavage above her sports bra. I shouldn't look down, but she's all fucking curves on her small frame.

My hand slips and she accidentally slams her fist into my chest.

She immediately halts. "Oh my god! *Sorry!*"

"It was my fault." I rub the spot knowing I'll be sore tomorrow.

She props her hands on her hips, her mouth flattening disapprovingly. "Should I chastise you for not focusing? *The way you do to me?*"

Another gymgoer walks up to the ropes. "Hey man, think we can get in the ring?"

"No," I bark, still rubbing the spot above my heart.

Scarlett laughs and spins around. "He's joking! We'll be done in fifteen minutes and then it's all yours."

"Thanks," the guy says, shooting me a sharp glare before walking away.

"Why do you have to be so mean all the time?" Scarlett asks, walking up to me and pushing me hard in the chest. "Stop being such a bully."

"I'm not."

"God, *you are*. You're so mean to everyone."

"I'm not mean to you."

"You are. Or...you used to be."

She's still going at me, pushing me so I have to keep taking baby steps back. She's right on me though, push for push, so eventually, I'm forced to reach out and grab her wrists to still her. She doesn't relent. My hands tighten and I can tell she's about to really let loose on me.

"Relax, will you? I'm still recovering from your last punch."

"*So?* Maybe this is a fair fight for once."

She gets one of her hands free from my grip. *Good girl.* Then she tries to reach her hand around to punch my damn kidney, but I recapture her wrist and spin her so I have her wrists cuffed together at her lower back. "You good?"

"No."

"Why do you have to be so difficult?"

"You like it," she taunts, bucking back against me, and her butt accidentally grinds against the front of my shorts.

Oh *shit.*

I immediately unhand her and take three steps back. My back hits the rope.

Don't look down, Scarlett. DON'T LOOK DOWN.

She does though, and her eyes go wide, her cheeks flushing bright red. She's so shocked and innocent. I look away and imagine bad, horrible things, anything but Scarlett in her matching leggings and sports bra set, the fact that it's so tight it might as well be glued to her skin.

She takes her bottom lip between her teeth as if she's the one who should be embarrassed. "Sorry. I took it too far."

I don't even say anything. What *can* I say?

I walk around the perimeter of the ring so I can climb down and head to the locker room. I need a cold shower, and I need it now.

Unfortunately, Scarlett's waiting for me when I'm done. She's showered too. She's washed off her makeup and let down her long hair. It's air-drying slowly, framing her face. She looks heartachingly young and sweet without makeup. Her brown lashes are clumped together from the shower. She's wearing a Columbia T-shirt and a new pair of leggings.

"Where's your coat?" I ask her.

"What? It's in my bag. But listen, I'm really sorry. I didn't mean to—"

I shake my head, not about to go down this path. This is why men my age should not have CRUSHES. I'm too old to be making excuses for anatomy I can't control. "Let's just forget it, okay?"

Her face falls. "Forget the training stuff?"

"No. Forget what just happened."

Her shoulders sag in relief. "Okay cool, yes." She smiles. "I can do that."

"How are you getting home?" I look toward the gym doors then back to her. "Jasper?"

Her face scrunches at the idea. "Oh. No. I was just going to walk. I live just around the corner."

"It's snowing," I point out dryly.

She waves away my concern. "Okay...so I was going to walk *fast*."

"Don't you have a car in the city?"

"I feel like we're getting into the weeds a bit here..."

I shake my head and motion for her to walk on. "Let's go."

"To your car?"

"No, to the moon, Scarlett. Yes, my car. I can't let a junior associate get frostbite on my watch. It'd look bad for the company."

"I could see if Barrett is still here. Or my dad?"

"Okay."

That'd be preferred. It's a stupid idea to put her inside my car.

But probably because I was so willing to relent, now she doesn't want to. "Whatever, fine. If you're willing to, I'd love the ride. Thanks."

A major perk of being a partner is that I get primo parking in the underground garage. Though when I make *senior* partner, my spot will be even better. Right up front. I'll get someone to shine my reserved sign every week. No, *every day*.

I unlock my Toyota Land Cruiser and toss my briefcase and workout bag in the trunk. Scarlett hovers near the passenger side door, her hand outstretched toward the handle.

"Up front okay?"

I don't even deign to give that question a response. I'm not going to *Driving Miss Daisy* her ass through the streets of Chicago.

"Up front," she confirms, tugging open the door and making herself right at home among my crap, though it's not fast food wrappers you have to contend with in my car; it's papers: files, documents, memos.

She has them all tucked neatly into a pile on the floor by the time I'm behind the wheel. Her scent is everywhere, hitting me like a wall when I close the door and buckle up. She's perched herself on my leather seat, her hands folded together on her lap. I flip on the seat warmers and show her where she can adjust hers.

"Thanks. I love toasty buns."

I shake my head and start to back out. My car started streaming music from my phone as usual. It's a Marcus Mumford live set, and Scarlett asks if she can turn it up.

I nod and she reaches over, ever so carefully turning the dial until she's satisfied.

I loop around to the back exit of the parking garage. "Tell me where to go."

Once outside, she points ahead. "Take a right here."

Then a moment later, "Left. *And*...home."

Okay, so her apartment is as close as she promised it would be, a laughable distance from the office, but it's snowing and the people outside look miserable. Like look at that smiling lady; I'll bet she wishes someone were driving her.

"You *really* saved me."

I look over at Scarlett with a droll glare.

"I would have been cold for like two minutes." She mock-shudders at the thought.

"Out."

She laughs, unbuckles her seatbelt, and leans toward me.

It's muscle memory that has me leaning back toward her, like my body knows what it means when a woman crosses over the console of a car with her chin tipped up and promise in her eyes. It takes everything I have in me not to take ahold of her chin, not to tip her face up toward mine and bend down to kiss her.

"Thanks for the ride, Mr. Rhodes."

Her dimple pops, and before I can chastise her about something, *anything*, she hops out of my car and hurries toward her apartment building, chatting with her doorman for a second before disappearing into the lobby.

Chapter Sixteen

Scarlett

"Any holiday plans?"

I'm at my desk on Wednesday, the day before Thanksgiving, working through emails when the question comes out of nowhere. First, I look around at the inanimate objects surrounding me, like maybe the West Elm lamp I brought in to spruce up the place has been a sentient being this whole time and I didn't realize it.

Across the room, Kendra looks at me expectantly. She's willingly asked me a question.

"Oh, just seeing family. You?"

I try to sound casual about it, like a dad testing the waters with his hormonal teenage daughters. You don't want to spook them into remembering they hate you.

"Same, yeah. My brother's visiting." She's looking at her computer again, scrolling with her mouse.

I nod like, *Cool, cool.*

Inside, I'm elated.

Since Halloween, Kendra has been neutral toward me, but there have been no conversations outside of work-required questions. *Did you send the so-and-so form back to Sophie? Have you heard back about any delays with the XYZ contract?* Maybe Kendra's just getting in the holiday spirit and she's happy she gets to see her brother soon. Maybe she got laid last night.

I have mixed feelings about the holiday weekend. On one hand, Wyatt is flying in from London and Conrad and his fiancée Hannah are coming in from California. They're supposed to get in this afternoon and we're all meeting for a late dinner at our family's favorite Italian restaurant downtown. Then we'll see a late-night screening of whatever superhero movie is currently in theaters—our Thanksgiving Eve tradition. Outside of stuffing our faces tomorrow, my mom has an entire weekend of wedding planning scheduled for Conrad and Hannah. It'll be one of the few times they're in Chicago before their March wedding, so my mom is in full-on strategy mode. I'm tagging along too, mostly to act as an impartial judge during crucial decisions (i.e. cake tasting). It's a thankless job, but someone has to do it.

Cooking for the holiday will be a team effort. My dad and mom usually tag-team the turkey. Wyatt and I will be on cocktail duty. Nyles and Barrett will handle the sides, and

Hannah and Conrad are on appetizers. Our group text has been insane this week with people sending and vetoing recipe options. Who knew there were so many ways to cook green beans?!

All in all, it'll be a fun weekend with my family, but it'll also be the longest I've gone without being in the office since I started at Elwood Hoyt. I don't know why I care. I guess I'm just really going to miss my office plant and adequate-at-best desk chair. And what am I going to do without the free Costco brand K-Cup pods from the break room?

Never mind that I won't see Hudson again until Monday.

That's beside the point.

Irrelevant.

Still, I can't resist going to check in on him in the afternoon. I know he's busy with the Zion Oil and SolarCo merger. A few hours ago, his office was filled with people. Now, though, he's solo.

I've gotten so used to seeing him dressed for the gym that it's jarring to take in his navy suit and tie. Behind his desk, he's Mr. Big Shot in all his glory.

"I can come back later if you're busy."

His dark eyes track my every step into his office. "Later isn't any better."

"Then I'll just leave this and go."

I set a coffee on the edge of his desk and am about to step back when he asks, "Why are you still at the office?"

People have been trickling out since noon to take advantage of the holiday. It's close to 4:00 p.m. now, and the place is all but deserted. I told my mom I was going to try to leave an hour ago.

I can't meet his eyes for some reason. I look down at my nude heels. "Oh, just ticking off a few last-minute things." Lingering is more like it… "Are you going to try to leave early?"

He checks his watch. "No later than 6:00. I have to make it over to Red's Bakery to grab pies for tomorrow."

I look up, watching intently as he rubs his jaw. My stomach tightens as if it's *my* hand doing the touching. I wonder what it would feel like. That scratchy stubble… "I take it the closing went well?"

"Without a hitch."

My smile is genuine when I congratulate him. "I'm surprised you aren't celebrating."

"I will be—*with pie*."

I laugh. "Right."

I rock back on my heels.

"Don't get soft on me over the weekend."

Considering there'll be no training for us because of the holiday…

"Oh please. *You're* the one I need to be worried about getting soft."

"True. I guess you could get in a session with Jasper."

Jasper. I almost choke.

"Eh…no." I concentrate on the windows behind him. "No Jasper."

"Not a boxing guy?"

"Not-my-boyfriend guy."

When Hudson doesn't reply, I'm forced to look at him again. I want to know why he's gone silent. He's frowning like this news upsets him for some reason. Maybe he's just confused. I feel compelled to add, *"Anymore.* And don't you dare say something crass like *Lucky him* or I'll steal back that coffee."

He leans forward and yanks the mug off the desk like he's scared I'll make good on that promise.

"You broken up about it?"

I'm surprised he's even asking. It's not like he and I usually have heart-to-hearts. This would be the first.

"The breakup? No. His parting words...eh." I shrug a shoulder and try to laugh it off. "Let's just say he gave me *a lot* to think about." I say the last part with emphasis so he'll catch my meaning.

Hudson does his signature scowl. "I don't want to hear it. It'll piss me off. No, never mind—tell me."

I chew on my lip, almost tempted to confide in him, which is wild considering I haven't told anyone about Jasper's comment. When I texted my law school friends to tell them the news of the breakup, they were bummed for me until I assured them it was truly for the best. My parents were strangely relieved, my dad especially. I thought they liked Jasper, but when I brought it up to her, my mom said she liked him because *I* liked him. The same couldn't be said about my dad.

"Nah. Never liked him."

To which I laughed. *"Dad!"*

He shrugged. "Eventually, if you two became serious, I would have told you my true feelings. But until then, I felt like it was best to just let it run its course."

Nyles has been the only one to try to dig for more intel. He doesn't buy that Jasper and I just outgrew each other. He thinks there's something more to it. I'll have to watch the wine at Thanksgiving tomorrow or I'll be spilling *all* the details, the good, the bad, and the ones I haven't even had the courage to admit to myself yet.

"It's nothing," I tell Hudson. "People say dumb stuff during breakups. That's all."

He doesn't say anything; he doesn't have to. His silence is the best interrogation tool there is, like he knows if he sits there stoically for long enough, eventually I'll crack like a pistachio, start to sob, and tell him all my deep, dark secrets.

It strikes me, suddenly, how strange it is that I'm here in his office just *chatting* with him. There was no reason for me to come see him. I didn't even think to come up with an excuse, and he didn't ask for one. I don't know how or exactly when it happened in the nearly two months I've been working at Elwood Hoyt, but somehow out of *all* my options, *all 700+ employees*, I've befriended Hudson Rhodes.

"Scarlett—"

"I—"

We speak over each other, and I'm the one to forge ahead. I point back toward his open office door. "I should get going. My mom's probably wondering where I am. Have a good holiday, okay?"

• • •

The Monday after Thanksgiving, we have a department-wide meeting. Everyone is crammed into the conference room where we got our team assignments on my first day on the job.

Sophie warned us what to expect, i.e. a lot of extraneous fluff better sent in an email.

I don't mind the fact that it's a waste of my time. Hudson will be here.

When I arrived, I took up a spot in the back, and I have the perfect vantage point; I don't even have to be sly about it as I watch him stroll in. There's a tightening in my stomach the moment he walks through the door, an infusion of adrenaline like I've been hooked up to an IV. Today, he's decided to torture us all in a dark gray suit with a pale blue-gray tie. He had a haircut over the weekend, just a trim, but that jawline seems especially fierce today. He props himself against the wall near the door like he's hoping to make a quick exit later. He crosses his arm over his chest, using it to prop up his elbow. He rubs his bottom lip, deep in thought for a few moments, and then he starts to scan the room, ever-so-slowly looking over his shoulder.

It takes him so long to reach me, and when he does, our gazes lock. His brown eyes soften. The harsh lines on his forehead ease. *Hi*, the look says.

A thousand butterflies fill my chest.

Hi.

It feels like he looks longer than he should, like we're just indulgently staring at each other while the world keeps spinning. I shift and peer down at my watch, wondering if he's still looking.

I want him to be.

The dangerous thought strikes me like a lightning bolt—a revelation I don't want.

I'm glad for the distraction as the meeting picks up. They

throw a lot of information at us, more than I was expecting. There's applause and acknowledgment of the merger Hudson wrapped up the Wednesday before Thanksgiving. It's so obvious how uncomfortable he is in the spotlight. He adjusts his collar and nods, not even looking around the room.

Afterward, when they release us, I don't feel like shoving through bodies, so I give people a chance to leave so I'll have a clear path to the door. Hudson hasn't moved from his spot. He's scrolling on his phone. I pass him, and he seamlessly falls in step beside me.

His shoulder bumps mine unintentionally in the shuffle. When my hand grazes his, I yank it away and wrap my arms protectively around my waist.

Everyone around us is rehashing their holiday weekend, but we don't say anything as we walk side by side toward my office. At the door, I branch off and walk in. My body is humming, and when Kendra comes in behind me, I almost can't look at her for fear she'll know everything. But what is there to know that's not locked inside a vault in my chest? So Hudson looked at me during a staff meeting? So he walked me back to my office? That's hardly enough to hold up in court. Both things could totally be written off, especially the last one. My office is *on the way* to his office. I wouldn't be surprised if I was reading too much into all of it.

Nyles kept pestering me about my love life over the weekend, like I expected he would.

"So you're telling me there's *no one* else?"

"I'm completely single," I told him. "I'm not even on any apps right now."

But the truth felt like a lie. I couldn't even look him in the eye as I said it. It's how I feel right now with Kendra in my office, like I'm harboring a big bad secret.

Fortunately, with how much time everyone took off over the last few days, the office is buzzing. A new email with a new task *pings* my inbox every five minutes. I restructure my to-do list a dozen times, trying to keep ahead of the things Sophie will want returned to her the fastest.

Kendra asks me if I want another cup of coffee, pointing to the forgotten mug on my desk. I've been so busy I forgot to drink the second half of the cup I poured for myself first thing when I arrived.

"That'd be great, thanks."

I finally take a break at lunch so I can head down to the food court, but I take my sandwich right back up to my desk and eat while I work.

It feels like I blink and it's 7:30 p.m. Kendra packs up her stuff and nods at me on her way out. I shut down my computer—heart racing—as I take my workout bag and head down to the gym. I never know if I'll arrive before or after Hudson. I never know anything about our encounters except that it feels like the rug could be pulled out from underneath me at any moment. For *now*, he finds me entertaining enough to toy with like a mouse, but for how long?

Each night is *the* night he might not show up, and each night he walks through the gym doors and comes to find me, it feels better than the last, like all the hope that's been building to a breaking point inside me all day hasn't been in vain.

I'm flat on my back, resting after a set of crunches when I see his shoes in my periphery. I turn and tilt my head. He has his hands on his hips. Today, TODAY, is a backward hat day.

"Are you going to lie there the rest of the night or are we getting in the ring?"

I hold up my hand, and he steps forward to take it. I feel his grip down in my toes. His hand is powerful and tight. He hoists me up so easily and then I'm on my feet in front of him, head tipped back. Our hands are still linked for one...two seconds... He lets go, and I smile before shoving him playfully on the shoulder.

"Let's go."

Maybe I didn't sleep well last night or maybe I didn't have enough caffeine today, but my concentration in the ring is shot. Hudson and I are working through drills, but it feels like I'm getting my ass handed to me more than usual.

Hudson notices too. "Where are you tonight, Elwood?"

I shake my head and try to focus. I throw a punch, and he easily deflects it. Another weak throw and he has me twisted around then down on my hands and knees.

I groan and stand up again, angry at myself for not being more focused, angry for letting this thing with Hudson burrow into my every waking thought...suddenly just plain angry. I growl and swing back around. Hudson isn't expecting it, but he still dips out of the way of my arm. My momentum's too much and I end up taking myself out. I land on the mat, flat on my back—a complete and utter fool.

I stare up at the ceiling. My heart might beat out of my chest. My breaths come hard and fast. My blood pulses through me. Everything feels raw, like in hitting the mat, I accidentally dislodged the tight tether I've kept on my emotions.

I'm not even aware that the truth is on the tip of my tongue demanding air, but suddenly my lips are parting like I have to say it. I have to get it off my chest. And if there's anyone I want to tell, anyone who might make this feeling go away, it's Hudson.

"Jasper told me I was boring in bed."

Hudson was already approaching me to check if I was okay. Now he crouches down at my side. "He what?"

I'm still catching my breath so my sharp inhales cut off my words. "He said...I'm boring in bed. The day we broke up."

Saying it out loud sounds so hilariously depressing, but the fact is, as a woman in the corporate world who's already been labeled things like studious, severe, intense, and Type A her whole life, I feel like my feminine prowess has always been in question. I didn't even quite realize what an insecurity it was for me until Jasper laid it out there and made it crystal clear. I'm a buttoned-up lawyer with nothing to offer.

Asinine or not, I've let Jasper's words replay in my head a thousand times a day, and I feel vulnerable now that the statement hangs out in the open again, between Hudson and me.

I hate this feeling, like suddenly I want to shake off my own skin. I have to do something, so I laugh, hoping to downplay it or, better yet, act like I never said anything at all.

Hudson says my name, trying to get my attention, but I can't look at him. He reaches out and nudges my side with his fist. Still, I don't turn my head.

"*Scarlett.*"

I squeeze my eyes closed.

"Forget it," I say lightly. "*God*, it's stupid."

He leans in, lowering himself close to me. For an eternity, he just stays there, not saying a word. When he talks, his voice skates across my skin like a tempting caress, sending goose bumps down my spine. "Scarlett Elwood, you could fucking *lie there frozen* and you'd still be the sweetest thing I've ever felt. If he was bored, it's because of his own damn issues."

His words are so gentle and heartfelt I can barely receive them. I just nod before rolling away and pushing up onto my knees.

We walk to the locker rooms, we shower and change, and we walk out of the building together, but we don't ever address the conversation we had on the mat.

He's gifting me the out, and I take it.

Chapter Seventeen

Hudson

"I went home and I slept on it. I think we should kill him."

At the sound of my voice, Scarlett abruptly stops typing and looks up at me with wide eyes.

It's early morning. Scarlett's the first associate in the office, and she looks like she's been here a while. Her coffee cup is bone-dry and there are already a few items crossed off the neat to-do list she keeps by her mouse pad. Every day she outlines tasks with precise strokes. I find that random fact sexy as hell.

"*What?*"

Her confusion makes it clear that she heard me but doesn't trust her ears.

"If not that, we sign him up for annoying spam emails. I looked into a few different options. My personal favorite is one with singing and dancing cats. We can have them sent to him daily, or even twice a day if you think it's necessary."

Realization dawns about who I'm referring to, and a second after, her face flushes with color and she drops her head into her hands. "I thought we weren't going to talk about it!" she groans.

I drape my shoulder casually against the doorframe and lean against it as I take my first sip of my coffee. "Frankly, it's all I *can* think about."

Her head jerks up and her dark eyes widen. "Hudson!"

Her hair is long and straight today, a perfect frame for her pretty face.

"So how do you propose we punish him?"

"We don't," she stresses. "We leave him alone and we move on with our lives."

"That's no fun." I pause mid-sip. "Good thing I already signed him up for those cat emails."

"HUDSON!"

"Relax. He'll never know they were from me. I listed your email address."

"*HUDSON!*"

I can't help but laugh. She couldn't be cuter than when she's exasperated with me like this. There's something so sexy about her feisty temper.

Jasper is now enemy number one on my shit list. Scarlett won't convince me otherwise. He should be glad he doesn't work here; I can think of a million ways to make an associate's life a living hell. Like, y'know, all the things I promised I would do to Scarlett when she first started here but never did.

She's made me soft, *for her.*

I don't think she realizes. She still treats me like she's wary of my every move, like at any minute I'll morph into the person she's been warned about. Little does she know, I'm her greatest ally and she's my biggest weakness.

"Is it still bothering you?"

"His comment?" She shakes her head vehemently, acting as if she's trying to get to work, tapping her pen on her to-do list. "No. It's getting better. I only thought about it fifty times yesterday..." She looks up at me with a teasing smile before adding, "It's *fine.*"

I push off the doorframe. "Well, murder is still on the table," I say mildly. "But if you're morally opposed, you let me know how else I can help."

"Will do. Now please leave me alone because I'm a very busy attorney and I don't have time for idle chitchat."

That day, I spend an hour of my precious time looking into Jasper Beringer like my job depends on it. He's squeaky clean (boring) and his parents are well-off (expected), so in some ways, he's untouchable. I'm offended that Scarlett dated him in the first place. If anyone seems like they'd be boring in bed, it's my boy Jasper.

Could I let his comment go? I could, and I *should.*

Will I continue to fixate on it like it was said directly to me? There's no other way.

Scarlett is...okay, she's not like a kitten in need of coddling. She's more like a lioness that could slice your head off with a single sharp claw, but even still, she doesn't deserve to have a lame dude fuck with her psyche like that.

I want to help—a rare feeling considering helping is not something I do unless it's accompanied by a hefty fee. I like minding my own business. Going home to my nice, clean house. Spending my hard-earned money on useless shit at Williams Sonoma in an attempt to seem like a well-rounded human who cooks and knows the difference between a strainer and a colander.

This stuff with Scarlett...what do you call them again? Oh right, *feelings*—they're screwing me up, distracting me from the simple cut-and-dry life I've always known.

I laughed at a senior associate's joke yesterday. Senior associates aren't funny. No one in this building is. We trade in our sense of humor for the honor of putting "esquire" at the end of our names. On top of that, lately I'm too distracted to screw with Lucy properly. Her power is going unchecked. Today, she took a two-hour lunch break to run down to a sale at Tuesday Morning and I just plum let her.

She did bring back a needle-stitched throw pillow for my office that says *If you don't have something nice to say, come sit by me*, so whatever, I forgave her.

We're inching closer to Christmas and the office has gotten, *sigh*, cheery. There are a variety of peppermint creamers in the break room refrigerator, and some cutesy office manager stuck a bucket of candy canes on my desk that I promptly swiped off into my trash can. Yesterday, "Santa" and a few "elves" strolled around our office for a morale boost, and, for some reason, we all just went with it? "Ha ha, Santa! You better have me on the nice list this year!" was said out loud by an adult with a fully formed frontal lobe. Also, I don't know if we didn't have much in the budget this year or if all the good Santas in Chicago were already booked, but this man was a geriatric bootleg Saint Nick at *best*. I could see the white elastic band holding up his beard, and when I sat on his lap and told him what I wanted for Christmas, he acted weird about it.

Kidding.

"Saw you flirting with Santa today," I tell Scarlett.

We're walking down to the gym together. Some days, Scarlett waits until she hears me locking up my office before she grabs her bag and meets me out in the hall, acting like it was a pure coincidence. *Oh, you just wrapped up too?* It's cute that she pretends she wasn't listening for my departure with her ear to the door.

"Funny," she says, referring to my Santa comment.

"Lookin' to become the next Mrs. Claus?"

"I'm sure I'm not adventurous enough in bed for Santa."

I look like I'm weighing this possibility. "You think Santa's doing some naughty stuff?"

"He *has* to be. With all those reindeer harnesses? And all that downtime in the summer?"

I have to pinch the bridge of my nose to keep from laughing, and even still, a chuckle slips out.

Dammit, Scarlett. Stop. Killing. Me. All. The. Time.

It gets worse though, because everyone knows that in life, a situation that feels impossible and dangerous can always, *always* get worse.

So far I've harbored my crush on Scarlett with steadfast determination, surreptitious glances, a fucking lot of—let's call it *self-care*, and reproachful reminders that I cannot under any circumstances sleep with Anders Elwood's youngest child if I want to make senior partner at this law firm sooner rather than later. One night with Scarlett and I could kiss my hope of a promotion goodbye forever. I'd be lucky if he let it go at that.

But it's one thing to *hypothetically* turn Scarlett down, quite another to really do it.

Later that night, I'm about to take her home after our workout. It's only the second time I've driven her, and she's trying to get out of it even though there's a foot of snow on the ground and more piling up every second. She's positioned herself between me and the passenger door. I'm about to just push her in.

"I thought we learned our lesson," she argues. "My apartment's only two seconds away."

"Scarlett. *In.*"

She maintains eye contact with me as she slides into the passenger seat, and I close the door on her before she can keep arguing. Ah wait, she's still arguing behind the glass. Oh well, I tried.

"I'm picking the music this time."

"Change the channel and you die."

She pushes those buttons with willful abandon. For all I know, she's reprogramming my radio stations.

Acoustic coffee shop music pours through my speakers and castrates my balls right off. She might as well put a beanie on my head and give me a tattoo of a crow taking flight on my inner forearm.

"Satisfied?"

She smiles. "Yes. This will help you keep your cool while I talk to you about something important."

I sigh like I'm exasperated by the sheer idea of her having anything to tell me. She knows to just ignore me and get on with it.

"So listen, I've been thinking about something you can do to help me with this situation with Jasper that doesn't involve murder, and you aren't allowed to outright shut me down." She holds her hand out like she's scared I'm about to cut her off already. "You *have* to think on it first...swear you will."

"No."

She crosses her arms and turns toward the window. "Okay fine."

It takes me all of one second to cave to her reverse psychology.

"I swear."

"Forget it."

"Scarlett, I *swear.*"

She turns around too fast, her pouty act gone in an instant. She's gleeful she got her way, and I'm sitting here in the driver's seat knowing I got fully played, not even all that bitter about it. She owns me.

"What did you say this is about?" I ask, missing my right turn on purpose so I can add five minutes to our drive. She notices but doesn't say anything. Soon, I'll be driving us out of the state just for the pleasure of being in her company.

"My Jasper problem."

I look over at her, surprised. "*Is* he a problem?"

"Not in the way you might be thinking. Don't start cracking your knuckles. Just his comment..."

"I thought we addressed the comment."

"We did, and believe me, what you said in the boxing ring a while back was very thoughtful and I haven't forgotten it. It's just..."

"Just what?"

"You *had* to say it."

I nearly drive the car off the road. "*I had to?*"

"Yes because you're nice—"

"NICE?!"

"One of the nicest people I know, yes."

Oh geez. Maybe I *did* drive my car off the road a second ago and this is the afterlife or something. That's the only explanation for this strange conversation.

I laugh and sputter. "That's *not* why I said it."

She waves her hand in a circle like, *Yeah, yeah.* Maybe I wasn't explicit enough two weeks ago. I should have gone into greater detail about all the ways she would never, *could never* bore me in bed.

"Anyway, I know how you can really help me. And here it goes. I want you to have sex with me for a grade."

I tilt my head like a curious chihuahua. "You want me to—*what now?*"

"Have sex with me and critique me."

"Critique the sex?"

She's so matter-of-fact about it. "Yes, I want a letter grade, A+, A-...B... If that doesn't prove exhaustive enough, I'm open to number grades too, that way you can be more precise."

Oh thank god, we're back at her apartment now. I don't have to entertain this absurd idea for one more second.

"Scarlett, get out of my car."

She throws her hands up. "I said you couldn't make your decision now!"

"Too bad, I have."

"See? I knew you would be too narrow-minded about this."

"*HR.*"

It's a full-stop sentence.

She rolls her eyes. "Yes, obviously no one at work could know. That goes without saying."

"It doesn't matter. I'm your boss."

Her voice lilts up as she continues. "So what better person to give me critiques? It's practically your job!"

I reach over and yank her door handle so the door flies open. Biting cold wind blasts into my car.

She starts to scoot off the seat. "Fine, Mr. Grumpypants. We'll talk about it tomorrow."

"No, we won't."

Her confident little wave over her shoulder says, *Oh yes, we will.*

Chapter Eighteen

Scarlett

This is another reason why I don't belong in the courtroom. On top of my hot temper, I have no powers of persuasion. If my goal was to have Hudson agree to my ludicrous plan, I should have really buttered him up first, maybe even spoon-fed it to him slowly over a few days—like the boiling frog metaphor—so he wouldn't even realize he'd agreed to have sex with me until we were already in the middle of the act.

My mistake was approaching him with austere simplicity. "It's just sex" and "What's the big deal" did little to convince him I am not absolutely out of my mind. I shouldn't have blurted it out like that, but I wanted to strip away all the fuss and make it seem very black and white.

Despite Hudson's initial response, I still am of the mindset that it's a simple proposition. I just need someone to confirm for me, definitively, whether Jasper was correct in his assessment of my sexual abilities.

I don't want to give Jasper this much power. Truly I want to write off his comment, but if for some reason he was right, well then maybe Hudson could also give me a few pointers and simple corrections, like "That thing you're doing with your hand really hurts" or "Yeah, not sure where you're heading, but that's my butthole."

I understand that I could seek help from another man, but Hudson is unequivocally the right person for the job. Not only is he, strangely, the only person in my life I trust to bring in on something this embarrassing, he's also—I'll just say it plainly: Hudson Rhodes looks like he knows his way around a bedroom.

You don't have confidence rippling off you like he does unless you can absolutely *make it happen* between the sheets. And if I'm wrong about that, well what better way to find out THAN BY HAVING SEX WITH HIM!

It's all I want for Christmas. The only thing on my list.

After the night I brought up my stellar idea and Hudson all but kicked me out of his car, I start to bring him coffee every morning for a week straight in an attempt to get back in his good graces, but if I so much as *breathe* in the direction of the sex conversation, he shuts me down.

"No."

"Not happening."

"*Scarlett*."

"Absolutely not."

You'd think each day his resolve would crumble little by little. I've been wearing my sexiest work dresses, which, *okay*, aren't all that sexy with their business-appropriate hemlines and sensible wrinkle-resistant fabric, but I still see him glancing at my body when he thinks he's being sly about it. On some level, Hudson wants me, and I just have to figure out how to make him act on that want.

Our company holiday party seems like the perfect opportunity to bring him to his knees, or at the very least, show him a new side of me. Physically, that is.

It takes me eight hours on the last Saturday before Christmas (aka the busiest shopping day in America aka *I had to fight your mom in Macys*) to find the perfect dress for the party. Good thing I had a secret weapon: Katherine Elwood.

My mom couldn't believe it when I called to ask her to go shopping with me.

"Is this an early Christmas present?" she teased.

"What? N—*yes*, it is. Surprise!"

Willingly partaking in one of my mom's favorite pastimes wasn't without risks. She wouldn't let us get started before we'd stood in a twenty-minute line to purchase an extra-large cup full of doughy pretzel bites glazed in so much Butter Sauce™ I swear I could hear my heart valves sigh in disappointment. When I suggested that we "just glance through the first floor of Nordstrom," she looked at me like she couldn't fathom how we share DNA then she thrust me onto the escalator with wild abandon. I could have died!

I didn't give her the full details of her assignment. Like a rookie detective only given the information absolutely necessary to do their job but nothing deemed classified, she assumed I just wanted to look my best for my first big company holiday party. She was completely unaware that I need to transform into a bombshell worthy of making Hudson throw caution to the wind, that I need to find the holy grail of dresses that will straddle the line between being sexy and remaining HR-approved. We're talking about a razor-thin margin here.

We settle, eventually, on a long silver halter dress that hugs my figure and seems to move like liquid across my body every time I take a step. It's a work of art, and the price tag reflects it. The only tricky part about the design is the open back, but my mom won't let that deter me from getting it. She has a white faux fur she offers to let me borrow. With that layered on top, the outfit will be perfect.

I have a hair and makeup appointment near my apartment. While I'm getting ready, my parents offer to swing by and pick me up for the party, but there's no way I can let that happen. I need Hudson to actively forget who I am if this is going to work. Reminding him of my last name, of who my father is— that's akin to throwing an ice-cold bucket of water onto the meager kindling I've managed to stoke between us.

So I arrive solo.

I deferred to the hairstylist and let her pull back my hair and pin it in this pretty knot at the nape of my neck. Beneath the faux fur, my entire back is exposed from my hairline to the little dimples above the base of my spine. Despite my mother's encouragement from earlier about my outfit being "totally demure" and "cute even"—I feel too provocatively dressed, but I'm already here, at the party.

It's a hell of a time to come to the revelation that I should have just gone with something understated and quiet. Everyone keeps looking at me, and I can't tell if they're good looks or bad looks or if there's even a difference between the two.

Good going, Scarlett.

Booze is the only thing that might make this better—or worse, but I'll take the gamble. Just like at the Halloween party, there are signature cocktails. No clowns this time though. The drink list is written on a gold-leaf-rimmed menu board sitting atop the bar, and I go with a Mistletoe Mishap, which just sounds plain fun and ends up being dangerously good.

"Come find me if you need another one," the bartender tells me with a wink.

I frown at him, then realization dawns, and *oh shit*. Like a superhero who's just recognized the terrifying extent of her new powers, I'm only now coming to terms with the silver dress effect.

I thought it was a suspiciously fast turnaround time between me walking out of my apartment building to me finding an available cab. And once I arrived at the bar Elwood Hoyt rented out for the party, an attendant from the valet offered to escort me into the building even though I wasn't confused about where I was going and there were people jingling their keys at him impatiently.

Dammit.

I really should go home and change. I made a grievous mistake, but just when I think I've totally lost my nerve and need to vacate the premises as soon as possible, Hudson walks in dressed in a black suit underneath a camel-colored wool coat and I almost pass out.

The sight of him almost knocks me out cold. Just straight heart attack levels of sexiness. I'm obsessed with his dark hair, the trimmed scruff along his jaw he's been sporting lately (ever since I made an offhand remark about liking it, actually), his sharp eyes as they come to rest on me. He doesn't even pretend to want to talk to anyone else.

I wave and point over to the food. He deposits his coat and comes to join me in line just as I pick up a festive plate and start to peruse the charcuterie selections.

"You're late," I say, keeping my attention down on the various cheeses.

Hudson falls in line a half-step behind me. I want to pause and stay where I am to let him creep gently closer, but I'm too scared to do it.

"I almost didn't come."

I smirk at him over my shoulder. "Scared of what the townspeople will do to you now that you've stolen Christmas?"

I'm teasing because a few days ago, I was in the hallway coming back from the break room when I saw a group of actors dressed like Whos of Whoville standing at Hudson's door, caroling and attempting to deliver a basket of Christmas cheer courtesy of Zion Oil. Lucy was clapping along and singing, really letting loose. Hudson shook his head.

"No. All right. Move along. Let's go. Get your props."

Their song trickled off awkwardly as each one of them stopped singing at different times. Hudson shooed them down the hall toward the elevators with little regard for their theatrical performance and the fact that they didn't get to finish it.

"It almost went on for fifteen minutes!" Hudson says now in an attempt to defend himself. "What was I supposed to do when the third person went for a solo?"

"It was impeccably done. My only regret is that I didn't come up with the gift myself."

"Don't think I didn't consider you as the culprit."

I smile warmly, like he just paid me the highest compliment. "Torturing you is my favorite hobby."

"I know. It's why you're in that dress…"

I turn and shuffle ahead in line, picking over the cheeses while trying to suppress my shit-eating grin. So he's not immune to me tonight.

Good.

As we continue on, I convince Hudson to try the brie drizzled with honey and he makes me take some of the jalapeño goat cheese I originally passed on. It absolutely melts in my mouth. I want to marry the goat.

"That was phenomenal." I'm already spinning on my heels. "I have to go back and get more."

"Relax. Let the other people have their cheese, you greedy thing."

Only Hudson could make "you greedy thing" sound that sexual.

God. This thing between us has got to just happen.

Yes, I want him to grade me and give me feedback under his strict tutelage, sure, but beyond that, I simply *need* Hudson in a way that's completely flipped my world upside down. I'm turned on all the time. Pretty much any time he moves or talks, I find some way to make it seem pervy and hot. I'm sweating here. And what has he done? He's shown up to this party in his custom black suit with all that lazy good-looking hair that I just want to *tug*.

"How long do you think we have to stay until we can blow this joint?"

"You're suggesting we leave?" Hudson says, devouring his brie as his eyes roll back in ecstasy.

"Say I was right about the brie."

"You were right about the brie."

I grin. "Yes, I want to leave. To do the grading thing."

The grading thing. What a hilariously casual way to proposition someone for sex.

Hudson's face takes on a new determined sharpness.

Oh dear. I made another mistake. I spoke too soon. I should have taken him to the bar, not the buffet. He's too sober for this conversation.

I hate the way he's looking at me now, all reproachful and disappointed.

"I won't change my mind, Scarlett. Your idea is absurd. You're wrong for me in every way imaginable, what with you being young and naive and *my boss's daughter*. You stand directly between me and my future goal."

"Which is?"

"To become a senior partner."

"Right. Okay—" I hold up my hand because I know he's about to cut me off. "I listened to your concerns, so it's only fair that you let me address them. As far as our age gap, well... you're exaggerating. You're not that much older than me. In fact, if I were considering getting a serious boyfriend, I would want him to be about your age, someone slightly older and established. Your age is actually a huge turn-on for me." I don't miss the fact that this comment makes him furrow his brows even more. "And about your future goals…I don't see why us having one night together should change that."

Hudson doesn't say another word, and I cave within ten seconds.

"Fine. I hear you. I won't keep pushing it."

"Just forget what Jasper told you," he adds sternly.

I shake out my shoulders. "Yeah, okay. I will. Poof—it's gone."

Chapter Nineteen

Hudson

Word to the wise: don't take time off for the holidays. Use the quiet office to be extra productive and get all your work done then take a few days off in early January. Go to some tropical island all by yourself. Ignore all the calls and text messages from your family, kick those feet up on a poolside hammock, and relax.

I didn't do this, you see. I went home for Christmas, and it wasn't relaxing. It was borderline insanity.

My mom started in on me the moment I walked into her house on Christmas Eve.

"No girl?" She leaned over, looking behind me as if expecting me to have a date. "All right. I'll clear the extra place setting at the table..."

"I never said I was bringing anyone," I pointed out, to which she responded, "Well...a mother can hope."

My dating life was the topic of conversation on Christmas Eve *and* Christmas morning. I was surprised to say the least. Since she brought up the subject during Thanksgiving, I assumed it'd be smooth sailing into the new year, but no.

It got worse.

She brought over a girl for me to meet on Christmas Day, the neighbor's granddaughter. I was minding my own business, scrolling through all the weird holiday programming on TV and eating my way through a cheese ball at an alarming rate when the doorbell rang.

I looked over my shoulder. "Mom, you expecting someone?"

My pregnant sister and her brood of children were already in the house. I knew they were present and accounted for because the noise level was at the usual crippling decibel. My brother-in-law was working up at the hospital until closer to dinnertime, so that left...the poor unsuspecting neighbor girl my mother had roped into her scheme unwittingly.

My mom got to the door before I did, and she whipped it open with a chorus of hellos.

"Everyone! *Everyone!*" she called, expecting a crowd of people to join her.

I don't know why she kept saying "everyone"; it was just me, standing in the foyer a few feet away from her. Corinne and the kids were upstairs in the game room.

"This is Emily," she said, ushering the girl into her house.

She couldn't have been a day over twenty. Younger even than Scarlett.

My mother looked at her with unabashed pride then told me, "Emily is a vet tech at the sweetest little animal hospital. She saves all sorts of critters every day, which I just find *so* admirable. Tell us about your work, Emily."

Emily, who up to this point had allowed my mother to lead her in and hold on to her arms with good-natured confusion, now made a point to step away and smile.

"Oh, it's...just like you said. I'm a vet tech." Her tone changed, hardened. "You mentioned you wanted me to come over and pick up a cake for my grandma?"

Poor, poor Emily. She had no idea she was being used as a lamb for slaughter.

I looked at my mom. "This is a new low."

My mom batted away my comment as her smile stretched bigger than ever. "*Cake!* Yes. I'll go get it. Hudson can entertain you for a moment."

She hurried away, and I wondered if she'd even made the cake yet. Surely she wasn't in there preheating the oven.

Emily looked at me for the first time and blushed, then looked down at the ground, the wall, the ceiling. She wanted out of there ASAP.

"Sorry about this."

My mom came back into the foyer faster than I expected, carrying a Tupperware cake carrier that, for all I know, wasn't even filled with a real cake. Had she thought that far ahead in her master plan?

"Here you go," she said, trying to hand it off to me.

I didn't take it. "She can obviously carry that Tupperware by herself."

It weighed a couple of pounds, if that.

She stepped closer and lowered her voice. "*Hudson Samuel Rhodes*, you will walk this fine young woman back to her grandma's house or so help me God—it's Christmas, Hudson! *Christmas!*"

Outside, I walked Emily back to her house, holding the cake. It was so light a baby bird could have carried it across the yard.

Emily looked sidelong at me with a tense expression. "I'm in a serious relationship, just to be clear."

Oh good grief. "That's fine. Ignore my mother."

She looked warily over her shoulder. "She's watching us through the kitchen blinds."

Of course she was. "I'm sorry. Don't be worried about your grandma having to live next door to her. My mom is relatively harmless. I think she's just had too much eggnog."

At Emily's doorstep, I passed off the cake to her.

"It's cool," Emily said. "You can go now. Tell your mom I'll bring her Tupperware back after my grandma's finished with the cake."

Inside her house, my mother was waiting for me with clasped hands and hopeful puppy dog eyes. "*Well!?*"

I walked right past her. "Congratulations. They're getting their locks changed. Maybe adding some steel bars to the windows as we speak."

"*Hudson.*"

"You're insufferable."

She threw up her hands. "*I'm a mother!* Of course I'm insufferable."

I plopped back down on the couch. "I'm perfectly fine on my own, you know."

Apparently, this speech didn't get through to her because later on, once we'd eaten all the traditional Christmas foods for brunch and we were hungry for something different, we placed an order for pizza.

I gave my mom more than enough cash to cover it, but when she answered the door to receive the delivery, she called my name like it was a question. "Hudson?"

Then I saw that she was gesturing to the man who was about my age, dressed in a Blackhawks jersey and hat.

It took me a second to register what she was asking. She didn't need more money.

Good lord.

I rubbed my eyes and said, "Just pay for the damn pizza!"

"Bad word! Bad word!" my niece shrieked, dancing around me on the couch until I picked her up and flung her back onto the pillows. She squealed with delight and demanded I do it again and again.

"I just wanted to cover all the bases," my mom said once she'd shut the door. "It's not too late to try to grab his number!"

Chapter Twenty
Scarlett

Is there anything sadder than the day after New Year's? Corporate America doesn't waste any time. They call in the worker elves in the dead of night to strip away the holiday decorations with all the efficiency of a Chick-fil-A drive-thru. By the time we make it back into the office come January 2nd, there's no more cheer, no more tinsel, no more artificial happiness of any kind. Now we've entered the bleak side of winter, the bitterly cold January days that seem to stretch on forever. I need to be on a beach in Maui; instead I'm in the Elwood Hoyt food court, battling seasonal depression and trying to pick between two sad-sounding proteins for my lunch salad. Hudson finds me just as

I'm handing over my credit card to pay upwards of $20 for wilted lettuce and chicken that was grilled sometime yesterday.

"I've changed my mind."

I frown at him over my shoulder. "You changed your mind? Because I asked if you wanted anything for lunch and you said Lucy already—"

"*No.*" He stands up straighter then fixes his already neat tie. "I changed my mind about the grading thing."

My stomach plummets then soars. I feel weightless for the length of time it takes me to realize he's pranking me. This is April Fools' a few months early.

"Why?" My tone implies I have zero time for his bullshit. I have cold chicken to eat.

He's looking over my head when he replies, "Because I need you to do something for me."

He sounds deadly serious.

My worry starts to compound on itself almost immediately. I accept my card back from the cashier and tuck it into my wallet before grabbing my food. Hudson falls in step beside me as I walk to a table in the corner of the food court. I'd love to take my meal out on the terrace, but seeing as the wind chill outside is hovering near -450 degrees, I'm stuck in here. "What is it? What do you need from me?"

He sighs and looks at me, finally. His eyes are so heavy when they land on mine. Two-ton boulders. "Listen, it's my mom's greatest wish, her last wish, to see me happily settled down."

I gasp. "Oh my god, your mom is dying?"

He shakes his head, unaffected. "No, but I figure it's better to get this out of the way now while you and I are doing each other favors."

Grateful I'm not about to have to Make a Wish, I pour dressing over my salad and then do the Kardashian shake. "So what does this favor entail?"

"I can't believe you're not outright agreeing."

"Can you blame me?"

Sure, I'm the more desperate of the two of us, but I need to know what I'm getting myself into. No lawyer signs a contract without reviewing it first.

He leans forward and drops his hands on the table, lowering his voice. "Listen, it's my mom's birthday in two weeks. I want you to come to the house with me and play along."

"So I just show up and pretend to be your date? Your girlfriend? *Wife?*"

He grins. "Easy there. Girlfriend will do. You'll smile and act like you absolutely adore me. Sing to my mom, eat cake, yada yada—then we'll be on our merry way."

I shake my head as I mull it over. "I'm not sure I'm the best woman for the job. I have a terrible poker face."

"Okay, just sit there and smile. No talking required. I'll tell her you're shy."

I frown, not sure I believe him on this. "And if I do that, you'll do the thing I want?"

He stands back up, suddenly uncomfortable with the conversation. He brushes invisible lint off his shoulder. "Yes. Fine. Whatever."

"Even if it'll jeopardize everything?"

His jaw tightens and he looks back at me with an unyielding, stern expression. "It won't. You convinced me of that. It'll be one time, and we'll take the secret to our graves."

I grin. "Fun. Okay. When?"

"What about tomorrow?"

I scrunch my nose. "On a work night?"

I'd barely have any time to get ready, and I desperately need to wax.

"What are you suggesting?"

"Saturday. You come to my place."

"Fine. Okay."

"Should we shake on it?"

"No. Eat your salad."

I shimmy my shoulders. "I'm excited."

His mouth is a terse line. He's really sucking all the joy out of this little arrangement of ours. "You shouldn't be. You have no idea how much my mom is going to hound you."

"I'm really good with moms. They love me. Well...Jasper's mom didn't love me, but the feeling was mutual there so who cares." Then my smile falls. "Wait—what's going to happen when she asks about me after the birthday party?"

He shrugs. "I'll play it off, tell her you're busy. Then in a few months, I'll tell her we broke up."

"Because you were incapable of giving me the emotional support I needed."

His brows arch. "Wow, you just think of that on the fly?"

"It's perfect. Your mom will buy it right away."

"Why can't we say it was your fault?"

I rear back. "No. I don't want your mom to be mad at me."

"She doesn't even know you."

"Promise," I insist.

He sighs. "Whatever. We'll come up with some excuse you agree with when the time comes, okay? How's that?"

I smile, satisfied with the result of our negotiations. "Fine."

"So Saturday?"

"Saturday."

Then he walks away, and the second he's out of sight, I drop my fork into my salad and sit there in a shocked stupor. Eventually, I take my untouched salad upstairs, put it in the fridge in the break room, and get back to work.

The week stretches before me like a never-ending black hole. I check my clock every minute, on the minute, for the next few days.

After work, I cram it all in. I book a facial, a massage, a wax. I get my nails done because for some reason sporting OPI's Funny Bunny seems crucial. I pull out the La Perla lingerie set I ordered months ago and hand-wash it, then steam it, then when that doesn't cut it, I iron it, then hang it up on my closet door so it taunts me for the remainder of the week. I rearrange my entire apartment on Friday night then wake up Saturday morning, decide I hate the new layout, and move it all back. Moira is emitting a cacophony of shrill meows. She'd like me to please chill out and stop moving her food bowl from one patch of tile to another patch of tile. She doesn't understand that we have a special guest coming this evening.

"A man, Moira, so I expect you to be on your best behavior!"

She hated Jasper, so I toyed with the idea of getting her out of the apartment before Hudson came over, but the cat sitter who watched her a few months back suddenly had no availability once I gave her my name. I also thought about stowing Moira in my room while he's here, but it took me a week of repeated washes to get the shrimp smell out of my pillowcase last time. And if I put her in there *without* shrimp, she'll probably shred my curtains in a blind rage. So, it is what it is. Moira will be a third wheel for tonight, and frankly she's the least of my problems.

I can't get out of my own head. My nerves are shot. A jog through the desolate, snowy streets in the late afternoon does nothing to burn off my excess energy, so I decide it's best to add alcohol into the mix. Before my shower, I pop the cork on a bottle of red wine my mom brought back from her most recent buying trip. The glass of Cabernet goes down a little too quickly, so I convince myself it was a light pour. A second glass seems necessary. Thankfully, it does the trick. By the time I sit down in front of my makeup vanity, I feel cool as a cucumber.

Once I've done a perfect no-makeup makeup look, I layer my daring La Perla lingerie set underneath a black slip dress that boasts a shorter-than-short hemline. I'm about to go in for more wine when the chime by my door goes off.

Hudson's right on time. I clear him with the doorman and then I wait at my door, swallowing down my last-minute jitters as best as possible before I hear footsteps out in the hallway. He doesn't get the chance to knock before I fling the door open.

He's wearing jeans.

Oh my god, I did not anticipate this curveball.

"Scarlett?"

I don't even answer him. He's wearing dark-wash denim and these beat-up brown boots, a black T-shirt, and a Cubs jacket. I barely resist the squeak of pleasure that wants to erupt out of me. He's glorious!

"You're being rude."

His tone implies he's teasing, but I don't even have the good grace to move aside and let him in. I'm so flabbergasted.

"I don't care," I tell him. My eyes zero in on his body. "You look…different."

"So do you. Now invite me in."

"Okay, but be forewarned, I will be checking out your butt when you walk by me."

My remark doesn't even faze him; he's used to me by now.

He doesn't wait for the formal invitation (realizing it's never going to come) and brushes past me—overwhelming me with the heavenly scent of his cologne—and then he walks into my apartment like he's been here a hundred times.

"I like your place."

"Thanks, I cleaned it all day. I didn't want you to think I actually live here, I guess. That candle is new. The throw blanket too." I step toward him and offer to take his jacket. He yanks it off in that sexy gruff guy way. Like can they not just remove a garment gently? With care? Apparently not.

I take his jacket to the hall closet, holding it high enough that I can steal another whiff of his cologne, just as I catch Moira hopping down from her perch on the windowsill. I issue an introduction-slash-warning: "That's Moira, she'll bite your hand off."

A loud, sassy *rawr* bookends my words, and though my back is turned, I imagine Hudson just barely flinching back in time. When I look to confirm this—expecting blood and carnage, fingers hanging by stringy ligaments—I find that Moira has LAID DOWN ON HER BACK and EXPOSED her fleshy pink BELLY to him. She's purring! I didn't think she knew how to purr. I thought the happiest feeling she was capable of was simmering disdain.

She squirms and bats her paws at him playfully. She is FLIRTING with him. In my apartment!

He bends down and scoops her up into his strong arms. "She's sweet."

My eye twitches.

I've never *once* been able to gently hold Moira like he is. If I have to get close to her for some reason, like to take her for a vet visit, it's an entire half-day ordeal to get her in her carrier. I start with treats that never work, then I go for the full-on chase-down method that ends with my arms being scratched raw and my nerves frayed and frazzled.

"She's a wild beast," I assure him.

"Really?" He nuzzles his nose against hers, and I just blink at them wondering if Moira somehow knows exactly what she's doing trying to steal my man.

Eventually, after they're done bonding, he sets her down and she winds through his legs before hissing at me as she walks back to her window of choice.

"Can I get you a drink?" I ask him. "Water? Soda? Iced tea? Hard liquor? A seltzer?"

He's still looking around my apartment. "Water's fine. Is this you?"

I've already started to head toward the kitchen island so I can't be sure which framed photo he's pointing to on the TV console. "Is it the one where I'm missing my two front teeth?"

"Yeah, and your hair's all tangled."

I laugh. "Yeah, that was the day after Halloween and I was hopped up on ten different types of sugar. Okay here's your water. Take it and sit down and we'll start."

He turns to me, entirely too amused. "We don't actually have to do this. In fact, we really shouldn't."

Rejection washes over me so swiftly it feels like a sucker punch.

"You don't want to?"

Chapter Twenty-One

Hudson

I wipe a hand down my face, trying and failing to come up with the right words here. Do I want to seduce and have my wicked way with Scarlett? Uh, yeah, would love to, actually. Thanks for asking.

Should I be doing this, though? Now *that's* the real question.

I know I've already agreed to it and I'm here, in her apartment, but it's not too late to talk some sense into her. She's standing in front of me brimming with pure innocence. She doesn't even have the capacity to mask her hurt over thinking I'm rejecting her.

"I can't be the best person for this. Surely there are a million guys lined up around the block. Here, let's get you set up with a dating profile. What app do you like?" I'm already holding my hand out like I'm waiting for her to pass me her phone.

She shakes her head. She's a lost sad puppy when she tells me, "I can't. It has to be someone I trust."

I squeeze my eyes closed, trying to channel some bullshit yoga mindset to conquer the raging desire coursing through my veins. In my current state, my brain mixes up yoga and Yoda so my inner thoughts sound like: *Want to fuck her, you do.*

Jesus Christ.

I look at her again.

She's chewing her bottom lip. "This is nothing serious. Okay? This is science."

Science, got it.

Wait, don't got it. "Explain."

She puffs out an exasperated breath. "Don't ask me to explain! I don't know. I barely passed my science courses. Just...it doesn't have to be all that intense, okay? No feelings, no tricky situations. One time. You and me and then"—she snaps her fingers—"it'll be like nothing ever happened." I don't say anything, and she puts her hands on her hips. "People have one-night stands all the time! We can be those people!" Her eyes take on a pleading look. "Can you just pretend I'm someone else for tonight? Not Scarlett Elwood, but a girl you picked up at a bar? A girl you really, really want to sleep with?"

Yeah, that's just it. There's no pretending required, and that's why this feels a little wrong.

"You don't need to do this," I tell her. "Jasper is—"

That sentence never makes it to the finish line. Scarlett—knowing full well where I'm headed—decides to take matters into her own hands. She suddenly starts to walk closer and then stops just when her chest barely grazes mine, arches up onto her toes, and kisses me with bold abandon.

Scarlett.

In mere seconds, I'm consumed by her taste, by the feel of her pressed against me. My hands reach out for her hips. I gather her close, bunching her silky dress in my fist as she moans. The sweet sound puts fire in my veins. I kiss her back, tilting my head as I band my arms behind her. I don't know if she planned on her kiss lasting this long, but now neither one of us is retreating.

I've been so good when it comes to Scarlett. Fantasies unspool one after another. My attraction to her is undeniable, and now I have her in my arms, her lips on mine. I decide all bets are off. For tonight.

She presses her hot little body against me. There's no denying how much I want her. She must realize how easily she winds me up. My hands move from her back down to her hips, lower until I have my palms curved around her ass, hauling her against me as our hips start to move, as we—

Suddenly she breaks away and pushes me. I realize the couch is at my back just before the back of my legs hit it. I sit while she stands assessing me with red lips.

"You can't take over like that," she chides.

"What?"

She's breathing as hard as I am. Those delicate eyebrows are furrowed in annoyance. "Usually, I'd want that. I would love nothing more than to let you do whatever it is you were about to do to me. It felt amazing, *believe me*, but I have to know if I can bring a man to his knees, Hudson. That's what this is all about. You have to let me lead, okay?"

"You're kidding me."

She throws her hands up. "That's the whole point! If we have great sex but *you're* the one in charge, I won't have the answer to my question. I'll just assume you were the reason it was so good."

I'm having the hardest time suppressing a laugh. "So what do you want me to do?"

"Let me seduce you."

The raging hard-on I'm sporting beneath my zipper must not be evidence enough. I wipe my hand down my face. "Scarlett, you could—"

She takes a step back and reaches for the strap of her dress. She's going to make good on her promise, and she only gives me a moment to realize that before she pushes her strap down off her shoulder and the front of her dress dips low enough that I catch a teasing glimpse of black lace lingerie cresting over her left breast.

Oh.

My stomach swoops.

My hands fist into the couch.

She's watching me, hungry for my reaction. I don't try to conceal it. I don't think I'm savvy enough to mask it anyway. She has to know how much I want her, how much this is killing me.

She lets her dress hang like that for a suspended moment as I just sit there, admiring her. Then with a shaky hand, she reaches up for her other strap, sliding it over her slender shoulder and letting it slip off before she pushes the top of her dress down to her hips.

So much of her skin is revealed so suddenly. I want to demand she slow down, let me catch my goddamn breath, but I can't speak as she slides her dress the rest of the way off, letting it pool in a silky heap at her feet before she steps out of it altogether.

I haven't taken a breath in what feels like five minutes. My chest is screaming for air.

Scarlett's in nothing but black lace. Her lingerie is delicate and sparse enough that I can see the pink tips of her breasts through the fabric. Even if she hadn't ordered me to just sit here, I wouldn't be able to move.

She's...exquisite.

I can't decide where to look. My gaze roves over her body with hungry abandon. I take in her full breasts over the top of her lingerie, the high cut of her black thong over her hips, her endless legs. A piece of her dark brown hair falls over her shoulder, casting a shadow over part of her face.

I can feel her nervous energy palpating between us.

"Am I okay?" she asks timidly.

I squeeze my eyes closed so I don't let out a string of expletives. When I think I've mostly managed to conquer the worst of my anger with Jasper, I blink my eyes open and look at her again.

Her gaze is wide and innocent. Her dark lashes frame the sweetest pair of dark brown eyes. Her face could bring me to my knees.

"Come here."

She hesitates as if she's scared, but when she eventually steps closer, right between my knees, I reach out to skim my hand up the outside of her right thigh, toying with the lace fabric, tugging it up higher until it rests over her hip bone. I swallow as my thumb brushes her skin. It's so soft she doesn't feel real.

"You're doing it again," she says with a weak voice.

Ignoring her, I bring my hand up to smooth it over the contours of her stomach, up higher, skimming her ribs and brushing the outside of her bra.

This isn't what a one-night stand is supposed to feel like.

"*Hudson.*"

Her teasing voice breaks me out of my spell, and I look up at her.

She's battling a smile. "You're not supposed to be the one doing the touching."

I can hear my pulse roaring in my ears. The way she looks, her body, her heart—she's so fragile, the gentlest thing I've ever held. Everything demands I sit up and take note of her. Fuck the agreement. Fuck her rules. I want to worship her. I want to splay her out on the floor of this apartment and not come up for air until daybreak.

But I surrender and sit against the back of the couch. I let my hands drop on either side of my thighs and I wait. I gave her my word, and I intend on keeping it, no matter what.

The humor dies in her expression as she realizes I'm relenting. I'm giving her exactly what she's asked for, without a fight, and now she doesn't know what to do with all her new power.

An order is on the tip of my tongue, but I resist just as she inches closer and—

"I'm going to sit down, okay? Like this."

And then she straddles me on that couch, her knees going to either side of my hips. My hands rise up—I'm about to seat her right where I want her—but I resist the urge and let her settle down onto me the way she wants.

Turns out she didn't need my help.

"Oh." She flushes when she feels me through my jeans. Then she smiles this delicious little smile I have to kiss away. She responds immediately to my lips on hers, settling down onto me farther, rocking her hips rhythmically. My hands move on their own, gripping her and helping her grind down on me harder. *God.* I kiss my way down her neck, lower. My lips graze her breast, over the black lace, *under* it. I suck her into my mouth and her fingers dig into my hair and tug.

"How am I doing?" she asks between heavy breaths.

"Scarlett."

"Because I can swivel my hips more, or how about—"

I kiss her again and shut her up. She kisses me back and works her hands down the front of my torso, down under my shirt so she can start to work it up and off me. I have that thing yanked off in a matter of seconds and then her hands are on my skin, wandering over every inch of my chest like she can't get enough of me.

"God, you're all man."

I laugh because I'm not quite sure how to take that.

She smiles and shakes her head. "I just feel like the guys I've been with...it's like they think women want these waxed figurines. I want..." Her eyes widen as she looks at me, looking down at my boxer briefs peeking out over the top of my jeans.

I'm glad she didn't finish the sentence. Everything we say tonight will make it that much harder to reset in the morning. It's why I'm being so quiet. It's why I'm holding back *some*.

For a few minutes on the couch, she's on top of me, but we're not kissing. Despite being turned on to the point of pain, we take each other in slowly. She undoes the button on my jeans. I push her hair back behind her ear so I can see the curve of her jaw and her flushed neck. She traces my abs with her pointer finger, getting accustomed to my body. It's like we know this is our one shot. We better make it count. I want to memorize every inch of her.

My finger loops underneath the strap of her bra. When she doesn't protest, I start to peel the black lace away from one breast, so slowly, and a shudder runs through me when I finally tug it all the way off. Her breast is perky and full and begging to be touched.

I oblige with my hand, then my mouth. Then...my teeth.

She hisses a curse under her breath and I chuckle and back away. She's looking at me, utterly incensed, her eyes shining. I can't just leave her like that, half exposed, so I slide the black lace off her chest completely and only bother to undo the clasp at her back after her bra is already hanging loose around her waist.

Scarlett's work clothes don't do her justice. Even those sports bras she wears to work out don't truly give the full picture, but now I have it as she sits on top of me, and she's unbelievable. I can't keep my hands off her. I cup her breasts and run my thumbs over the tips, getting her worked up. She starts rocking on me again, slowly dragging her panties over my jeans to create friction.

She wants relief. She's as desperate as I am. I loop my hands up around her neck, threading my fingers through her hair, and then I bring her mouth down onto mine.

I want her to come apart like this, like we're two teenagers in high school, overloaded on hormones and desperate for any release we can get. I want to watch. I break our kiss and take my hands off her, laying them on the back of the couch on either side of me.

For a moment, she stills. I shake my head. "Keep going."

Her nostrils flare and I look down to where her lace thong has slipped to the side, revealing just the barest glimpse of her. I tilt my head as she continues this maddening lap dance and the fabric slips even more. I reach down and help it along, hooking my finger on the left side and pulling it over.

My gut clenches tight. I shiver with pleasure at the precise moment she decides to be bold. She tips back and touches her hands to my knees, holding herself stable as she continues rocking. I know what this is doing to her. I can feel her shaking. I should be patient, but desire wins out and I have to feel her. I have to know what it's like to brush my thumb over the center of her thighs, to tease and stroke her. I rub concentric circles as she continues grinding down onto me and then I know the exact moment she tips over the edge—that sharp inhale is followed by an earthquake of pleasure. She can barely contain it, and I don't let her off easy. I want every last shake and tremble. When her eyes peel open, she looks at me like she's just woken up from a trance, hotter now than ever.

Fire blazes in her gaze and she launches forward, kissing me in a frenzy as she lifts herself up so she can tug down my zipper. She pushes the denim down only enough that she can successfully slip her hand down into my boxer briefs, to cup and fist me, pumping up and down as if I'm not about to die from the feel of her hand gripping me.

A *"fuck"* falls from my lips just before she pumps again, tightening her fist, working her hand up and down on me. Our tongues tangle and then I feel myself about to break. I yank her hand away a bit roughly and she looks at me crestfallen, like I could possibly find fault with anything she's doing right now. No.

"Did I—"

"I need to get a condom."

Lightning quick, she recovers from her worry. With a timid smile, she nods toward the side table. "I put some in a decorative bowl over there. I bought four different kinds."

She's not kidding. She must have run down to the corner store and swept every condom off the shelf and into her basket. Then she thought to display them in a cute ceramic dish like she was serving up some peanuts.

I almost laugh. "Just grab one."

She leans over to root through the bowl, and I'm a bastard for staring between her legs, at that black thong that's not doing a damn thing to cover her up anymore. I reach my hand out and stroke her inner thigh, just below that sweet spot. She freezes and then goes slack, arching her back ever so gently to let me know she likes what I'm doing. She wants more and I oblige, teasing my hand higher, running my palm up and down her soft skin. Each time, I go a little farther, but never quite to where she needs. I know she's in agony, but I'm in no hurry.

The view of her perched on her hands and knees on her couch is something I'd like to burn into my memory. I could die right now and feel confident that I've seen all I need to see.

To hell with the panties. I tug them down to her knees.

"*Hudson.*"

Her chiding tone is half-hearted. She wants this. I take her all in while she shimmies her hips impatiently. Just when I think she can't take another second of being on display like that, I lean over and bury my face between her legs without warning. It's the most tantalizing angle. I can taste all of her, *feel* all of her. She cries my name like I'm torturing her, and that's *before* I slide my middle finger inside her.

I feel like a bastard taking from her like this, demanding she arch even more, flare her hips, let me stroke her. I know she's overly sensitive. I know she just came, but I also know how easy it'll be to make her come again. Scarlett doesn't stand a chance when I add another finger and start pumping in and out. There's nothing sexier than the way she feels pressed up against my face. The taste of her on my lips. Her *scent*.

I feel that second wave of pleasure crash over her and I'm relentless, cruel, on the verge of feeling dangerously out of control.

"*God.*" She breathes the word out over a long, excruciating exhale, like she's just been wrung out to dry.

When she's capable of speaking in full sentences again, she turns back to look at me over her shoulder. She's flushed. Her eyes are wide and glassy. "Two? TWO? Jasper used to complain about how long it took for me to…"

Something in my expression makes her sentence drift off.

Jasper.

"I hate him. Don't bring him up again unless you want to hear his name on the six o'clock news."

She laughs, and it must be nice to be able to laugh at a time like this. I'm in physical PAIN over here. I'm one feather-light touch away from coming in my fucking pants like a fourteen-year-old in his mom's basement.

Scarlett's at the condom bowl again. What's she going to do with that thing after I'm gone? Put it on her nightstand?

She picks one at random. It might not fit.

"Hand it to me."

"I just about have it."

Burning up with impatience, I rip the condom wrapper out of her hands and have it out of the foil and rolled down onto my length in record time.

She smiles, impressed.

Then she glances down and swallows.

"Right. Maybe I should lie down on the couch and we'll take it slow...or..."

I want to laugh again. She looks genuinely concerned.

"Just come over here, will you?"

She kicks off her panties and then climbs back on top of me. This time, she holds herself up on her knees. My hand goes to her waist and I hold her steady, lowering her gently as her eyes widen.

"Relax," I tell her with a half-laugh, half-groan.

"I'm scared."

"You're overreacting."

"Hudson, YOU WOULD BE OVERREACTING TOO if you were in my position."

Now I'm laughing, which is ridiculous because this is the most exquisite feeling of my life and I should be savoring it with every fiber of my being.

"Slower," she hisses, gripping my shoulders. Her nails dig into my skin.

I almost want to pull her down onto me hard, just to end this beautiful misery. Maybe I would in another life, but in this life, Scarlett has me over a barrel. I'm so obsessed with her, so in awe, I press into her slow inch by slow inch. Anything she wants, I'll give her.

"So I'm doing well so far? Like if you were to grade me right now..."

Her question falls on deaf ears as I finally work her down onto me most of the way and I go still, savoring every overwhelming sensation.

"I'm passing at the very least, right?" she prods impatiently.

"*Scarlett*," I bite out in warning.

I lift her up off me and thrust into her again, and her hands tighten on my shoulders so she doesn't tip over. I do it again, easing her into a faster rhythm until she's scratching her nails down my arms, bending down to find my mouth, kissing me with wild abandon.

Her questions don't matter anymore. There's nothing but what my hands can feel, what my eyes can feast on. I can't comprehend anything else beyond *her*. My hands hoist her up and down harder as I thrust at a maddening pace. She transitions between kissing me and peeling back to watch what I'm doing to her, like she's just as enamored by it as I am. We're wrapped up around each other, as close as two people can get.

I'm panting and trying to stave off the inevitable, skirting the edge of oblivion. When I come, I buck off the couch and press my fingers into her skin. I'm surely leaving marks. Black stars pop behind my closed lids.

Afterward, I settle beneath her with the weight of the world. It was so good. So, so achingly good, but the post-sex high doesn't last. Insidious guilt must have been waiting in the wings because already it starts to weave through me. Overtaking the vestiges of lust. Popping the happy-go-lucky bubble we've crafted for ourselves.

I keep my eyes closed for so long she laughs and kisses my cheek. "Wake up."

"I'm not sleeping."

I don't mean to sound so gruff, but I can't help it.

"What are you doing then?"

"*Processing.*"

"Did I break you?" She taps her finger against my chest, right over my heart, like she's a comedian doing a mic check. "This thing still working?"

I blink my eyes open to see she's smiling down at me. Earnest. Sweet. Scarlett. I find I'm completely speechless.

I'm scared, actually.

I peel her off me and set her down on the couch like she's a rare antique I should have never been handling in the first place. She's so naked and so young and I immediately lean down and grab her black dress and tell her to put it on. I watch the excitement of the last few minutes slowly start to drain from her face as I stand and get dressed myself.

"Hudson?"

I can't look at her. What can I even say?

"Hey." She stands and grabs my arm, forcing me to turn back and look at her. "Did we just ruin everything? Can we still be friends?"

Her pained expression breaks my heart.

"Sorry," I say, hauling her toward me and tightening my hold on her. "I'm sorry."

"For what?"

I can't say it.

My silence does my talking for me though, and Scarlett's too smart not to pick up on the seismic shift that's happened between us.

She steps back forcefully. She's already wearing an angry scowl.

"I wanted that," she says fiercely. "So don't you dare ruin it with some apology now."

She doesn't get it. She doesn't feel what I'm feeling inside, like the world's biggest pig, the worst user. I wanted her like I've never wanted anything, and I let that blind me.

Now, that fog has cleared enough for me to feel sick to my stomach.

"I'm sorry, Scarlett."

"Stop saying you're sorry!" she erupts, stepping away from me even more. The distance seems crucial. "God, just stop. Why are you doing this? We could have just laughed it off and ordered dinner. Watched stupid TV and then parted ways." She points an accusatory finger at me. "I could have seen you on Monday and everything would have been fine. Why are you looking at me like that?! Like you're scared I'm about to start crying."

I *am* scared she's about to start crying. It's like we're inside an emotional vortex. Everything feels too raw.

I knew this was wrong. I knew it on every level and I just couldn't let common sense guide me. I wanted her too much, and now I can never go back and do the right thing. I can't go back to before, when I hadn't touched her.

I've always joked that I'm a villain at heart, but I've never truly felt like one until right now.

Chapter Twenty-Two

Scarlett

For once, Moira and I share the same mood. All day Sunday, my apartment is the perfect backdrop for my misery and heartache. I don't bother drawing the curtains back or changing out of my pajamas. I order breakfast, then I order lunch, then I order dinner, all from the comfort of my cozy spot on the floor onto which I've piled every comfortable blanket and pillow I can find in my apartment. I'm unwilling to sit on my couch. If I didn't stand a high chance of going up in flames alongside it, I'd have already set it on fire.

If it's not perfectly obvious, I'm angry with Hudson, and unfortunately, my anger with him is only eclipsed by my anger with myself. I knew on a molecular level that it was a very dumb idea to sleep with him. I knew without a shadow of a doubt that I'd already developed real feelings for him despite him being my older boss. Oh, and look at the dumbass who still got hurt when things didn't pan out exactly as I hoped they would! Feel bad for me! The girl who walked into the arms of a villain!

Did I think he was going to tuck me in and read me a bedtime story after sleeping with me on that couch!? It's Hudson Rhodes! My brother warned me about him on day one, and I was too stupid to listen.

I'm unwilling to think about or reimagine everything that happened before he left my apartment last night. My full attention is focused on the way I felt after that door closed behind him: like complete trash. The shower I took didn't suffice. I also threw away the lingerie and dress I wore for him. Sent them both down the trash shoot with a satisfied slam of the metal door.

Despite Hudson fleeing my apartment as fast as his feet could possibly carry him, I hoped, as silly as it sounds, that he would reach out to me on Sunday. *Hey, Scarlett! Sorry about my weird-ass exit last night! Just realized my body was possessed by aliens for a little while, but everything is all good now! Want to meet for lunch?*

I would have also even accepted a simple "Hey."

I kept my phone by me all day, and the despair of realizing, at around 7:00 p.m. Sunday night, that I would not be getting a phone call or text or email from him made the situation sear through me as fresh and painful as ever.

On Monday, I barely want to get out of bed, but I'll be

damned if I skip work and get fired because of him. I reach for whatever clothes my fingers touch first, pull my hair up into a ponytail, and apply as much makeup as I would on any other day in the hopes that I look semi-human despite getting horrible sleep the last two nights.

My stomach is twisted into a tight knot a seasoned sailor would be mighty proud of as I take the elevator up to the 70th floor. I don't want to see Hudson first thing. I'm not sure how I'll react, what asinine thing will slip out of my mouth. I've got a "Screw you" locked and loaded.

The hallway near my office is crowded—thankfully. I didn't get in as early as I usually do, didn't want to run the risk of bumping into Hudson when there weren't other people around. Just him and me and an empty hallway? Trouble.

I set my things down in my office and then head into the break room for a coffee. I need it more than ever. There are a few first-year associates in there that pay me no mind, but I'm used to it by now. Usually, I don't let them bother me, and today should be no different.

I make Kendra a cup of coffee too. She was already at her desk when I went in, but she was on the phone so I didn't get the chance to ask if she wanted anything. I decide to err on the side of caution.

Back in our office, I set down her coffee and offer a short hello. I mean, I haven't gotten too carried away in our fledgling friendship, but she doesn't even respond or look up or acknowledge me in any way. *Okay...*

I don't know if it's the fact that it's only the second Monday into the new year or if maybe Kendra woke up on the wrong side of the bed, but over the course of the morning, it feels like all the progress we managed to make before the holidays has completely come undone.

When I get back from lunch, I ask her if she had a good weekend, and she replies with a curt, "Fine."

Have I gone back in time? This is how it felt the first week we shared an office together. Why the extra cold shoulder *now*?

I get my answer, later, in the restroom. I'm fixing my dress, about to open the stall door and head out to wash my hands when I hear someone talking.

"I just think it's weird how much time she spends with Hudson."

"You know they work out together. Dilan says he sees them in the gym *all* the time."

"Yeah, he told me. Did you see her following after him like a lost puppy at the holiday party?"

"Oh my gosh, *yes*! She didn't even try to hide it. It's so obvious she's sleeping with him! Or *trying* to more like—I doubt he'd go there. He doesn't seem like the type to make that mistake."

"Not for someone like her! Are you *kidding*?"

I feel sick listening to these women gossip about the two of us. Without seeing their faces, I can't confirm, but I'm pretty sure it's Makayla and Ramona, Kendra's best friends. Kendra might have started to thaw out before the holidays, but her friends never came around at all. They still shoot me annoyed looks in the food court and during meetings. If I cross paths with them in the hall or if I happen to forget my place and accidentally speak in their presence, they make it very clear they want nothing to do with me. In return, I've given them a wide berth. Now, I'm extra glad I did because clearly, they super suck!

First of all, I wasn't following Hudson around at the holiday party like a lost puppy! He and I spent most of the night talking to Lucy, and then at one point, Hudson chatted with my mom, which was hilariously funny because she was pretty slack-jawed at how handsome he was and when he walked away, she said, "*That man*," all exasperated and with a southern accent for some reason. I wasn't even offended on behalf of my father because I KNOW, MOM. I KNOW.

Beyond that, well yes, unfortunately the rest is true, more or less. I *have* spent a lot of time with Hudson and I *have* opened myself up to gossip and ridicule. While it's not actually against company policy to date coworkers, it's still not encouraged, especially considering Hudson is my superior. No matter how we'd gone about it, us being together was going to invite a lot of commentary, good and bad.

Of course these women don't *actually* know the truth. They don't know we only slept together for the first time over the weekend. They're being nasty and hateful based on nothing but speculation. Unfortunately, that doesn't make me feel better. They've managed to hit their mark beautifully.

Their assessment of how things look between Hudson and me only frays my emotions that much more. Even with everything going on between us, my initial worry isn't about how complicated these allegations might make my work life; it's about whether or not this will get back to Hudson. This might affect the promotion he's so desperate for, and I'd never forgive myself for that. Hudson is the hardest working attorney at this office by a mile.

So I fling my bathroom stall door open and walk directly toward Makayla and Ramona, who, by the time I reach them, have stopped talking and are just staring dumbly at me.

"Excuse me." I indicate the soap dispenser Makayla is blocking like, *You mind?*

She opens and closes her mouth, guppy style, but she doesn't apologize to me. Maybe she's playing naive about the whole thing.

Makayla looks at Ramona. Ramona looks at Makayla. Makayla laughs, and then they flee the bathroom about as fast as Hudson fled from my apartment.

When they're gone, I lean over the counter and try not to throw up from all the adrenaline. I can't look up and meet my own eyes. It'll zap the last bit of courage I'm working with at the moment, and we're talking about a microscopic amount here. It could dissolve at any minute and then what? How will I possibly finish this work day?

My eyes cut to my trembling hands gripping the side of the counter. I try to take a deep breath. It helps, so I do it again, slower this time. I concentrate on the sound of air leaving my lungs as my vision softens, then blurs.

After I leave the bathroom, I go straight to my office. The second I walk through the door, I look at Kendra despite every instinct telling me not to. She rolls her eyes, answering every question I needed answered.

I want to go right over and snatch the untouched coffee cup from her desk, but I withstand the urge, instead taking a seat behind my desk and willing myself not to cry. I end up having to YouTube a bunch of cute videos of dogs just to get through the initial ten minutes of panic. But can you imagine? *Me* breaking down in front of *Kendra*? I'd rather step on a nail.

I see Hudson for the first time at the end of the work day. When I walk out of my office to head toward the elevators, he's in the hall talking to Sophie. I see him, freeze for the quickest instant, and then breezily continue on, brushing past him without saying a word. Every hair on my body stands at attention, begging me to look back, but I resist like a champ.

"Scarlett, did you finish that second draft for me?" Sophie asks just when I think I'm in the clear.

Ugh.

I squeeze my eyes closed, take a deep breath, and then turn with a perfect smile. "I did, but I was going to glance over it one more time at home before I send it back to you. I'll have it back no later than 8:00 p.m., if that's okay?"

She nods in approval. "That's fine. Thanks."

Hudson watches this entire exchange, his eyes fixed on me. I don't look at him once before turning on my heels and heading toward the elevators.

It feels wonderful until it doesn't. That comedown happens so fast my shoulders actually slump. By the time I kick my apartment door closed, I feel utterly defeated.

Moira senses how little fight I have left in me. She doesn't even swat me away when I try to pet her head. She just sits there, probably thinking I'm pathetic, but at least I get the comfort of touching her for my allotted three seconds.

"Hungry?"

She meows, and I get to feeding her. Then I shower and put on my softest pajamas and text my trainer to see if it'd be possible for him to rework me into his schedule again. It's not ideal, but if I leave the office around dinnertime and get in a session with him at his gym, I could work from home afterward to maintain my billable hours and not have to bump into Hudson in the Elwood Hoyt gym anymore. It's the only way forward.

The next day, there are flowers sitting on my desk when I walk in. I don't even know what to think when I first see them sitting there, an overwhelming mixture of green hydrangeas and pink peonies that must have cost the sender a fortune, that's for sure. I frown as I step closer and inspect them.

There's no note, which I find incredibly annoying because they could be from anyone. My mom and dad? Jasper? (Ew.) Hudson? (More ew.)

Kendra's no help, of course. I ask if she saw who delivered them.

"No" is the only response I get, and there's a lot of attitude infused in that single syllable.

Because I don't yet know if they're the embodiment of good or evil, I put the flowers on the floor in the corner. I can't throw them away, but I also can't look at them all day.

At 2:00 p.m., I have to join Kendra and a few other associates for a conference call with one of our clients. McNealand is a large shipping company interested in acquiring an equally large maritime manufacturing company. If they pursue the deal, we'll all be part of the acquisition team.

Hudson is already sitting at the head of the conference table talking to Bethany and Sophie when I walk in. I claim a seat far away from him.

"You won't be able to hear way over there."

Hudson's voice sends a cascade of goose bumps down my spine.

My initial instinct is to argue, and for the record, I do have about ten comebacks on the tip of my tongue, but then I dutifully scoot down a few chairs and take a seat in the middle of the conference table instead. Kendra—who walked in behind me—steals the spot beside Sophie and strikes up a conversation like she's the nicest person in the world. Who is she really? *This* person? Or the vile being I have to deal with day in and day out?

As I stay perfectly still, my attention down on my hands, a few more senior associates trickle in and the conference table fills up. A guy named Nathan, who I've met on a few occasions and seems harmless enough, sits beside me and accidentally nudges my elbow with his chair as he sits down.

"Sorry."

I smile. "No, it's fine."

A second later he curses and thunks the table with his fingers. "Damn. I forgot my coffee."

I hesitate for a moment. Then, "How are you ever going to survive?"

He chuckles, and Hudson clears his throat. I roll my eyes. We haven't started yet; it's not like the conference room is dead quiet.

I peer up to see Hudson looking at me. Navy suit. Matching tie. Crisp white shirt. Annoyed expression. Perfect lips. Scruff.

I wish he'd shave.

I wish he'd stop looking at me like that.

Like *I've* done something wrong.

I mouth, "Stop," and his expression only darkens.

"How are you settling in?" Nathan asks me.

I turn away from Hudson and smile at my seatmate. He has to be in his early thirties, but he's still hanging on to a perpetual baby face, ruddy cheeks and all. "Oh...fine, I suppose. How long have you been here?"

His brows shoot up when he realizes the answer. "Eight years."

"Was your first year rough?"

He laughs as he remembers it. "It was the hardest year of my life. I gained like ten pounds and broke up with my girlfriend and nearly got fired a few times."

"But you survived," I point out with a supportive smile.

He nods and smooths his hand down his tie. "And you will too."

His encouragement makes me feel a little lighter right up until Hudson takes charge of the meeting, and for the better part of an hour, I'm forced to listen to his discussions with our client. Everyone in the room is furiously taking notes, and I do the same. Even in the current circumstances, the acquisition sounds exciting, and I won't slack off. I have to separate my work from my real life.

I wish I could avoid Hudson altogether, but he's the one talking, the one in charge. It'd be weird if I kept my head down the whole time, so I brace myself then peer down the conference table. Getting to look at him for so long, uninterrupted, makes me elated and enraged all at once. It would be satisfying to find him tired and pale, a shadow of his usual self. But he's so healthy-looking, robust and strong, like he could withstand anything. In certain moments, when his jaw tics or his hand brushes his lips absentmindedly—despite trying my hardest not to—I can't help but recall blips of

Saturday night, fleeting memories that carry so much emotion
with them. Each one makes me wince and fidget in my chair.

Like he knows exactly what I'm thinking, Hudson meets
my gaze on one such occasion. He looks so frustrated now,
but I know what he looks like when he's drugged with lust,
soothed and sensual. I know how those lips turn up at the
sides in moments of joy, how that mouth feels between my
legs.

I blink and look away, ashamed of my dirty thoughts. I
was doing so well until now. It's Hudson's fault.

Thankfully, the call with McNealand doesn't last much
longer, and I shoot to my feet the moment Hudson dismisses
us. Nathan is saying something, asking me a question, but I
don't hear it because Hudson has just called my name.

"Scarlett."

It slices through the air and lands like an arrow in my
heart.

There's no reason he would need to talk to me, no reason
to call me out in front of everyone. But I can't ignore him.
That would look even more strange, so I steel myself with a
deep breath, nod goodbye to Nathan, retrieve my laptop, and
head down toward Hudson's end of the conference table.

He's finishing up a conversation with Bethany. It's clear
I'm meant to wait in the background like a servant until he's
good and ready to talk to me. I decide the flowers in my office
are getting shredded no matter who sent them, just on the off
chance it was him.

Bethany walks away, and Hudson turns to look at me.

The air whooshes out of me. I can't stand the effect he has
on me. It's too much power for one person. Does he realize?

His expression has cooled. Not that it matters—I have enough anger in me for the two of us.

"The flowers. Were they from you?"

He looks to the door, confirming we're alone.

There's a glass wall on the hallway-facing side of the conference room, so even though the door is shut, people can look in and see us. I'm glad we're not behind an opaque wall. It's better if we have to behave like we're in public.

"It's the start of an apology," he confirms. "I owe you flowers and more."

I narrow my eyes, wanting to be crystal clear. "For sleeping with me even though I *asked* you to?"

His mouth tightens into a disapproving line. His gaze rakes over me, not lasciviously but with reverent care, like he's looking for physical signs of distress. He won't find any. I'm practically dressed in armor. I've picked my blackest dress—the one I feel most powerful in.

"I need to apologize for taking advantage of a situation. I should have never gone to your apartment."

My breakfast turns sour in my stomach. I don't want to hear any of this. "Right. Well, good talk."

I'm about to turn and leave, but then he stops me dead in my tracks when he says, "I need you to hold up your end of the bargain."

Excuse me, sir?

A caustic laugh bubbles out of me. "Hold up *my* end of the bargain? Be glad I haven't mowed you down with my car."

Oddly, my threat eases the worry lines on his forehead. He likes when I'm sassy. Unfortunately, I can't force down the urge just to spite him. I am who I am.

He ignores me and continues, "My mom's birthday is Saturday. I'll pick you up around lunchtime."

"I'd rather eat glass."

"I'll see if she can add it to the menu. Be ready at 11:15 a.m."

"No. You didn't hold up *your* end of the bargain either, asshole. Where's my grade, huh?" I hold up my finger as if just now remembering something. "Oh right! You ran out of my apartment before you gave it to me!"

He looks so troubled, so remorseful. It's the last expression I want to see on his handsomely smug face. Doesn't he realize that?!

"I would take it all back if I could."

He doesn't understand how much those words wound me.

"Great," I respond flatly. "Thank you for that. I feel so much better now. You mind if I get back to work now or would you like to keep annoying me?"

He doesn't balk at my attitude. He stays resolute and firm. "Saturday."

"*No.*"

"Saturday, Scarlett."

If not for that glass wall, I'd flip the cocky bastard off as I walked away. As it is, I just have to imagine doing it, which is only half as satisfying.

When I get back to my office, I look down at the flowers and notice the tip of a tiny card poking through the top of the blooms. I didn't catch it before, but now I bend down and yank it out.

There's no signature, just three handwritten words in scratchy black ink on thick cream cardstock.

You were perfect.

My lip wobbles.

My chest squeezes.

Fuck him.

I tear the note in two and then throw it in the trash.

Kendra's looking over here because I guess I've been muttering to myself or something, but I just stare at her like, *What?!* and she quickly returns her focus to her own desk.

I'm not going Saturday.

Hudson will have to find some other idiot to take home to meet his mommy.

Chapter Twenty-Three

Hudson

I royally messed up with Scarlett, but that doesn't mean we can't fix things. I'm certain of that. She might want me to walk off the face of the planet, never to be seen or heard from ever again, but I can't let that happen. I'll fight for us. I'll right my wrong and get us back on track...whatever that track may be. I'll know it when we get there, I think.

I knock on Scarlett's apartment door at 11:15 a.m. on Saturday morning, just like I promised I would. Moira meows on the other side as Scarlett's footsteps draw near.

"Did you order something, Moira? I swear to god if you pressed buttons on my phone again when I was in the shower—"

Her lock unlatches and then she whips open the door.

She's standing there in a thigh-length ratty T-shirt and no pants. Her hair is mostly falling out of a lopsided bun on top of her head, and her face is completely makeup-free. If the circumstances were different, if she wouldn't drive a knife straight through my heart if I tried it, if we weren't all wrong for each other, I'd lean in and kiss her. That's my first impulse upon seeing her like this, disheveled and cute.

She doesn't even say anything. There's not a hint of shock on her face. She looks at me standing there like she's bored to tears by my presence, then she promptly tries to shut the door in my face. I block it and push it open.

"Security," she shouts half-heartedly before giving up altogether and walking away. "Or better yet, I'll just call the cops. Moira, where's my phone?"

Moira comes right to me, meowing at my feet until I bend down to pick her up.

"Moira, *attack*."

Moira doesn't listen to Scarlett. She nuzzles her little head underneath my chin, using my scruff to her advantage. I scratch her right behind her ears until she purrs.

"God, you two are pathetic," Scarlett sneers.

I smile. "She likes me. Does she like everyone?"

Scarlett doesn't answer that. She crosses her arms over her chest, props her hip against the kitchen island, and waits for me to explain myself.

I set Moira back down on the ground then deliver the news. "I'm here to take you to my mom's birthday party."

She doesn't miss a beat. "Give her my condolences."

"Scarlett, you're going."

"I'm not."

"I see you got my flowers."

They're on her kitchen island, in a place of honor.

She sees me notice them, walks over, and swipes them right off the counter into the trash, vase and all. "I forgot to throw them away the other day."

I smile. "Get changed."

"Are you hard of hearing, old man? *I'm. Not. Going.*"

I walk past her into the bedroom on the right. It's neat and tidy and it smells just like her. There's more personality in this one room than there is in my whole house. She has framed artwork covering a whole wall, stacks of coffee table books beside framed family pictures. She has that white fluffy bedding that looks like it'd be as soft as a cloud. I'd keep looking around, but I'm on a mission.

Her closet is as orderly as the rest of her apartment. I pass over her work clothes and land on a section of dresses. I have no idea what she'd prefer to wear, but I know I love her in blue, so I grab a pale blue dress off its hanger and bring it out into the living room.

Scarlett's on the couch, underneath a throw blanket, watching a recorded episode of *Dateline*, totally unbothered by the fact that I'm in her apartment. On screen, the reporter tells a gruesome story of dismembered bodies found stuffed into wooden barrels on some farm in Arkansas. I suspect Scarlett is getting ideas for what to do with me, and she confirms it when she asks how tall I am.

"Six three."

She frowns at the screen. "Right. Well I'd probably need two barrels then."

I toss the dress at her and it lands on her lap with a plop. "What's this?"

"Your outfit. Where's your hairbrush?"

"Are you saying my hair isn't fine the way it is?"

I narrow my eyes like I'm studying it. "I'm saying it's fine if *you* think it's fine."

She reaches for her remote and turns up the volume.

"*Authorities assumed the murders took place the night of November 5th, but—*"

I check my watch. "We need to be in the car in fifteen minutes if we're going to be there on time."

"Well good." She points to the door. "If you leave now and hurry down the stairs, you should have no problem."

"Scarlett. I will haul you out of this apartment over my shoulder if I have to."

"I'd like to see you try."

I arch my brow, and she groans angrily and throws the blanket off her legs so she can stand and confront me. I'm so used to dealing with her in high heels at work I forget how small she actually is. She walks right up to me and pokes me in the chest with her finger.

"Listen up. You don't get to wreak havoc on my life and then expect me to hop to it when you come calling. You can drag me to your mom's house kicking and screaming, but I'm not going to play along with your schemes. I'll tell your mom the truth."

"Fine. Do it. Now get dressed and let's go."

I'm not worried about her threats. Oddly enough, I don't really care what she does. I just want her in that car, whatever way I can get her there. I know it might be more respectful to give Scarlett the space she's asking for, but it feels imperative that I push for more. We're at a crossroads, and if I let her have her way, that might be it. Whatever we are, it'll be done, for good. I can't let that happen.

"Give me one good reason why I should do anything for you after the way you left things on Saturday night."

"Scarlett, I—"

She holds up her hand. "No, actually, don't start. I don't want to hear your pathetic excuses. It'll only enrage me and Moira. She hates bullshit."

"Fine. I won't get into it. But truthfully, I need you."

My solemn tone gives her pause. I can see her weighing her next words, trying to decide if she wants to put in an order for some wooden barrels or not. She owes me nothing. I know that. I've thought a lot about Saturday night, and I regret so much. But the crippling guilt I felt immediately after sleeping with Scarlett has given way to a convoluted, tangled mess of longing and regret and remorse and, worst of all, desire. I know I should stay away from her. I should right this wrong, and yet here I stand, in her apartment, my hands fisted at my sides, my attention pinging off every one of her delicate features I wish I could touch. An apology is on the tip of my tongue, but I hold my breath and stay quiet, giving her a moment.

She looks away and frowns at the TV. Then, with a sigh that seems to originate from the very depths of her soul, she reaches down, grabs the remote, and turns off the show. I listen to her mumbling under her breath as she walks away. She's really not happy with me, but she relents to my request, and by "relents", I mean she gets ready and allows me to lead her downstairs without causing a scene that would draw the attention of local authorities.

"I don't have a gift," she says, crossing her arms in the passenger seat. As if that will be the thing that finally tips the scales for me. *Oh, in that case, get out.*

"I have more than enough." I nod toward the pile of presents in the back seat. Lucy helped me order a few things online, and I think she got click-happy at one point when I excused myself to use the restroom. I don't remember buying my mom and Lucy matching Louis Vuitton bags, but Lucy assures me that I did. *"And next year, you'll be getting us—I mean her, the matching wallet."*

Scarlett's brows shoot up when she looks back at the gifts, but she doesn't say anything. I pull away from her apartment building and join the traffic.

Scarlett folds her hands neatly in her lap and looks out the window, seemingly lost in space until she feels the need to inform me, "Just so you know, people are gossiping about us in the office."

I'm not surprised. I expected there to be speculation the moment Scarlett and I started working out together in the Elwood Hoyt gym. I didn't make a point of staying away from her at the Christmas party either, and we've eaten lunch together a time or two down in the food court. Our friendship was going to invite gossip no matter what.

"So you shouldn't talk to me or look at me or bother me anymore," she continues, keeping her gaze out the window. "Not if you want your precious promotion."

My fingers tighten on the steering wheel. I want to say so much. A novel's worth, really. Instead, I offer a simple "Noted."

"To practice, I think we should start now."

I smile.

God. Even now, I like her so much.

I flip my blinker on and change lanes, trying a normal conversation on for size. "My mom is turning 62, but she's going to lie and tell you she's turning 52."

I pause for questions but don't get any.

"My sister will be there too. My brother-in-law is on call and will be late if he can make it at all. He's an emergency medicine doctor and his schedule can sometimes be erratic."

She hums.

"You'll also meet my nieces and nephews, all seventy-five of them."

This catches her attention. She whips around to face me.

"Kidding. There are only three of them, but sometimes the noise level makes it feel like there's a whole lot more, and another one is on the way. My nephew just started potty training last week, so sorry in advance if he pees on you. My oldest niece *will* ask you if you have any makeup she can use. *Do not let her.* She'll never leave you alone after that. I'm warning you."

Scarlett crosses her arms and turns her attention back on the road.

I don't push my luck. For the rest of the drive, I crank the radio and stay quiet in an effort to keep this intensely fraught peace intact. It feels like at any moment, we'll implode.

My mom lives in a one-story house in a suburb near Chicago with tree-lined streets and bikes littering front yards. I come here on Halloween and pass out candy with her. Last year, we had so many trick-or-treaters we ran out of candy, and my mom started giving out the cash I had in my wallet. I've considered what it would be like to move out here one day. The commute into the office wouldn't be too bad.

"*Oh*, I like that house," Scarlett says, more to herself than to me. It's a two-story colonial with red brick and neat hedgerows rimming overflowing garden beds. I've always liked that house too, but I don't dare agree with her because I know it'll only piss her off.

A minute later, I park in front of my mom's house, and then I open the back door. I'm prepared to Tetris the gifts in my arms in lieu of making two trips, but Scarlett starts loading her arms up too.

"Thanks."

She ignores me and closes the door. I lead us up the front walkway knowing without a shadow of a doubt that my mom has already clocked our arrival. With her motherly intuition, she probably knew the moment we exited the highway. The front door is flung open before we reach it and—oh god, her eyes are welled up with tears.

"Hudson! Who do we have here?!"

She ignores me and goes straight for Scarlett, pressing her hands to either side of Scarlett's cheeks and looking her over. Personal space does not exist for my mother. I wince and expect Scarlett to wrench away, but she laughs and smiles.

Scarlett and my mother are about the same size, though my mom is all blonde—"*It hides the grays!*"—and dressed in bright pink.

"Hi, Mrs. Rhodes."

My mom guffaws with a laugh and a teasing smile. "Mrs. Rhodes?! What am I, *80*? You can call me Renee."

"Mom, this is Scarlett, and you can let go of her now."

"Oh hush, you." My mom loops her arm around Scarlett and scoops her inside. I'm left, forgotten, on the front porch.

"Happy birthday, Mom!" I add with dry sarcasm.

Again, no one pays me any attention. I could leave them and go get a Starbucks if I wanted. Wouldn't matter.

"Scarlett," my mom says with an admiring tone. "That is *such* a gorgeous name."

"Thank you, it's a family name. Scarlett was my grandmother on my mother's side."

My mom lays a hand over her heart like she's completely enchanted by this information.

"You named me after your dad," I point out.

Crickets.

In the foyer, my mom takes the presents out of Scarlett's arms and dumps them in mine. "Are you hungry, Scarlett? Here, come in the kitchen and I'll make you whatever you want."

Scarlett laughs as she follows after her. "It's your birthday—I should be making *you* something to eat!"

"No, no, come on."

She bands her arm around Scarlett's shoulders and starts to lead her down the hall, but Scarlett stops abruptly in front of the landscape painting that has hung there in the same spot since I was a child. If I lifted the frame, I'm sure the paint behind it would be three shades lighter than the surrounding wall. It was the first piece my mom ever did, a lot moodier than the ones she paints now.

Painting has always been her hobby of choice. And though she's never listened to my sister and me when we tell her how talented she is, how much people love her work, she did relent and let me commission a dozen pieces for my corner of the Elwood Hoyt offices.

"Oh, these are just like the ones Hudson has at work," Scarlett notes. "I *love* them."

My mom looks taken aback for a moment. "Oh." Then she laughs. "They're nothing. Little abstracts."

"Did you..." Scarlett turns to her with nothing short of awe. "Are these *yours*?"

A shake of her head, a bashful little laugh. My mom is so used to slithering her way out of a compliment about her art, but Scarlett won't let her.

"I love them, truly."

She nods, taking it in. "Well thank you. I do like this one in particular."

"You'll have to show me any others you have around the house," Scarlett insists before continuing on into the kitchen.

Before she follows, my mom looks at me over her shoulder and gives me an emphatic thumbs-up when Scarlett isn't looking.

For the record, I do try to go into the kitchen to join in their conversation, but my mom makes it clear she wants one-on-one time with Scarlett. "Hudson, can you go see why that toilet in the hall upstairs won't flush?"

Sure.

Then, "Also, there're some flowers outside that need water, I bet."

Surprised she didn't say, *And you might as well mow the grass while you're out there.*

My sister, Corinne, arrives thirty minutes late with a cacophony of screaming children and a slew of apologies. "It took us forever to get on the road and then my gas light came on, and then Wren had a blowout that almost got all over her car seat." She suddenly grips her baby bump. "Holy *shhhh*—if I don't make it to a bathroom in the next five seconds, I'm going to pee all over Mom's floor."

I point up. "Upstairs hall bathroom is working again."

"Oh thank god."

My nephew, Jack, already dashed past me and beat her to the downstairs one.

Then, from the kitchen, I hear my niece Annabelle ask Scarlett, "Who are you?" Then, "Do you have any makeup?"

Scarlett should have listened to me when I warned her about this. I hop up to save her, but it's too late. She opened Pandora's box the second she agreed to check her purse. She's lucky she only had a tube of lip gloss and some powder because they both belong to Annabelle now.

My sister is absolutely mortified when she makes it down from the restroom. My family is probably under strict orders to impress Scarlett by any means necessary. I can imagine my mom running everyone through drills: "He's finally brought a woman home! Places! *Places*, everyone!"

Instead of being the perfect family with perfect manners, we're five minutes in and Annabelle's already rooting around in Scarlett's bag.

Corinne tries apologizing, but Scarlett laughs it off. "Truly, had I known, I would have brought more."

Annabelle's eyes light up. Her newly pink glossy lips split into a smile. "There's more?!"

Corinne sighs and tries to shoo her out of the kitchen. "Annabelle, *go*. Be a kid. Find a stick or something."

"Later, Mom." My six-year-old niece refuses to leave the barstool next to Scarlett. She's looking my date over with a shrewd eye. "What kind of eyeshadow palette did you use this morning?"

She's inspecting Scarlett's makeup carefully, getting right up close to her face. *Too* close. Kids have no concept of personal space.

Scarlett has to think for a second. "Oh. It's just one I picked up at Sephora. I can't even remember the brand. You like it?"

Annabelle scrunches her nose and tips her hand back and forth like, *ehh*. "I think you should go with more of a matte finish for everyday."

Scarlett, immediately trusting the judgment of a first grader, pulls out her phone. "Okay. Which one should I buy?"

I have no frame of reference for whether this is all normal or not, the way Scarlett just assimilates into our family as if she's always been a part of our gatherings. She helps my mom with lunch, insisting she'd rather be put to work than waited on hand and foot. My mom puts her on drink duty and Scarlett asks if there are any oranges or lemons. My mom has both, and Scarlett whips up a citrus-infused iced tea that blows my mom's socks off.

We sit around the table at lunch, and Scarlett voluntarily puts herself within firing range of my youngest niece, Wren. At one point, Wren reaches out and gets a good chunk of Scarlett's hair in her hands, really making sure to rub her sticky chicken salad fingers onto every strand.

My mom almost has an aneurysm. "Scarlett! Oh no, I'm so sorry. Here, come over to the sink and let me help you rinse that out."

Scarlett smiles and rolls with the punches, gently untangling her hair from Wren's grip and replacing it with her pinky finger instead. Wren is just as satisfied, kicking her feet and smiling a big gummy smile that Scarlett returns.

"I grew up with three older brothers," she explains to everyone. "This isn't the first time I've had chicken salad in my hair at the dinner table."

"*Three* older brothers?!" Corinne sounds horrified by the concept. "Hudson was bad enough on his own."

Naturally, this turns the conversation toward our childhood. Scarlett is desperate for stories of my adolescence (likely for blackmail purposes), and my sister delivers.

"Oh he used to love playing with Barbies. Yeah, he'd get really into it—"

"As most anyone would!" my mom cuts in, defending my honor and trying to ensure that nothing my sister says will change Scarlett's good opinion of me. Little does she know there's no good opinion left. Corinne can talk away.

"He went through a phase where his favorite color was purple. He was *obsessed*. He'd wear this purple shirt of mine that said 'Girl Power!' across the front until he had his first growth spurt and…" She has to pause here to laugh. "He couldn't even fit his little head through the hole. Oh my god, do you remember that day? You cried and made Mom take you shopping to find another purple shirt."

"No, no, I don't remember that," my mom chides, shooting Corinne harsh glares and miming her pointer finger slashing across her throat.

Scarlett just laughs, looking over at me, likely trying to reconcile the man she knows now with the child who cried over a purple T-shirt. I shrug and go back to eating.

"He was *such* a good little boy," my mother adds, derailing the fun conversation with a list of qualities she thinks will win Scarlett over. "Very respectful and smart. So smart! Tell her, Hudson. Tell her how you were always on the honor roll in school."

Corinne cracks up. "Mom! She knows Hudson is smart. They work together."

"Oh fine. Can't a mom brag on her son a little bit?"

I stand up and slap my hands down on the table, drawing the attention of my nieces and nephew. "Who wants cake?"

I'm surprised the responding ear-splitting squeals don't shatter the windows.

While my mom is opening her presents, Scarlett sneaks around the kitchen, tidying up, quietly gathering plates so my mom doesn't have such a mess to contend with once we're all gone. By the end of the party, everyone's about ready to trade me in for her. None of the kids understand exactly why she isn't just a part of the family from now on. While I'm outside on the trampoline with the kids, they hound me with questions.

"Are you like married now?" Annabelle asks with a deeply serious expression.

"Nah, kiddo."

"But you're *going* to get married?"

I snort. "Not even close."

Jack asks, "Do you love her?" but because he's three it comes out sounding like, "Do you luff hewr?"

"Luff hewr! Luff hewr! Luff hewr!" Jack repeats, going on and on with it so that I have no choice but to double-bounce him and send him careening into the air in a fit of giggles.

"Do that to me! To me!" Annabelle demands.

By 4:00 p.m., the kids are exhausted, the cake's been eaten in multiple waves, and everyone's on the downward slope of their sugar high. When I nudge Scarlett and let her know it's time for us to hit the road, everyone demands a hug from her. Annabelle wants two, but I think the second time around she was using the embrace as a ploy to whisper in Scarlett's ear what kind of makeup she wants Scarlett to buy her for *her* birthday in June.

"Thank you for having me in your home," Scarlett tells my mom.

My mom rushes forward and squeezes her tightly. "It was so *so* nice to meet you. Don't be a stranger, okay?"

Scarlett steps back and nods.

Outside, everyone gathers on the front stoop to watch us head down the path to the car.

"Bye, Scarlett!" Annabelle shouts.

"Luff hewr!" Jack adds, now programmed to repeat the phrase because it gets a laugh from Annabelle every time.

The tableau is so wholesome it looks like the end of a made-for-TV movie. It's not until we're in my car, safely tucked behind closed doors, and halfway down the block that Scarlett whacks me on the arm.

"OUCH!"

"That is for duping your mom, you a-hole. That woman is a saint, and she deserves better than that!"

I rub my bicep. "Oh please. She's doing just fine, I assure you. I paid off the last of her mortgage, and that fancy car in the driveway? Yeah, bought her that too."

"She doesn't want your *crap*, Hudson! She wants you, happy and in love, and we made her think you were!" She drops her head in her hands like she's in agony. "Oh my god, turn the car around. I'm going to go back and apologize."

"No can do."

I reach over to hold her in her seat just in case she gets any ideas.

She looks at me with a wide-eyed expression. "What are you going to tell her when she asks about me?! Because she *will* ask about me. She and I really connected!"

"Relax." I shrug, trying to act calm about all this. "In a month or two, I'll break the news to her that we broke up."

She drops her head in her hands again. "God, that's going to devastate her."

"She'll recover."

She cocks her head to glower at me. "The story stands. *I* broke up with *you*. That's the way it goes. Because you were an arrogant jerk and didn't deserve my love—that's what you're going to tell her."

"Should I be writing this down?"

My sarcasm isn't appreciated. Scarlett wants to kill me more than ever, but she doesn't understand how intense my mom has become about my love life recently, and this way, at least, I can buy myself a month or two. *If I'm lucky.*

"It's really not a big deal, Scarlett."

"Maybe not to *you*…"

She murmurs the words toward her window, and I realize I'm really the lowest of the low in her book. This mess has gotten too out of hand. I want to apologize to her again about Saturday, but I know it won't go over well.

If I could go back in time...

No. That hypothetical game won't work, and it doesn't matter. Even if I rewound to before last Saturday, even if I never showed up at her apartment, never kissed her, never gave in to my desire—I'd still be in this mess, trying to navigate this complicated relationship.

"I'll text her when I get home and tell her we're just friends," I promise solemnly.

Scarlett's shoulders sag. "Thank you," she says with a small voice.

Very few people have the ability to burrow deep down inside me, but Scarlett is one of them. All I want to do is make her happy, and I've yet to figure out exactly how to do that.

"For the record, Scarlett—"

"*Don't.*"

I have to. I can't sleep knowing she might have the wrong idea about our situation.

"I was the only person in the wrong last weekend," I trudge on resolutely. "I should have never put you in that position."

"Pull over."

I can't. I'm on the highway.

"Scarlett."

"Just forget about it, Hudson!" she explodes. "I'm not dumb. I know why you feel weird about everything that happened. I know you're worried about the implications of us sleeping together, and in case you haven't noticed, I've backed off, haven't I? I've given you space. No more working out. No more strange little friendship."

244 MR. BIG SHOT

What do I say to that?

Was there ever a world in which Scarlett and I slept together and then continued on with our normal lives? Because I can't even imagine it. Saturday night was too important. Having her for that brief moment—it upended everything.

I'm so angry at myself for letting things get to this point with Scarlett. I went into that night with a sense of wild abandon, almost like I couldn't rationalize the consequences. My judgment was clouded by need, a need that had transformed into a vicious never-ending pain. At least it felt like that for me.

I can't even comprehend how I let this relationship get so far away from me. There's no one on earth with a tighter grip on their emotions than me. I've always been practical and by the book, stern, unfeeling to a fault, even. But had you asked me if that was a problem before, if I was looking to change, I would have laughed in your face.

So then how did I get here? How have I screwed this up so badly?

"For the record, I liked our strange little friendship."

This actually makes her chuckle sadly. "Yeah...me too."

Chapter Twenty-four

Scarlett

Hudson and I put our friendship on ice, but it doesn't mean we aren't acutely aware of each other 24/7. I try my hardest to avoid him in the office, but it just isn't possible. Working on the same floor, in the same department, means I bump into him *all* the time, and that's not even including all the mandatory meetings about the McNealand acquisition that's getting underway.

The Monday after his mom's birthday, he and I happen to end up on the same elevator first thing in the morning, and there is no way to avoid the weird tension and awkward eye contact. To make matters worse, the pack of people buffering us thins out by the 55th floor, and then it's just Hudson and me! Alone in a stainless steel box! If it were flammable, we'd be nothing but ash, that's how much tension burns between us.

I stand facing the doors, holding my breath. I don't want to get so much as a whiff of his cologne. My plan is to flee the first second I can.

"Scarlett."

He says my name with this exquisite pain in his voice, like I'm torturing him, just as the doors are about to slide open, and I squeeze my eyes closed, hold my breath, and dart out of the elevator as fast as possible.

He's not allowed to *Scarlett* me! Not even now, a week into our weird exile from each other. I'd be lying if I said my anger hadn't started to simmer down. There's only so long I can hold a grudge. It's harder than it seems! I don't have the emotional bandwidth for it. I'd rather spend that time, I don't know, stalking *Real Housewives* forums on Reddit.

On top of my non-anger issues, I'm lonely! Work has been as isolating as ever. Makayla and Ramona avoid me like the plague ever since the bathroom incident, and Kendra continues to be cruel every chance she gets. Something will happen and I'll accidentally find myself wanting to tell Hudson about it, only to get this huge lump of feelings stuck in my throat once I realize I can't go to him for any ol' thing anymore. I realized it'd gotten particularly bad when, last night, I had a full-blown conversation with Moira.

"Honestly, I didn't expect him to be good with kids. And he wasn't in the typical sense, you know?"

I paused there, like she was going to contribute something, then seamlessly trudged on when she didn't miraculously develop the ability to speak English. "He wasn't afraid to be silly with his nieces and nephew. I watched him on the trampoline in his mom's backyard, double-bouncing Jack and Annabelle, seeing how high he could get them before Corinne shouted at him to be careful."

Moira just yawned and looked at me like, *Sweetie, this is embarrassing. Move on.*

But I can't move on. That's become crystal clear. I didn't even agonize over my relationship with Jasper like this. I mean, sure, I was hung up on his asinine assessment of my lovemaking abilities, but I never once found myself missing his company. Not like I miss Hudson's.

So I'm going to forgive him.

Starting now.

"Hi. *Morning.*" I pause and clear my throat. "Can we talk?"

I'm standing at his office door first thing. There are other associates here; Jansen and Bethany said hello to me when I was in the break room just now. Lucy is at her desk too. But this is okay. I'm allowed to talk to Hudson at work. I'm allowed to bring him a cup of coffee.

Hudson shoots to his feet, blinking through his surprise. "Yes, of course. Come in."

We've endured two weeks of separation. It feels like I've punished him as much as I've punished myself, and I don't want to do it anymore.

"I'm not upset with you anymore."

He points to the coffee I brought him. "So that's safe to drink?"

I smile. "Yes."

I venture farther into his office, and he quickly curves around his desk to take it from me. We almost get too close, but I step back and so does he. It's a silent agreement. We both realize how important it is to keep a healthy distance.

"I'll apologize again if you'll let me. I can maybe help explain why I acted like such an idiot—"

I shake my head. "No. Let's not go backward. I think... maybe it'll only make it worse. I've thought a lot about our situation, and there are only two paths forward."

He listens intently, nodding for me to go on.

"We could let this be the end."

His eyes widen and frustration clouds his face like a dark mask.

"Or..." he presses, making me smile.

"We can continue on as friends."

The tension in his forehead eases. "Friends."

"I like you too much to do the first option."

"I like you too," he says, sounding relieved to get it off his chest.

"I missed you these last two weeks."

His responding smile is so warm, so beautiful, I have to blink and look away, just for a second.

"I missed you too."

If there's a tightening in my chest, if his words seem to unfurl this happy little feeling inside me, I don't think too hard on it. It's better, I've realized, to not give in to my feelings for him. That road proved tricky, and I'm certain if we head in that direction again, it won't end well. I'm not certain of Hudson's feelings for me, but I know I don't want to lose him for good.

Simplifying things is better. For now.

But if I'm being honest, I know this thing between us hasn't been put to bed. I know it in the way his attention strays to my lips when we talk in his office. I know it when his hand accidentally grazes mine when he walks me to the door. I know it, later that night, when I wake up in a sweaty panic after having yet another sexy dream about him.

Unfortunately, there's no way this is over.

Chapter Twenty-Five
Scarlett

"Listen! *Listen!* Is everyone listening?" The chatter dies around the table as we all look over at the tipsy brunette wearing a skintight pink dress and a coordinating pink *BRIDESMAID* sash. "Tonight, everyone who's single at this table is getting laid!"

The other women raise their champagne glasses in the air in a raucous toast to this declaration, and no one notices that my cheer is a little lackluster.

It's the first weekend in February and I'm out celebrating my future sister-in-law. Hannah's bachelorette party is in Miami. I wasn't sure I'd be able to make it. It took a herculean effort to get here, and while everyone else has been livin' it up in the MIA since Thursday night, I flew in this morning and will be flying out at the crack of dawn tomorrow so I don't miss any work. I'll be back at my desk, fresh as a daisy come Monday morning. On top of that, I brought my laptop and toiled away like a worker bee on the flight down here. Hannah, knowing this, stopped me as soon as I walked into the beach house.

She reached out then opened and closed her hand twice in quick succession: *Hand it over.*

"Where's your laptop?"

I screwed up my face. "Laptop?" What is that word you speak?

"Is it in your carry-on or your purse?"

She started yanking my purse off my shoulder, and I stepped back and held my arms out to buy myself a little time to come up with a good excuse.

Instead the truth spilled out. "You can't take my laptop, Hannah. I might get an email!"

"No! No work for twenty-four hours, Scarlett."

"You can't do that. I'm a doctor!"

"No, you weirdo. You're an attorney and no one's life is on the line—"

"Mine will be!"

"—if you don't answer a stupid email until tomorrow morning. I mean it! It's my wedding wish."

Irritated, I replied, "That's not a real thing."

"It is now!" And then another bridesmaid swooped in with a can of hard seltzer adorned with a sparkly pink penis straw, and that was that. Even if Hannah hadn't confiscated my laptop, I'm too drunk to work now anyway. I've consumed enough alcohol to rival a freshman fraternity pledge. These people are trying to kill me.

We spent all day at the beach picking up as much color as we could manage. Then we headed to the pool. I *think* I had a sip of water then, so that's good, but now we're at dinner at Carbone in these slinky pink dresses someone picked out for all of us to wear. They're from Amazon and I'm pretty sure they're for small children because I could barely get this thing over my butt. I feel like I'm barely wearing anything at all.

Hannah has gone for an understated bridal look: feather boa, Miss USA crown, and over-the-top bridal sash. The pièce de résistance is the blown-up picture of my brother someone has made into a necklace for her to wear around her neck. It's huge.

She's just as drunk as the rest of us, as she should be. I love seeing her let loose. She's usually as uptight as I am. Blonde, demure, and reserved, she's an accountant at the Elwood Hoyt offices in Los Angeles, which is how she originally met Conrad. When she first joined the family, she and I bonded over our workaholic tendencies, which is how she knew to take my laptop away from me back at the house.

Even now, if I so much as attempt to reach into my purse, she shouts at me from across the table.

"No phones, Scarlett, or I'm going to make you do a shot!"

One more shot and my liver will become sludge. Quickly changing course away from my phone, I hold up my hands in innocence and reveal to her the tube of lipstick I was digging for. *Ha!*

She purses her lips then points her pointer and middle finger toward her eyes, back toward me. *I'm watching you.*

She doesn't really have to watch me. I'm not going anywhere. After fifteen rounds of heavenly but heavy pasta dishes, I will need to be wheeled out of here on a trolley.

I don't think anyone's in a rush to get up and try to wibble-wobble ourselves out of here, which is how we got started on truth or dare in the first place. This is a game I have not played since my twelfth birthday when Lindsey Gee dared me to lick her brother's toilet seat.

"Truth or dare. TRUTH OR DARE!"

"Do we have to?" Gabriella asks. "I mean isn't that a little juv—"

Jordy holds up her hand. "Boo, don't be boring, Gabriella. Tell us who gave you the best orgasm of your life, and don't bother trying to say it was your husband—we'll know if you're lying."

I crack up listening to them all together. Since the women around the table are Hannah's friends, I'm sort of the odd man out in the group, but they've been so welcoming. *Too* welcoming.

"Scarlett, you're up! Same question. When did you have the best orgasm of your life?"

A laugh bursts out of me. "I can't answer that!"

"Yes you can! Don't be coy. We know you aren't a prim-and-proper attorney all the time. Gotta take those sensible slingbacks off sometimes!"

Hannah promises to cover her ears, and I shrug. "It was a few weeks ago."

Hannah frowns. So much for covering her ears...

"With Jasper?" she asks, looking personally offended by the notion.

I nearly spit out my champagne. "*After* Jasper."

Her eyes alight with excitement. "Who!?"

I shake my head and look down. "Just...a one-night stand."

I reach for the Dom and fill up my glass, hoping that by the time I'm done, everyone will have moved on to someone or something else. But when I set the bottle back down, I look up to see eight pairs of eyes blinking at me expectantly—a parliament of curious owls.

"This one-night stand gives you the best orgasm of your life and *that's it*?" Jordy asks me. She's the one who originally wanted to play the game, and as Hannah's most outgoing friend, I know she'll die before she lets me off the hook on this one.

"Do you know him?"

"Where'd you meet him?" someone else asks.

I shrug and drink. "Doesn't matter."

"Umm, it extremely matters," Jordy says with righteous indignation.

"He wasn't a stranger," Hannah smartly guesses with a confident smirk. Her astute gaze is focused on my reddening cheeks.

"Let's move on!" I blurt out. "Jordy, I dare you to give the waiter your number."

She looks bored. "I already did that a half-hour ago."

Right. "Go lick the toilet seat."

The more I want to put the topic to bed, the more they want to resurrect it. I apparently look guilty as hell.

"Do you have his number in your phone right now?" Jordy asks.

At this point, lying is getting me nowhere, so I answer truthfully, hoping the karmic boost will help me out of this. "Yes."

I shamelessly added it from the company directory the morning before we slept together. I wanted to be sure I had it saved in case he needed to change or cancel our plans. Oh my god, I'm pathetic!

"If you called right now, would he answer?" Hannah asks. "Yes."

I know without a shadow of a doubt if I called Hudson, he'd answer.

Jordy claps her hands now, drawing the attention of everyone at our table *and* the surrounding tables. Management wants us out of here yesterday.

"Let's call him!" Jordy suggests.

"Let'ssss *not*."

I think my Ss will be convincing enough, but not for Jordy. "Oh, we really have to. We have *got* to let this man know he gave you an orgasm to end all orgasms."

I'm tipsy enough that I can't immediately remember why that would be a bad idea. It seems like Hudson *should* know the truth, right? *I'd* want to know if I were him.

"Call him! Call him!"

The chant carries around the table until I feel like the entire restaurant is looking at us. I hate all the attention.

"Okay! Oh my god. Stop. I'll do it if you all just stop."

I reach into my purse and get my phone. My hand trembles as I try to come up with some excuse to get out of this now that I've already agreed to do it. I could say my phone's dead, but Jordy's sitting right next to me and she can clearly see it's alive and kicking.

"You know what? I just realized maybe I *don't* have his number."

"Boo!"

"Don't be a coward!"

"Call him!"

"You don't have to," Hannah tells me from across the table, trying to protect me from her friends. "But if you don't, I will."

Some sister-in-law she is!

It takes me longer than normal to figure out how to navigate to my phone's contact list. The champagne has fully gone to my head, and I laugh as I run through a list of Hs that seems a mile long. "Oh my god, *Ms. Higgins*! She was my favorite AP art teacher—"

"Don't get sidetracked!" Jordy snaps.

Finally, I reach Hudson's name, and without a moment's hesitation, I press call and hold the phone to my ear. Everyone's grinning and whispering excitedly as the phone rings...and rings. Oh my god it's going on forever. Slowly, my initial *zing* of adrenaline dwindles down to nothing.

I hang up just before it cuts to voicemail. A pang of sadness fills my chest and I try to shake it off, though I know it's futile.

"There, I tried. He didn't—"

My phone screen lights up with an incoming call.

Hudson.

I feel lighter than air. I might float away. His name alone sends a fissure of excitement down my spine.

"Oh shit! He's calling back," Jordy tells the table. "Shh! *Shh!*"

She quiets everyone just as I answer. I'm smiling like a girl absolutely smitten over a man who has confused and annoyed and intrigued her for the better part of four months.

"Hello?"

"Scarlett. Hey." He sounds sort of in awe. "Did you just call me?"

I hadn't realized how much I missed his voice. Not just a lot, but *a lot* a lot.

I look up at Hannah's friends as they wave their hands encouragingly.

"I did..."

He waits for me to go on, and I register how noisy the restaurant is in the background just when he asks where I am.

"Miami."

"*Miami?*"

His shock makes me laugh. "For Hannah's bachelorette party."

He hums in understanding.

"And I'm at the dinner table with all the bridesmaids right now."

"Hi!"

"Whattup!"

"Hiii!"

They all lean in and bellow into the phone, making him laugh.

"So you're at a bachelorette party? Got it." A brief pause ensues, then, "Why the call?"

I flatten my sweaty palm over my napkin.

"Well, it was part of a truth or dare game."

"Okay..."

"It was really silly and I should let you know I've had lots of cocktails today, and some gross shot thing they made me do before we left the house, and now I think I've had most of this Dom Pérignon by myself. Anyway, what are you doing?"

He laughs. "I'm at home, in bed."

Oh right, it's nearly 11 p.m.

I wince. "*Sorry!* Oh my god. I'll let you go."

Jordy rips the phone out of my hand, sensing that I'm not at all close to revealing the truth.

"Mystery man, don't hang up!" She turns and covers the phone to keep me from grabbing it. When she's assured he's still on the line, she continues, "We made Scarlett call you for a dare just like she said. Yeah, we asked her what guy gave her the best orgasm of her life, and I'm delighted to inform you that *you sir are the lucky winner!*" She drops the gameshow host voice when she adds dryly, "We thought you'd want to know."

By this point, I have my arms crossed on top of the table and my forehead resting down on top of them. Embarrassment on embarrassment on embarrassment, that's what this feels like. I won't be able to get up. To walk out of here. To ever show my face in the Elwood Hoyt offices ever again.

Jordy holds the phone back up to my ear. "So here, tell him."

"I'm sorry" is all I can muster.

Hudson chuckles. "Don't be."

"This is weird. I shouldn't have called. I'm sorry."

I can't seem to stop apologizing.

"You think you'll be able to get home safely?" is what this peach of a man asks me after everything Jordy just told him.

I take the phone from Jordy and sit up. "I think so."

"Are you going anywhere after dinner?"

"Maybe to a club?"

"Can you call me when you get home?"

"Won't you be tired?"

"Scarlett." God, I love his no-nonsense tone. "Call me when you get home."

Jordy hears this and, loudly enough for him to hear, responds, "Okay, *Daddy*."

The girls around the table burst out laughing, but Hudson doesn't. I can't even begin to imagine what he's thinking right now. We haven't had a full-fledged conversation since we spoke in his office and now I'm drunk-dialing him from Miami?!

"I'll let you go," I say timidly.

"Love you!" Jordy quips.

"Bye! Love you!"

"Bye, Daddy!"

I hang up before the girls can say anything else.

"Dude, he sounded HOT," Jordy says, fanning her face.

"He is, isn't he?" Hannah asks.

I just nod, helpless.

We do end up at a quintessential Miami club, and it's filled with the most beautiful women I have ever seen. They should be making us take out the trash or clean the urinals or something—we do not belong here. Even still, Jordy somehow gets us into the VIP section where she's chatting up a legitimate NBA basketball player! He's so tall she has to shout her questions up at him.

I'm so excited about the scene until I'm not. I hit a brick wall somewhere between the 28th and 29th Calvin Harris EDM remix blasting straight into my ear canals, and I'm dead tired, about to fall asleep on the couch when a cute guy approaches me.

Okay! He's scruffy and blond and looks very well-dressed. I should recognize him maybe. Was he on *Summer House*?

I barely get his name. I think it's Jared or Jerry. I'm about to ask him to repeat it when Hudson calls me. I've been clutching my phone on the off chance he called, which felt stupid right up until he actually does.

I answer straight away, right in the middle of this new man asking me a question. "Hi."

"Are you home yet?"

"No, are you?"

He laughs. "Where are you guys now?"

"I'm in a loud club and I'm talking to some guy and I don't know his name. What's your name?"

Again, I can't tell if it's Jared or Jerry. He really needs to enunciate.

"Hand him the phone," Hudson demands.

"The guy?"

"Yes."

I do as he says, watching on as Hudson talks to Jar/Jer. The guy's blond eyebrows shoot up in surprise and then they clamp down in anger before he hands the phone back to me and stands up to walk away without another word.

"Okay...bye?" I hold the phone back to my ear. "What'd you say to him? He looked annoyed."

"Doesn't matter. Stay with the group."

"The group is kind of spread out..."

I look over to see Jordy making out with the basketball player. She has to stand on the couch just to reach his face, but they seem to be just fine with the arrangement.

"Where's Hannah?" Hudson asks.

"Behind the DJ booth."

I look over to see she's stolen the poor guy's headphones and is making Gabriella take multiple boomerangs of her. We look like a bunch of moms.

"Sorry I called you. I didn't mean to drag you into this."

"I'm not upset."

He says it so emphatically I'm inclined to believe him.

"That's good. I'm not upset either."

He laughs.

There's a natural lull, and I feel compelled to continue our conversation by any means possible, even if that means saying something stupid. "You really screwed me over by scaring away that guy..."

"Oh really?" he replies dryly.

"Yeah, everyone is supposed to get laid tonight, and he was my only option."

"What?"

"It's like a bachelorette party rite of passage."

"Scarlett—"

"But here's the thing, I'd rather not have sex with anyone else—"

"*Scarlett—*"

"Why'd you leave my apartment after? Was it because you were scared I'd be clingy or something?"

"Fuck."

God I love the way the word sounds coming from his mouth. It's like he's absolutely drained of energy. It's just the way he sounded after we had sex.

"You said I was perfect."

"You were. *You are.*" He sounds absolutely resolute about that fact.

I smile a dopey drunk smile.

"*Perfect*," I repeat.

And when he doesn't say anything, doesn't chastise me for bringing up this subject, I decide I should keep talking.

"I have dreams you know."

There's nothing but silence on the other end of the line, but I know he's listening with bated breath. I can picture him sitting there, hoping I'll continue despite the wrongness of it. We've been so good since I went into his office and offered a truce. We haven't gone back to working out together. We don't hang out outside of work at all. We're nice to each other in the office, we make small talk when the option is available. I'll bring him coffee, he'll invite me to lunch with Lucy and him. But everything from before—all the ways we were trying to sneak by fate—has been carefully avoided until now.

"About you," I finish. I hear his sharp intake of breath and I know I've struck a chord. "They're rated R. Very, *very* risqué and troublesome. You see...every time it happens, when I wake up from one of these dreams, I feel *empty*." I smile a salacious smile. "Do you ever feel that way, Hudson?"

"Yes."

The word is stern but honest, and I love it.

"What do you do?" I ask, wanting to test this drunken power while I've still got it.

"You don't want to know."

I tsk. "I really, *really* do."

"You're playing with fire here, Scarlett."

"Aww, don't leave me hanging...or I might have to go track down that guy you scared off."

I can imagine how lethal his eyes look right now, how out of control he feels to have me so far away testing the boundaries like this.

"What do I do?" he repeats. "I think back on the way you looked on your couch. I reimagine the entire night. I torture myself with every tiny detail."

"Sounds painful."

"It is."

"I wish I could help. I *could* help."

"Tell me the name of the club and I'll order you an Uber."

Ugh. I want to pout at the change in subject. "You don't have to..."

We could go right back to imagining ways to torture each other.

"I'd rather know you'll get home safe than have to worry about some drunken fool hitting on you again."

"Maybe I *want* to be hit on."

There's a sigh on his end of the line, but it doesn't sound like exasperation so much as desperation. "I thought we agreed on our path forward. Strictly friends."

"Yes, and then I got drunk and lonely and now here I am, practically *begging* for a morsel of your attention." I know I've taken things too far, know this conversation will come back to bite me in the morning, but for now, I have to know one more thing. "If you were here, and I wasn't drunk—"

"Yes." He cuts me off before I can even finish.

I laugh. "So *impatient.*"

"You have no fucking idea."

I love the gruffness in his voice. It does something to me, twists up my insides, makes me shift on my seat. I tip my head back and look up at the strobe lights on the ceiling. Everyone in the club falls away. The blaring music mutes to nothing. "I wish you'd tell me more..."

"I don't want to make things harder for us come Monday. I have no excuse."

"I'm not making it easy on you. There's your excuse. I'm practically begging you. And I won't remember a thing, promise."

He goes quiet.

"Tell me one fantasy," I plead. "*One.*"

"You. In my office. Bent over and holding on to the edge of my desk. You're in that black pencil skirt you wore your third day on the job."

"And what are you doing?"

"Tasting you again."

I swallow past the intense rise of desire threatening to choke me. Before, it was teasing and fun. Now, it feels so raw and real I can barely force a laugh. I lift my head and root myself back in the here and now. When I speak, my voice is wobbly. "Ah, there. That wasn't so hard." And then, "Goodnight, Hudson."

I hang up.

It's a bold move, of course. I know full well Hudson is in Chicago, staring down at his phone, hot and bothered by our conversation. Or worse, completely pissed off.

Poor, poor Hudson.

But more importantly, poor, poor *ME*!

Chapter Twenty-Six

Scarlett

On Sunday night, I'm splayed on my couch, recuperating with a gallon of water, a rerun of *Dateline*, and a random collection of junk food from my pantry when my phone pings with a new work email.

I reach for my phone right away, but I don't bother sitting up to read it. It's a meeting invitation, which doesn't spark any sort of reaction because I get those all the time. I only go rigid once I see who it's from.

Hudson wants to meet at 7:30 a.m. tomorrow morning. No one else is on the invite list.

Bright and early the next day, I stroll into the Elwood

Hoyt offices with treats for Lucy.

"Oh, look at you, spoiling me," she says with a laugh of delight.

I point to the brown bag. "Pastries from a little bakery right by my house, the one I was telling you about the other day. You have to heat up the cinnamon roll before you eat it. It's so much better."

"Where's my cinnamon roll?" Hudson asks from behind me.

My back stiffens.

Lucy winks at me. "Ignore him."

"Did you have a good weekend, Scarlett?"

I can't look at him. I focus on Lucy as I nod. "Sure. Great."

"It's 7:29."

"So I still have a minute."

Lucy looks between us, confused.

"We have a meeting this morning," I explain to her.

Her eyebrows shoot up. "Ah, right. Better get to it then."

She opens up the crinkly brown bag as I turn away and head for Hudson's office. This must be what it feels like to walk the plank.

I don't look at him on purpose. No sense in losing my nerve on the way to the lion's den. Better to steel myself now and freak out in there, behind closed doors.

Though there's likely no reason to freak out. This meeting could be completely work-related. It could have to do with the McNealand acquisition or something. It's not out of the question...well, not until Hudson shuts the door behind him and asks, "How was your trip?"

It's disconcerting to have him at my back, so I turn to face him.

He's standing with one hand tucked into his pocket. Relaxed and confident. He's wearing a white button-down underneath a dark gray suit. He shaved this morning, and though I love the scruff, I realize I've been dramatically underrating his clean-shaven jaw. He's not smiling, though that's the norm with him. I doubt he's mad, but I can't be certain.

"Should I apologize?" I ask gently, testing the waters.

If he's mad at me...I don't mind, actually. I like him when he's a little grumpy.

"Are you sorry?" he fires back.

My smile is slow to spread. "No."

His dark eyes drift over me. "I worried about you getting home."

"I managed just fine."

His jaw tics.

"I shouldn't have called," I blurt out. "Blame it on the alcohol and the other women. The silly dare..."

"So you regret our conversation?"

My answer is rushed, "Not at all."

"And you remember what we talked about on the phone?"

"Every word."

His gaze catches mine. "You promised me you'd forget it."

I don't mean to—it's not that I'm doing it intentionally—but my attention drifts to his desk. His secret fantasy comes to mind, completely unbidden, raw and tantalizing.

He knows that's what I'm thinking about. My reddening cheeks are a dead giveaway.

I swallow and look down at my high heels.

He starts to walk toward me, closing the space between us with precise, efficient steps. I don't have time to back away, to retreat even an inch before he has his hand gently around my neck, tipping my chin up with the tip of his thumb.

"Where is the line?" he asks, his gaze flitting between my eyes. "Where am I supposed to stop?"

My hands stay limp at my sides, and though I try to hold perfectly still, suspended in this moment with him, I can feel myself trembling.

"It's not supposed to be this hard..."

His voice is nothing but anguish. His gaze drifts over my lips, staring for a prolonged, agonizing second before he leans in and steals a kiss.

I gasp.

He inches even closer, his hips bumping into mine.

Where is the line? It's a good question. Is it here, with our mouths yearning for each other? Or here, as he parts my lips and takes our kiss further?

Our location isn't lost on me. I'm not so far gone that I don't consider all the acute dangers lurking around us. This is completely inappropriate and dangerous yet I moan and draw closer to him. I yank the lapels of his jacket and arch up onto my toes and kiss him back with a ferocity I don't recognize. I want like I've never wanted. I need him, and the idea of not having him, of putting a stop to this now feels earth-shattering.

It's the fastest string of wrong choices I've ever made in my life. One bad decision tips us into another. I have his jacket pushed off his shoulders like it should have never been there in the first place. His hands yank my shirt out of my skirt (*the* skirt) and then the buttons go, one, two, three, four. The material gapes and his hands slide inside to cover my breasts. Thin silk tingles against my sensitive skin. He slides his hand past the material, covering me with his warm palm. I bite his bottom lip, kiss him again, harder this time. Our tongues touch then tangle, and then I feel everything, all at once. It's a sweet kiss of death. I might not make it past this moment. My chest might expand past the point of no return, but it'll be worth it.

I don't register that he's walked us back to his desk until he has me propped up on top of it, right on the papers, knocking over a container of pens, shifting his computer screen a few inches to the right so that it bobs and *almost* tips over.

I laugh, but Hudson doesn't. Can't. He looks down at me with an expression that's hard to discern at first. It's so close to anger, but then I see it for what it is: fear. His brown eyes swim with it.

He leans down and kisses me again, almost like he wants to hide it from me, wants to erase the feeling behind our wild actions. We're so desperate for here and now, but I know there's nothing beyond it. I know he'll leave me after, just like he did last time, and even knowing that doesn't draw me up to the surface. I let him spread my legs. I let him trace his hand up my inner thighs. I make it easy for him to tug my panties to the side and sink his fingers into me and that first orgasm comes so quickly it's like it's been building since our conversation on the phone.

I sink my teeth into the base of his neck, that secret patch of skin his collar will hide once this is all said and done, but I'll know I've marked him. I know later, he'll press his fingers there and remember what it felt like when he unbuckled his pants and thrust into me with wild impatience. His aggressiveness is almost scary, almost too much. The way he kisses me to muffle my cry, his begging for me to wrap my legs around his hips. He needs to take me like this, thrusting harder and harder, coaxing until I come again, tightening around him, digging my fingers into his hair, making it painful because there's no other way to curb the intensity, no other way to channel it other than to make him hurt like I hurt.

He breathes my name against my neck and we're panting together, barely human.

He can't finish like this, not without a condom, and though there's no discussion, no request from him, I slide down off the edge of his desk and take him in my mouth and finish him on my knees. While it's happening, it feels like I'm on top of the world, untouchable. I stare up at him with all the adoration of a devout worshipper. He doesn't understand what I've already come to realize.

There is no fighting this.

I'm careful when it's over. I stay on my knees, breathing through the rising tide of emotion. I stand up and I hear myself telling him, "That was some fantasy," in a voice filled with light and laughter.

He'd never know I'm on the cusp of crying, never suspect his tender touch on the top of my elbow, his way of helping me up off the ground to ensure I'm all right and cared for—it's too much. We have to cleave it here, immediately after the fact. Continuing to touch will lead to something like hope, and I'd like to avoid that at all costs.

He tries to get me to look at him, but I won't. "Can I use this bathroom?"

"Of course."

I clean up as best as possible, and though everything tries to race forward—the guilt, the fear, the shame—I conquer it all with forced, deep breaths. Good sex can just be good sex. That feeling in the pit of my stomach doesn't have to take precedence.

When I'm done in the bathroom, I'm surprised to find Hudson is standing on the other side of the door, his forehead wrinkled with concern, his mouth a sharp, disapproving line. He's cleaned himself up too. He looks perfectly put together again.

"Scarlett—"

I have a good idea of what he's about to say—because I've heard it before—and due to the chance that it will devastate me, I cut him off. My laugh sounds like it's coming from across the room, that's how outside of myself I am.

"Don't get soft on me now," I tease.

His expression doesn't loosen. He's wound tight. He looks like he's shouldering some huge burden. "I know that was a lot."

I smile. "But nothing I didn't ask for."

He reaches out to smooth my shirt and fix my collar. Gentle, reverent touches.

"I have to get to work," I tell him.

It feels like a petty game I'm playing with myself, to be the one to shut it down first, to nip it in the bud before he can.

He straightens and holds up a finger, remembering something.

"My mom wanted me to give you this."

He hurries to his desk where he picks up a frame with a yellow satin ribbon tied around the middle. When he holds it out for me to take, I realize it's one of his mother's landscape paintings, no bigger than a piece of paper. It's her signature style, sweeping blue skies and saturated green hills.

I don't even know what to say.

"She painted this for me?" I almost sound troubled by the idea.

He rubs the back of his neck, staring down at it. "I'm sure there's subliminal messaging incorporated into it somehow. The words 'Marry Hudson' are probably swirled into the clouds."

I laugh and fight the urge to clutch it against my chest. "If I write her a thank you note, will you pass it on to her?"

"Of course."

My tone shifts. "Did you ever talk to her about us? Come clean and all that?"

"I tried to."

He sounds guilty about it.

"Hudson!"

He laughs, and I'm wholly unprepared for his boyish dimples. "She was really taken by you."

"I told you she would be! You know she friended me on Facebook after that lunch. Wrote me a message and everything. I had to print it out to read, it was so long."

He groans in agony. "The woman cannot be stopped."

"I like her."

He nods, processing everything. His gaze is down on the painting again. "I'll break the news to her soon," he promises.

Right.

I nod. "I guess there's no rush. I don't want to burst her bubble. Whenever you think it's time."

There's a natural lull in our conversation, and both of us look away. Then, like we've rehearsed it, we look back and our eyes connect again at the exact same moment, and we laugh. We're shy like we're eighteen, on the cusp of adulthood, unarmored and soft. The innocence is so foreign to me. I haven't considered before now all the ways I've lost this ability to feel so purely.

"I think we've found ourselves in a bit of a pickle."

Hudson laughs again. "For the record, I didn't call you into my office to have sex with you."

"No?" I feign disappointment. "*Damn.*"

He studies me so intently I worry I'm telegraphing every thought. Does he see it? The truth? I'd like to know it for myself.

"What are you looking for, Scarlett?" he asks.

I wasn't expecting the candid question.

"Me?"

What do I want? What have I always wanted?

"I'm looking to add my name to that little plaque out in the hall. Scarlett Elwood, *partner.*"

His eyes spark with interest. "And in your personal life?"

"I have no personal life."

"Good." His reply is curt, quick. "Neither do I. You know I'm the least eligible man in this building. Ask anyone. I have no heart, no head for anything outside of law. I'm a real villain, actually. Before you came, Lucy was my only friend, and I'm not sure how that friendship started anyway. I don't want any distractions. I want my promotion and then I want to keep working. No sailing off into the sunset for me."

"You're a villain?"

"Don't you see it?" He points to the painting. "Look what I did to my mom, lying to her about being in a relationship."

"You're a real bastard," I laugh.

I can't reconcile how he sees himself with how I see him. I mean, sure, no one would say he's the most personable man alive, but he's so warm, down deep.

"Exactly. Ask your brothers. They'll confirm it."

I nod, glad I already steeled myself for this conversation. "So is this some big warning to stay away from you? Because I'm no fool. I'm not head over heels in love with you, Hudson. I'm married to my work too. I don't want any distractions."

"So we understand each other."

Do we?

The door to his office opens while we're still looking at each other and Lucy walks in without knocking. She's holding a stack of papers for Hudson to sign and she's talking a mile a minute.

She doesn't even take note of how we're standing, too close for coworkers, though at least we aren't touching. I'm holding the painting, and a quick assessment of Hudson's desk proves there's no damning evidence, but it's not in its usual orderly state either. His computer monitor is about to tip off the edge. Another inch and it'll be lying on the floor, a crack splintering the screen right down the middle.

There's no conversation to be had now that we have an audience. I have to get to work and Hudson is already late for a conference call, and that's the way it goes in big law.

I'm an attorney first and a person second and I don't feel sorry for myself. I relish it. I love my work and I'm good at it and I'm going to make a name for myself in this company despite everything.

I don't want Hudson. He was a means to an end for me, someone to help me get my mojo back after Jasper the Lame Ghost. And now I have it.

So there.

We can move on.

Chapter Twenty-Seven
Scarlett

I've put the Kendra issue almost completely to bed. She sucks and she always will suck. I know it in my heart of hearts, and yet I can't seem to stop holding out hope that she'll wake up one day having undergone a full-on personality transplant overnight. It's why I still put in the effort to be cordial even though I know it's futile.

Every morning, I walk into our office with the understanding that I can project all the sunshine and rainbows I want but that doesn't mean it'll change anything. I've come to terms with this purgatory I've found myself in with her, which is why I'm beyond shocked when I enter our shared office after my meeting with Hudson to find her standing behind her desk, loading up a cardboard box with her personal belongings.

She's not dressed in work attire. She's in a T-shirt and sweatpants. When she sees me, she just nods in greeting. But then she tacks on a mild, "Well you win."

I drop my work bag on my desk. "I win what?"

Has this been a game the whole time? If so, it's been the most awful one I've ever played.

"I'm leaving."

"What?"

"Yeah, I hate working here. I thought it would get better. I've tried, but it's just not worth it. Not for all the money in the world."

I didn't realize she was struggling. I mean now that she mentions it, I can think back on a few instances where it seemed like Bethany or Sophie was frustrated with her about something, but I never thought it had anything to do with Kendra herself, more so just the intense workload in general.

"Where are you going?"

I figure she'll name another big law firm, maybe Pierce Hughes in New York City or LMD in Boston.

Instead, she says, "Bali."

Her answer is so out of left field, and I try to place the word within the confines of law. Is Bali a firm in LA or...

"Bali?!" I erupt, finally understanding.

She's unfazed by my wide-eyed reaction. "Yeah. I've always wanted to live there, and it's kind of now or never. I'm going to pursue my jewelry line."

Jewelry line?

"Wow...that's—"

She can tell I don't know what to say. She shrugs. "Yeah, whatever. My parents are outraged, but I don't care. And hey, at least you'll get the whole office to yourself now."

She seems lighter now that she knows the end is near, like her hate for me was intrinsically tied to her struggle with this job. That might well have been the case. Every time she was particularly grumpy or excessively rude, she might have just been struggling to stay on top of her work. The stress might have been eating away at her.

"I'm sorry it didn't work out."

And the sentiment is genuine, oddly enough. I didn't like Kendra, but I also didn't put much effort into hating her. I thought we might have a reckoning of sorts one day, a final battle royale that would end in us either murdering or befriending each other.

Her just up and leaving, for Bali no less, was never on my bingo card.

"Eh, whatever." She picks up a stapler, studies it for a second, then shoves it in the cardboard box. "What's a crap ton of student debt compared to happiness, right?"

I chuckle.

She starts to empty her top drawer, picking up the pace with pens and paper clips—shoving it all in with little care or attention. "Anyway, since it doesn't matter anymore anyway, here's my two cents. Makayla and Ramona probably won't last here much longer. Ramona's trying to get knocked up by her boyfriend who's some big finance guy. She'd much rather be a stay-at-home mom than schlep to work here every day. And Makayla can barely stay on top of her workload. The girl is dumb as a box of rocks. She told me she got called in for a performance review a few weeks ago and they essentially told her she was on the chopping block."

"Wow."

"Yeah. I doubt she lasts the month."

I can barely keep up. First Kendra, now Makayla and Ramona too? I sort of thought everyone was settling in the way I was, loving the work as much as me. With everything I had going on, I forgot the warning Bethany gave us on our first day on the job. *By this time next year, a quarter of you will be gone. In two years, only half of you will be left standing.*

Turns out, she was right.

"Can't say I'm particularly sad about that news..."

She's unbothered by my honesty regarding her pseudo-friends. Then she picks up her mouse pad. "Want this?"

I look down at mine. "I'm good."

She drops it unceremoniously into her box and tosses in her mouse for good measure.

"Did you guys actually hate me?"

"Oh yeah, for sure."

There was no pause, no hesitation.

Her candidness makes me laugh. "Because of my dad?"

She shrugs. "Eh, maybe at the beginning, but then it just became the status quo. Kind of a brutal necessity. Makayla's actually pretty annoying when you get to know her and Ramona and I would never be friends in any other setting, so we needed a common enemy to unite us. And honestly, it *was* pretty annoying that you had everything made."

"Can't you see how hard I work though?"

She looks at me for a second as if weighing my question, then she waves it away. "Sure. Whatever."

She yanks the paper calendar off the wall and drops it in with the rest of her stuff, thumbtacks and all.

All right then, so we're not really going to have a nice, happy reconciliation. I get it.

She checks her drawers, slams them closed, spins her chair one last time, and grabs her laptop on the way out.

"Good luck in Bali."

She pauses and looks over at me. Her face has never seemed so open and friendly. "Yeah. Good luck here." She tips her head, offers a small smile. "Surprisingly, after everything, I'm kind of rooting for you."

Then she walks out, and to be fair, I give it a *full* half-hour before I move my stuff to her desk. *Oh my god*—her chair is so much better than mine. I swivel around in it three, four times before I get ahold of myself. Her desk drawers are way deeper too, and they slide in and out like a dream. So smooth I'll be wanting to reach in for files every chance I can get.

I call down to maintenance and request they move my old desk and chair out of the office, and then before the man leaves, I ask if he happens to have a hammer and a nail. I want to hang the painting from Hudson's mom on the wall near my desk.

My dad comes to visit and to eat lunch with me in my office.

He whistles when he walks in. "Look at this place."

His reaction is unwarranted. It's as bare and boring as it was on my first day in October. Neither Kendra nor I cared to spruce it up with personal items. Me, because I didn't want to give her any more ammunition. Her, because...well, maybe she wasn't planning on staying all that long.

My dad does one of his customary photo shoots where I have to sit behind my desk and smile awkwardly while he exhausts the camera on his phone.

"Pretend you're talking to a client," he tells me, giddy with his brilliant idea.

I do it because Kendra's not here to make fun of me anymore, and truly, it's not that much effort to make my dad happy. I draw the line at pretending to type an email though. You give this guy an inch, he'll take a mile.

"Sending these to Mom," he tells me before taking a seat and proceeding to do it right then and there.

Five whole minutes pass where he studies each picture and picks the very best one. He sends them and then my phone buzzes on my desk. Oh the joys of being a member of the Elwood family group text. Never a dull moment.

"I'm sure she'll have an interior decorator in here by tomorrow morning, jazzing the place up," I say wryly.

He sighs like, *At least you know the score.*

While we eat, we talk about my mom's upcoming buying trip. She booked it for two weeks after Conrad and Hannah's wedding. She's on the hunt for antiques in Venice this time, and my dad is planning to join her.

"You could come too. I'd approve the time off."

I shake my head.

Venice sounds great. Who wouldn't want to go to Venice? But I'm in my first year at the firm and it's important that I stick with my current schedule. I know that might seem crazy to some people—to pass up opportunities like extra time off—but this is the path I've chosen, the life I want.

My dad sets down his nearly finished salad on the edge of my desk, wipes his mouth with his napkin, and then leans back in his chair. He looks around the office, studies me, smiles. I can tell he's getting contemplative even before he starts. "I'm proud of you."

I roll my eyes, trying to deflect.

"I mean it. I'll be the first to admit I underestimated you, but you've really started to make a name for yourself here. On Hudson's team, no less. That's no easy feat."

I busy myself by picking at the remaining feta cheese left in the corners of my to-go container. "It hasn't even felt like a hardship. I like this job."

He studies me long enough that I'm forced to meet his gaze. "I know. Sorry for not realizing that before."

Emotion tightens my chest. "So you approve of me working here now?"

He frowns. "My concern was always about your happiness. I didn't want you sticking it out here out of some misplaced need to impress me. Barrett's a little bit like that. I think had I gone easier on him, given him the chance, he would have taken a different path. He loved filmmaking in college, and I squashed that dream." He grunts as if there's nothing he can do now but shake his head and move on. "I regret it, and maybe I was trying to right that wrong through you...keep you from going down a difficult path you didn't choose for yourself."

It's a good point. I'll never know if I was born with an innate love of contracts and legalese or if my interest in the law profession is intrinsically tied to my relationship with my father. I don't consciously feel a burning desire to please anybody but myself, but I'm also the youngest child, the only girl, and I know that comes with consequences, good and bad. Either way, there's no way to separate myself from my profession now. It's in me, of me, the way anybody loves anything. There's never one specific reason why you enjoy something.

I'm considering this when Hudson comes to mind. We were in his office together just this morning. Ripping clothes off, sinking our teeth into each other. Even still, I walked out of there feeling confident in our ending, and now, hours later, it's already started again. The hunger. The hope.

"You okay, kiddo?" my dad asks.

I shake my head, force a smile. "Yeah. Just thinking…"

Chapter Twenty-Eight

Hudson

It's been twenty-four hours since Scarlett and I had sex in my office, and I can no longer ignore that I've come down with a case of something pretty serious.

Even still, I put on my big boy pants and get my ass to work. I never take time off. I don't even know how someone would go about doing that. I did have Lucy postpone my 9:00 a.m. meeting though. I'm lying flat on the couch in my office, and she's at my desk, typing my symptoms into WebMD for me.

I have her really worried. I once had the flu *and* food poisoning at the same time and I worked straight through, no complaints. I just barked orders at people through my closed office door and holed myself up in my bathroom whenever it was required. I was probably *more* productive actually because no one could come in and bother me.

What I have now is worse. Bad enough that I'm laid up on the couch, *not working*—which must mean I'm on my death bed.

Lucy has taken the necessary precautions. She's wearing yellow oversized cleaning gloves she found under the sink in my bathroom, a face mask she dug out of the bottom of her purse, and sunglasses.

"When was the onset of symptoms? Within the last twenty-four hours?"

I think on it. "No. It's been gradual."

She hisses like that's not what she was hoping to hear. "And you said your stomach is hurting?"

"Yeah, and my head is a little fuzzy. It's hard for me to concentrate. General malaise, issues with sleeping—"

"Slow down. General mala-*what-now*?"

I say it all again, slower, spelling things out when I need to.

I never realized how slow Lucy types. Every keyboard click comes with a ten-second delay. She must be falling asleep between each one.

"Right. Looks like you have GERD," she says definitively. "Great."

I'm not even upset about the could-be diagnosis. GERD is an ailment millions of people have, right? It's curable. And if not, I'll dedicate my life to finding a cure.

"Now hang on. Sorry, was reading the wrong thing." She pushes her sunglasses on top of her head and looks around my computer at me. "Have you gone swimming in freshwater lately? You might have one of those slithery parasite things, the ones that crawl up your—"

I wince. "No. I haven't."

She shrugs. "Just trying to be thorough."

I throw my arm over my eyes and heave a deep, worry-filled sigh. This is worse than I imagined.

"Let's go back to the start. There has to be something we're missing. Maybe I need to have my pancreas removed."

There's a hum on her end, and then I hear the telltale sound of latex squelching as Lucy yanks off her gloves. To her, the worry has subsided, but I'm in the exact opposite camp. WebMD couldn't diagnose me; this must be extremely serious indeed.

"You ever consider maybe these symptoms aren't related to an illness?"

I furrow my brows and slide my arm up enough on my forehead that I can look over at her. I'm confused by her question.

Lucy pushes away from my desk and stands up. She pulls her mask down as she continues, "It could be emotional pain."

I bark out a laugh and sit up. "I don't endure emotional pain. I inflict it. Big difference."

She comes to stand in front of me, looking down with a cheeky expression.

"Just...thinking over your symptoms, it really only points to one thing."

"What?" I ask, suddenly on the edge of my seat. Did she find the answer and I missed it? Was it GERD after all?

She points her finger out at me. "You, Mr. Big Shot...*are feeling*. Maybe for the very first time."

I rub my chest. "Not possible. Go back to your post. Let's keep searching. I did drink water straight from the tap the other day—could that have given me that weird parasite thing?"

She barks out a laugh. It's obvious she pities me. I hate this—her thinking she knows better than I do. I'm the one living in this body, having to endure this torture. It's one thing to acknowledge my enduring crush on Scarlett, but to go beyond that, to contemplate—

I can't go there.

Lucy's about to leave my office. She's whistling a peppy little tune, having completely moved on from my troublesome woes. She's *that* confident she's right about what I have.

"What's it supposed to feel like?" I call out just before she takes her first step out the door.

She looks back and smiles, happy for me. "Like the best and worst thing you've ever endured. Butterflies one second, shittin' bricks the next."

Great.

I'm fucked.

My morning with Lucy has only made matters worse. Acknowledging the elephant in the room has now made it so I no longer know how to act around Scarlett. I feel like I'm a bumbling buffoon.

I see her in the break room just after lunch.

"Hey. Hi. Coffee?"

She already has a mug in her hand. She furrows her brows, smiling. "Yup. Got some right here."

"Cool. Yeah. Love the stuff."

I turn away and cringe. *Love the stuff?* It's like I've never conversed in the English language before.

"Same. Yup." She laughs and looks at me funny. "Word on the street is you're sick."

I force a cough for some reason. Then I clear my throat. "Yeah, it's...a developing condition." I sound like a local newscaster with a breaking story.

This earns me a frown. "You okay? Do you have a fever?" She's about to step forward and press the back of her hand to my forehead, but I freak out and step back. She takes the hint. "Right, well, if you need anything, let me know."

The next day, I'm walking down the hall from the conference room, and Scarlett is walking toward me in the other direction. I break out in a sweat. I blow out air. I stop walking, just plain freeze, and then she notices me, so I narrow my eyes down on an arbitrary spot on the paper I'm holding, acting as if it's really important for me to review it right this moment.

When she gets closer, I look up.

"Scarlett, hey."

She was walking with Bethany, talking about something, probably work-related and important. She nods to let Bethany know she'll catch her in a bit, then she stops and turns to me expectantly.

Right. I was meant to have something to say to her other than "Scarlett, hey."

There's a little smile on her lips she's battling to suppress. She likes this.

"Are you uhh...you going to the wedding next weekend?" I try to make it sound cool, like I'm indifferent about her answer, a high schooler asking about the party after the Friday night football game. *Yeah, whatever, I might stop by. Like if I have nothing better to do.*

"My brother's wedding?" Scarlett asks, sounding like it's the dumbest question she's ever heard.

I blush for the first time in my entire life. I'll have to nab the security camera footage from this hallway and light it on fire in a trash can to destroy all the evidence.

"No. Thought I'd skip it," she adds with playful sarcasm.

I scratch the back of my neck, unable to fumble for a funny or witty or—let's not kid ourselves, at this point I'd even take a semi-articulate—response.

"You're a bridesmaid?" is the question I land on.

"One of about twelve." Her eyes widen with the statement. "There are a lot of us."

"The girls that were with you down in Miami?"

She half-laughs, half-blanches. "Afraid so."

"That's great. Yeah, I'll be there too," I say stiffly.

WRAP IT UP! my brain screams. *This is horrible! You're acting like a robot!*

"With a date?" she asks.

I stutter a response. "N-no. Wait." I step back. "Are *you* bringing a date?"

She shrugs and glances down the hall, cooler than cool. "I mean, I'm not *opposed* to the idea."

"Right. Yeah, whatever. Same." Then I do a jerky step forward, nod, and say, "Anyway, bye."

I storm straight for my office. Lucy perks up when I pass in front of her desk.

"How's it going?" Lucy asks.

"Terribly."

"It'll get better!" she promises, just before I slam my door, rattling it on its hinges.

This has reached emergency status. DEFCON 1. I can't be around Scarlett, not until I feel like I'm on top of things again. I've totally lost myself. Yesterday, I paid for a junior associate's lunch when he realized he forgot his wallet at his desk. Today, I held the elevator for someone. Willingly! A little while ago, a partner from our corporate litigation department called to ask me a question, and I asked how his day was going. If this keeps up, people are going to start liking me.

I can't imagine a worse fate.

Chapter Twenty-Nine

Scarlett

It's the wedding day. The blissful sounds of birds chirping and bells ringing have been totally drowned out by *"Who stole my sticky boob bra? The one I got from Target. I swear to GOD!"* and *"Hurry up at the makeup chair! You were supposed to be starting hair fifteen minutes ago!"*

I'm getting my eye shadow done when Jordy comes around with an open bottle of champagne.

"I thought that was for the mimosas" is the last thing I say before she forces me to down a mouthful of it.

"It's for whatever we want, ladies. Drink up!"

If Jordy had it her way, we would be teetering our way

down the aisle, tipsy and giggly and sloppy *but fun.*

Conrad has six groomsmen, a respectable number, but it's nothing compared to Hannah's roster. Not every one of us will walk down the aisle with a groomsman, but I somehow made the cut. I'm surprised I don't get paired up with Barrett or Wyatt, but I realize later that Hannah finagled it so that all the single people are grouped together on the off chance she can help sparks fly. It's sweet of her, but I've been paired with Hugh, Conrad's good friend from undergrad. We've met a handful of times over the years and I always thought he was really nice, but he's not really my type. He's a nerdy gamer (just like Conrad), which I could totally be into, don't get me wrong. Someone who enjoys fantasy novels? Sure! I like them well enough, but not on Hugh's level. And then there's the anime and board games. Not the generic ones, mind you. He only plays indie board games, created and produced in small batches. When we're taking pictures, he tugs up his pant leg to reveal his *Lord of the Rings* socks.

"Killer," I tell him.

"Right? Like who doesn't want Gandalf on their ankle?"

"Gollum too," I say, my eyebrows shooting up. "I mean, the likeness is eerie."

He chuckles and adjusts his bowtie. It's black, though he wishes Conrad had gone with the R2-D2 pattern Hugh found on a *Star Wars* website. My mom would have had an aneurysm.

"Later, a few of us have these Chewbacca outfits we rented. We're going to run out in them during the reception."

"Oh god." I laugh. "Conrad is going to love that."

"Could everyone look here please?" the photographer asks, putting the kibosh on our conversation.

We smile and pose, and afterward, Hugh sort of lingers near me as if hoping to get a conversation going again. Then Gabriella walks over and notices Hugh's socks and freaks out—"Oh my god! Those are *amazing*!"—and I promptly slink away to give them the chance to get to know each other better. I don't see Hugh again until it's ceremony time.

Hannah's family and my parents have spared no expense for this wedding. We've basically taken over the Langham. The ceremony is outside on the terrace overlooking the Chicago River, a ballsy move considering how cold it can be in early March, but that's nothing money can't fix. Cashmere throws have been draped across the back of every chair, not that they'll be needed thanks to the space heaters end-capping every row. If anything, guests will be sweating.

Later, the reception will take place inside the largest of the Langham's ballrooms. I poked my head in earlier to see how it was coming along. My mother was standing in the center of the room in a cute coordinating sweatsuit with her hair pinned up in rollers, ordering people around, polite but panicky.

Her attention to detail has no doubt paid off. I can't wait to see it.

"Okay, you know what you're doing here?" Hugh asks me, nodding toward the aisle.

We're standing with the rest of the bridal party and groomsmen just inside the hallway off the terrace, awaiting our cue to get this show on the road. Hannah's at the back, taking a few photos alongside her father. It makes me wistful looking at them. I can't imagine what it will be like when I walk with my dad down the aisle. Oh, he's definitely going to cry. *I'm* going to cry. It'll be a mess.

"It's easy. Just like we rehearsed," I assure Hugh. "We just follow the people in front of us."

The aisle is made from a white silk runner that's been hand-embroidered with Hannah and Conrad's signature wedding monogram. A thick white floral arch sits at the end where Conrad stands, handsomely waiting for his bride.

"Not too fast though," Hugh confirms.

"Right. We have to be cool about it. Pace ourselves."

"Okay, you do the leading. I'm a great follower."

I chuckle. "Noted."

There are close to 300 people in attendance—small by my mother's standards—but Conrad and Hannah were insistent that they didn't want it to get too out of hand. The terrace is packed to the gills as the pianist begins to play.

Guests shift in their chairs, turning back to look at us. Thankfully, Hugh and I are toward the end. I get the benefit of watching most of the bridesmaids walk in front of me as I hang back at the edge of the doorway, mostly out of sight. I scan the sea of chairs, searching like I'm on a *Where's Waldo?* assignment.

Hudson's surprisingly easy to spot in the crowd. He's tall, which helps. Also, most of the Elwood Hoyt employees have banded together in the back rows. Lucy sits on the aisle seat wearing a cheery yellow dress that I instantly love. Hudson sits to her right, his head slightly bowed.

Lucy sees me and waves. I smile and give her a little wave back. She turns, murmurs something to Hudson.

He lifts his head and shifts in his chair to look over his shoulder. His brown eyes meet mine. My stomach flips. The easy joy I felt seeing Lucy is inflamed and turned to ash, replaced with heart-racing, nausea-inducing nerves. Seeing him makes it so every other man feels inconsequential, boring, lackluster. Hugh says something and I smile because it feels like I should smile, but I'm not listening. I'm looking at Hudson.

It's a formal wedding and he knows how to dress. I love his black tie, black jacket, the slope of his broad shoulders, the sharp contours of his handsome face. He's still looking back at me but he hasn't smiled, hasn't given me any sign of *anything*.

The last two weeks have been a new kind of strange for us. He hasn't been avoiding me, but our encounters have been stilted, condensed down to small talk, really. He's seemed almost nervous around me, though it's hard to believe Hudson Rhodes has the capacity to be nervous around anyone.

The bridesmaid and groomsman in front of me link arms and start walking down the aisle. Hugh steps up, offering me his bent elbow, and I smile and take my place.

There's an uptick in murmurs as I appear in the doorway. It's not surprising considering how many people I know here.

"*...haven't seen her since she was a baby...*"

"*...looks just like her mother...*"

"*...Barrett's twin...*"

I smile down at Lucy as I pass her by, but I resolve to not look at Hudson, at least not until I'm safely up front, standing in line with the other bridesmaids, holding my smile, calming my nerves. The flower girls and ring bearer trickle down to a chorus of laughter and oohs and ahhs. The cutest little things. And then Hannah steps up with her dad and everyone stands. In the chaos, I look at Hudson, and while everyone's looking at Hannah, he's looking at me.

He looks troubled by something. I keep waiting for a smile or some kind of nod, a secret word or mouthed joke. It doesn't come. His eyebrows stay furrowed. His mouth keeps to a flat line, leaving me with an ominous feeling of dread, but at the very least, I console myself with the news that he didn't bring a date. Bethany and her husband are sitting on the other side of Hudson. Unless you count Lucy, Hudson's here alone.

I turn to watch Hannah take her final steps toward Conrad. Her father lifts her veil, grips her arms, and kisses her cheek with a final thoughtful parting word. Then the ceremony begins. I didn't think I'd get choked up and emotional during it. Conrad is so stoic, the most serious one out of the bunch of us Elwoods, but I watch him turn to Hannah and absolutely crumble. His eyes brim with tears as he smiles down at her. *I love you*, he mouths, and I reach up to swipe a tear from my cheek, overjoyed for Hannah and my brother. Maybe also a little envious, though the feeling is so foreign I don't recognize it for what it is right away. I've never been someone particularly in a rush to be married, or even in a rush to be in a serious relationship. It's why I didn't immediately notice the red flags with Jasper. I thought it was perfectly reasonable that I wasn't interested in moving in with him just yet. The burning desire to be with him all the time, the need to check in, the yearning for that connection—all of that would come later, I thought. Now I realize I have all of those things, all for the grumpy man sitting near the back of the crowd. The man I was warned to stay away from. The one I never saw coming.

I can't look back at him, not again. This overpowering well of emotions building up inside of me feels like it might blow at any minute. It's made worse by the swell of music as

Conrad and Hannah kiss for the first time as husband and wife, the celebratory applause as everyone cheers.

I'm grateful that once we proceed down the aisle after the newlyweds, the guests are invited to a cocktail hour and I have time to compose myself, to refit the airtight lid on my blaring thoughts while I smile and pose for photos, both with the bridal party and with my family.

"You look stunning," Barrett tells me, dropping a light kiss on my head as the photographer snaps away. "Doesn't she, Wyatt?"

My brother shrugs, unbothered by the question. Wyatt has always been the shy, quiet one.

"Any promise with that groomsman you walked down the aisle with?" Nyles asks out of the corner of his mouth, still smiling for the camera.

"None whatsoever."

Nyles pouts. "How boring. I love a wedding meet cute."

The reception begins with a formal dinner. I'm seated at the front of the ballroom with the rest of the wedding party, sandwiched between Gabriella and Hugh, who for the better part of the meal lean in front of or behind me so they can continue their conversation with each other. I offer to switch places with Gabriella more than once. Hugh too, but they don't budge. Either they don't want to make me feel bad or they don't want to seem too interested. It's such a waste of time. The two of them are made for each other. Right now, they're dissecting the plot points and directorial style of a particular *Mandalorian* episode while I pick at my chicken. I can't see Hudson from where I sit. Or rather, I can if I lean heavily to the left and practically drape myself on Gabriella's shoulder. I tell myself it serves me right. I shouldn't be so focused on him. There are speeches to pay attention to, good company to enjoy, *Star Wars* cinematography choices to discuss.

I'm unable to fully be present in any of it. When the final course is winding down, Hannah and her dad take to the dance floor for their father-daughter dance. I couldn't tell you the song choice or how long they're out there. I didn't even realize Conrad and my mom had taken their places. I blink and realize everyone has stood from their tables to join the bride and groom on the dance floor at the DJ's urging.

I'm not drunk. I have no real excuse to feel the way I do. I keep waiting for the effects of the wedding ceremony to wear off, like a drug with a three-hour lifespan. I should be able to shake this, but I can't. The profound newness of my current state doesn't feel quite real.

The song to wake me up out of my trance is "Take a Chance on Me" by ABBA, for two reasons. Firstly, it's an irresistible bop no matter what anybody says, and secondly, it's the first time I've really been able to clearly spot Hudson since the start of the reception. He's standing just to the left of the dance floor talking to Lucy and my mom. His hands are tucked into his pockets. He's bent over slightly toward them so they don't have to raise their voices quite so loud. I watch my mom ask him something, and he smiles and shakes his head, and I love him.

This is not a profound thought. It's not revolutionary or shocking. It's Saturday; I'm at a wedding; no, thank you, I don't want any more wine at the moment; and I love Hudson Rhodes.

I don't get up, don't move from my seat. I'm the only person from the wedding party still at the banquet table at the front of the ballroom, and one of my aunts sees my dopey smile and my little laugh and she gives me a pitying look on her way to the bathroom. She doesn't realize what's going on here. She doesn't know I'm newly in love.

Oh my god.

My brothers don't let me get away with being a wallflower for long. Barrett and Nyles come find me during "Lay All Your Love on Me". Side note: I think Hannah and Conrad might have requested the DJ play ABBA and *only* ABBA for the entirety of this reception. Which, that's amazing, but also bold.

"This song," Nyles says indignantly. "*This song*, Scarlett. Get up. You have to get up and dance. I feel like I'm in college again, studying abroad in Greece, dancing on tables, wishing your brother would email me back."

Barrett laughs. "I don't remember stringing you along."

"Are you kidding? You were the worst. *The. Worst.*"

They have me by the hands now, dragging me behind them as they reminisce about the start of their relationship and how it really went down.

Everyone is losing their minds over this song, bouncing and singing at the top of their lungs, and I find Hudson sitting over at a table by himself. He's hunched over, his hands clasped between his knees. His brow is furrowed and his lips are pursed as he worries about something.

Dancers move around me, and I have to crane my neck to keep my view of him. I just get him in frame again when Nyles takes my hands and starts to spin me around.

I laugh and placate him, shimmying along with everyone else. It's become clear that they are not going to let me off the hook with this song, and it's easier to just give them what they want. But I still take any opportunity I can to look back at Hudson. I arch up on my toes in time to see him shoot to his feet and take two determined steps toward the dance floor then shake his head, turn on a dime, and head out the side door.

"Let's do a conga line!" someone shouts.

There are audible protests.

"Already?"

"It's never too early!"

Conga lines are to weddings as the "Cha Cha Slide" is to middle school dances. You're simply not getting out of it. My shoulders are grabbed. I'm thrust forward and then Barrett and Nyles join in behind me.

"I never can resist a conga," my brother comments.

"There is something so kitsch about them. I love it. Scarlett, you're supposed to be kicking your feet out to the side," Nyles admonishes, seemingly embarrassed by my lack of conga skills.

I'm ignoring them, looking at the door, hoping Hudson's going to reappear any minute.

Surely he didn't leave. They haven't cut the cake. The night's barely half over. We haven't even YMCA'd.

I break off from the conga line and head for the side door before I can fully register what I'm doing or what I'll say once I bump into Hudson. "Are you okay?" seems too serious, too invasive. It conveys the fact that I've been watching him all night, that I know something is wrong, but what else am I left with?

I push through the side door and let it bang shut behind me. The music stays in the ballroom. Out here, it's almost deafeningly quiet. To the right, the hallway dead-ends. To the left, I loop back around and find the entrance to the ballroom. There are more guests out here than I planned for. I have to endure a five-minute catch-up with two of my cousins, then another forced conversation with a few of my mom's friends. "I could just pinch your cheeks! Where are you working now? Oh, look at you go! I'm so impressed!"

Hudson isn't out here. Just to be sure, I walk the length of the hall again, all the way from one end to the other.

A waiter from the wedding sees me and asks if I need help.

"Have you seen a guy out here?" I ask. "Black suit, black tie, pretty tall, brown hair."

He shakes his head. "No. Sorry."

I can only muster a dejected smile. "Right. Thanks anyway."

Left with no other options, I'm forced to turn back toward the ballroom. I don't want to feel like this, shoulders slumped, completely heartbroken over the idea that Hudson might have left the wedding without even talking to me.

Have we stooped so far from where we once were as friends?

I almost turn an about-face and head up to my hotel room. Face-planting onto my bed sounds like a welcome alternative to putting on a bright smile and reentering the fray, but I'd regret not being here for Hannah and Conrad, my parents, everyone.

I make it back to the reception in time to see Hannah belting out Beyoncé lyrics, and I almost succeed in forgetting all about Hudson. Beyoncé's powerful in that way. I can't just mope in a corner, so I dance myself back into happiness. My parents join me, along with Nyles and Barrett. Even Conrad gets out on the dance floor, though Wyatt continues to refuse. "No one dances like this in London" is his excuse. As if fun doesn't exist in that part of the world.

"Oh my god, you *can* dance! Stop being so stubborn and get out here." I take his hands and start to drag him toward the DJ.

He puts up a good fight. "I mean it, Scarlett. I'm horrible."

"So am I!" I insist.

In hindsight, I should have believed him. Poor Wyatt is as bad as he promised he would be, and I can't contain the laugh that bursts out of me once he starts to pair a side-to-side shuffle with a limp-armed shimmy. I throw a hand over my mouth, but it's too late.

"What in the hell are you doing?" Barrett asks, coming up behind Wyatt.

"I'm dancing!" Wyatt says, tossing his arms up before walking off the dance floor entirely. "Screw you guys. I'm going to the bar."

"Get me a Jack and Coke, will you?" Barrett calls.

"Get it yourself!" Wyatt calls back.

Barrett shoots me a wink and then trails after our brother, leaving me on my own on the dance floor. Not for long, though. All the bridesmaids are out here and a Rihanna song is starting up just in time. I'm almost out of breath by the time it's over— we all are. The DJ recognizes that it's time to transition to something slow, and here we go again with ABBA. It's "The Winner Takes It All" and everyone immediately knows the drill. Pair up or scram, losers.

Jordy and Gabriella jokingly start to spin around me, dramatic and slow. Then, before I know it, I'm added to their circle. Those iconic crooning vocals pick up as we clutch hands. We spin fast enough that the room starts to blur, the crowd blends together, and even still, I catch the shift—the approaching black suit.

I gasp and break off from Jordy and Gabriella, a little off balance, my vision still swirling until all at once, Hudson cuts into view. I straighten myself and face him as he takes the last few steps toward me.

Jordy bumps my shoulder as she comes to a stop and curses under her breath. "*Shit.* He's hot."

Gabriella inhales sharply and leans in. "It's him, isn't it?"

I ignore her question and stare at Hudson while my heart beats out of my chest. There's so much on the line—a heart suspended. I love him, and that realization has hit me like a freight train. From this point on, if he only wants friendship, it'll feel like death. We look at each other as I hold my breath.

Then he holds out his hand for me, palm up. "Dance with me."

Like a besotted fool, I can only nod.

It occurs to me that I should warn him that people are going to see us, but he already knows that and he's still here. So I swallow my nerves and let him lead me deeper into the crowd, right to the dead center of the dance floor where the bodies are dense enough that we disappear among them.

He turns and faces me again, and I'm unsure of what to do, where to touch. He's never seemed so tall, so intimidating as he does now. I stare at his chest as he steps forward and takes my hips, and instead of awkwardness, there's recognition and possession, a smooth claiming. He doesn't sound polite when he orders me to put my hands on his shoulders. I do it so gently I can barely feel the smooth material of his black suit jacket, the suit jacket I've been eyeing all night. He looks devastating in it. Devastating, always. The most handsome, kind man. Kind. I smile at the floor thinking of telling him that. He'd snarl at me.

When I work up the courage to look up again, I realize he's studying me. His dark eyes start at my feet and travel up in the span of a slow, intoxicating breath. When our eyes meet, awareness settles over me. I somehow sense everything he's not saying. I'm drowning in the sincerity of his silent compliment.

He tightens his fingers at my hips, gathering the material so it's easier for him to bring me closer. We're listening to ABBA croon away, and it shouldn't be so good, this 1980s song, but it just says it all.

I open my mouth to ask him a million questions. Why have you seemed so sad tonight? Why did you leave a moment ago? Why did you wait so long to find me?

Nothing makes it out though. I feel paralyzed by the realization I had during the wedding. This feeling, choking me up, it's the stuff of fairytales, and I've been completely closed off to it, immune, or so I thought.

Scared, I look away. Then before I can think of the consequences, I lay my cheek against Hudson's chest. He stiffens, and a beat later, he drops his chin to my head. We're totally wrapped around one another. We barely move, swaying side to side, slower than the beat. It's my favorite part of the entire night. My favorite moment...ever.

I close my eyes and embrace it.

Everything will come after this song, the unknown consequences. But for now, we hang suspended in the simplicity of holding each other. All I feel is Hudson's broad chest, his arms wrapped around me confidently. I can't think of who's seeing us, of what they're thinking. What is there to say but the truth?

I love him.

It's a moment I'll never forget. A moment though—that's the painful part, knowing I'm only in his arms for the length of this song.

It's over before I realize. People are starting to shift apart, talk and laugh, and prepare themselves for a new song. No one is holding on to each other like we are, resisting the end. Hudson's the one who steps away first, fissuring my heart in the process.

He looks so pained when he looks down at me. "Scarlett—"

"Ladies and gents, I'd like to direct you to the table on the left over here. Our bride and groom are ready to cut the cake! *Oh*—careful with that icing!"

The crowd surges around me. "Scarlett, come on," Nyles says. "If Hannah's about to shove cake in Conrad's face, I want a front-row view."

Nyles has my hand and he's tugging me, not realizing I'm looking back at Hudson, willing him to ask me to stop.

Hudson just stands there.

His feet rooted to the floor.

Chapter Thirty

Hudson

Everything is happening right now.

Life rushes past me and I can stay where I am, feet glued in place or—

"Scarlett, wait."

She stops and shifts out of her brother-in-law's grasp. Nyles looks back at Scarlett, then sees me. His brows shoot up in understanding and he leaves her there, following the crowd to where Conrad and Hannah are getting ready to cut their cake.

Scarlett and I have been left all alone in the center of the dance floor. It's not my location of choice. I could ask her if she'd like to come talk to me somewhere else, somewhere more private, but then I run the risk of a million things getting in our way.

She doesn't realize what I've already had to go through to get here. For the better part of two weeks, I've tried to reconcile my feelings and build the courage to actually act on them. Tonight is the night, though I couldn't have picked a worse occasion. Scarlett is part of the wedding; she has a role to play, a place to occupy. This is the first time I've had her completely to myself all evening.

A moment ago, I was panicked that the opportunity to talk to her had passed me by. I almost took the coward's way out. I dipped out of the ballroom to get some air, to continue the back-and-forth argument in my head. It wasn't an argument over how I feel about Scarlett; that's set in stone. It's everything else that's the issue.

I came back from outside to find Scarlett's parents talking with Lucy near the ballroom doors. I didn't even pause, didn't think.

"Have you seen Scarlett?" I asked the group.

Katherine frowned and shook her head. "I thought she was on the dance floor a moment ago."

Anders looked over his shoulder, searching for his daughter. "Is it something for work?" he asked. "I could—"

I turned to him, stared him boldly in the eye, and tossed away my future at Elwood Hoyt, not with a gentle remark but with a bold finality. "No. It's not work-related. Sir—Mr. Elwood. I'm in love with your daughter."

Katherine gasped.

Lucy laughed with delight.

Anders just smiled, no shock evident at all.

Then he nodded approvingly. "Okay then."

Okay then!?

I forged ahead. "I understand this is a bit unorthodox and it's nothing that I planned—"

Anders held up his hand. "This is partly my fault."

Katherine gaped at her husband. "What in the world are you talking about?"

"I did this," he said, straightening his bowtie with a smug smile.

"You what?" Suddenly I sounded angry.

"Oh relax. I didn't do anything nefarious. I played Cupid, put you two in each other's path. It was my hope that you would come to care for each other. I love my daughter more than...well more than most everything on earth, and I wasn't going to let her end up with a man like Jasper." He shuddered at the thought.

"Why would you want her to be with me?" I asked, frowning in confusion.

Anders looked at me with an expression made of pity and maybe even a little humor. "I can't think of a better man for her."

Katherine clutched her chest. "I can't believe this. I really cannot believe this." Then to me, "Does Scarlett know!?"

I stiffened. "Not yet. No."

"Well what the hell are you waiting for?" Anders asked me. "Why are you standing around talking to us?"

And so I went to find Scarlett on the dance floor. I wrapped her up in my arms and held her one more time before everything changed for better or worse.

Now, she looks at me expectantly, worry eclipsing every other feeling.

"I need to speak with you," I tell her.

"Now?"

"Yes. Now. Yesterday. Last week. Last month. But not tomorrow. It's now or never."

She swallows and nods. "Okay."

"If I don't..." I shake my head. "I don't know. I'll make a scene, cry by the wedding cake or something."

"Hudson. *You'll cry?*"

"I—I don't know what this is supposed to feel like, but it's kind of horrible." I sound desperate. "I could throw up."

Concern mars her delicate features. She rushes toward me. "Did you eat something weird?"

"No! *I'm in love!* I thought that was perfectly obvious."

She gasps.

Steps back.

Shakes her head. "That's...no. That was not clear in any way." Her brows tug together in consternation. "Who are you in—"

I bark out a laugh. She's kidding. She has to be kidding. I thrust my hand out toward her. "You! Scarlett. *You*, of course."

She smiles, her eyes already welling with tears. "Oh." A short laugh. "I wasn't sure. Are you sure?"

"Absolutely certain of it. I just told your parents."

"YOU WHAT?!"

The question bursts out of her, drawing a few curious stares from nearby wedding guests.

"I didn't plan it like that. It just happened. I felt it was important that your father know."

"But what about your promotion?" She covers her mouth in horror. "Oh no, Hudson." She shakes her head adamantly. "No. I won't let you suffer because of this. Your work is all you care about." She's already taking my hand like she's going to tug me over to her father and fix things this very second. "I'll explain everything to him, take full blame. We're going to get you that promotion if it's the—"

I resist her tugging and instead, loop my hand around hers, keeping us where we are. I wait until she looks back at me, to be sure she's listening. "I don't care about it."

"You what?"

"It's absurd." I laugh. It's pure joy like I've never felt. Oh my god, I've gone horribly soft, and worse, I don't even care. "The promotion doesn't matter, Scarlett. It's you I want, with profound, unwavering certainty. Please say you want me too, say this isn't one-sided. I really will cry. It feels like the worst agony. Lucy said it's supposed to get better, but—"

"You've discussed this with Lucy."

"Yes. I thought I had the flu at first."

Scarlett considers this. "Is that why you were sick the other day?"

"Yes." I shrug. "Lovesick, I guess."

"Love..." She mulls the word over like it's still shocking to hear.

"Love," I confirm.

I watch her hard facade splinter. Those steely eyebrows, that determined set of her jaw—*gone*, in an instant. Her chin wobbles, and she releases a weak little "Oh."

And though it's insane and hokey, I get the sudden realization that I would—if I had the ring in my pocket already—drop down to my knee on this dance floor and ask her to marry me on the spot. Later, when I do propose—because I know I will—I'll tell her that. I'll tell her I wanted to do it right here and now.

"I love you too, actually," Scarlett tells me, her voice full of bewildered surprise.

"Is it so shocking?"

She nods. Then, weirdly, reverses course and shakes her head instead. "No, actually. Not at all."

"I'm not exactly lovable."

"You *are* though," she says, coming toward me until we're chest to chest. She tips her head back and stares up at me. "You're *so* lovable. I couldn't resist you even if I tried."

Then her gaze slips down to my lips and I bend down and kiss her, and though we don't know it, won't hear the story until tomorrow morning at breakfast, Katherine, Anders, and Lucy are standing just to the side of the dance floor with a perfect view of the cake and a perfect view of us and when I kiss Scarlett, the three of them start to clap. Anders even whistles.

It seems the Elwoods are about to add one more to their ever-growing family.

Epilogue

Scarlett

"Think your parents mind?"

"That you're walking me back to my hotel room?"

He looks at me sidelong, a glance so chock-full of charm I'm surprised my knees don't give out. It's a look that says, *I'm not simply walking you back to your hotel room.*

I hum and pull out my key from my clutch then hold it to the door until the light turns green. Once I'm inside, Hudson follows me into the room and shuts the door quietly behind us.

My heels are the first things to go. I toe them off with a long sigh. *Oh my god.* Sweet relief. I toss them clear across the room and look over to see Hudson watching me. He doesn't look distressed now, not in the least. All the worry he's been carrying is gone now.

We spent the last hour out on the dance floor together. For a corporate lawyer, Hudson has major moves. Lucy was out there with us, my parents too. I watched Hudson spin and dip Lucy while she laughed. My dad and I danced together near the end of the reception.

"You're happy?" he asked simply.

"Beyond" is the one word I was able to form. Anything else would conjure a flood of tears.

"Good. I like you two together. It fits. I thought it would."

I reared back. "*You* thought it would!?"

He smiled and angled me out so he could twirl me back toward him. "You'll have to ask Hudson about it."

I plan to, some other time. Now, I walk toward him and turn to present my back. I pull my hair forward in front of my shoulder so he can access my zipper. He knows what to do, tugging it down and kissing my bare shoulder before pushing the material apart and helping me step out of it.

"Will you move in with me?"

I still then turn to look at him over my shoulder.

"Into your place?"

He nods. "I have a house close to Elwood Hoyt. Plenty of space. Close enough for you to walk to the office, though I could easily drive us."

"Sudden, no?"

He shrugs. "Sudden? I don't know. When have you felt like this before?"

I consider it then smile. "Never."

He absorbs that with a solemn nod. "Then we're on the same page. I don't want to keep doing this. I'm all in, Scarlett. I've just admitted to your family that I'm in love with you. I'd like you to move in with me. I'd like to spend as much time with you as I can, and I know neither of us will cut down our time at the office, not really, so I've been thinking through that problem already."

I smile and tip toward him, propping my arms up on his shoulders. His hands go easily to my hips, toying with my panties.

"Have you?"

"Yes," he says, bending to kiss me. "You'll give me every night and all your weekends. If we need to work, we'll go in together. I'll add a second desk in my office if I have to."

I laugh and kiss him again. "Everyone will talk."

"Fuck everyone."

He steals a heavier kiss, tracing his tongue over mine. I feel my desire burn deep down inside me.

"And on these nights you have me..." I start to work his dress shirt up and out of his suit pants. I unbutton it from the bottom, taking in his toned stomach, the hair on his chest, his masculine build. "What will we do?"

He smiles. Right now, I wish I had a camera. I want to snap a picture of his face like this, so open and at ease, happy and dimpled.

"We'll watch TV, make dinner, drink wine, cuddle with Moira," he promises, helping me take his shirt off.

Then before I can get his pants unbuttoned, he's walking us over to the bed. He hoists me up by my hips and positions me in the center of it.

"You'll rub my feet..."

I snort. "As if!"

He laughs and comes up and over me.

"I'll rub *your* feet," he amends. "I'll do whatever you want." His brow furrows only slightly, like he's troubled by a new thought. "You haven't said yes."

Oh.

"Let's move my stuff tomorrow." I say it like it's that simple because it feels that simple. Wild how easy it can be when it's right.

My answer makes him happy. He kisses me again, trailing his lips down my neck.

"I'll help you pack," he promises.

"I'll treat you to dinner. You like pizza?"

"Of course. Don't you remember feeding me a few months ago? The first night you stayed late? You brought me pizza at my desk and we shared dinner."

He's worked his way down my body and now he's kissing near my navel. I slide my fingers through his hair, touching him lovingly. "I thought it was nice that you let me use your desk."

He looks up, his chin pressed to my stomach. His eyes darken. "I wanted you then, but I didn't allow myself to even think it."

My finger glides over his cheekbone, back and forth reassuringly. He returns his attention to my body, peeling down my panties, letting them slip to the floor. I scoot back, trying to reposition myself, but he doesn't allow it.

He tsks and keeps me right on the edge, tracing his finger between my legs so I arch up in response. I can't help it. He knows just how to touch me, toy with me, until I'm writhing while he watches, bewitched by the sight of me.

When Hudson settles over me, his eyes locking with mine, his hips weighing me down, there's not a feeling like it. It's more than joy; it's serenity.

His eyes catch mine. He smiles.

Most importantly, whatever you do, avoid Hudson Rhodes at all costs.

That was the warning I was issued, and I wonder what would have happened if I'd listened and steered clear of him. I could have asked my dad to place me on a different service, and maybe Hudson and I would have never crossed paths after that first day. He wouldn't be here now, bending down to seal his lips to mine.

It's unthinkable to imagine never having found Hudson, the only man to value every side of me, to understand my drive as an attorney, to push me to be better.

I pull his face toward me and kiss him back. I let him pin me to the bed, slide into me, thrust. I arch my head back and cry out, and Hudson looks down at me in awe.

"I love you."

The conviction in his voice makes it hard to bear.

"I love you too, Hudson."

In a thousand ways.

I'm the first to admit that falling for Hudson wasn't easy, but I'm a girl up for any challenge. Now I'm grateful for the warning label he's carried for so long. He's too perfect. If people had access to his sweet side, someone would have snatched him up a long time ago. If the world knew Hudson was a big teddy bear beneath the scruffy jaw and angry eyebrows? All hell would break loose.

This is perfect, the universe ensuring balance.

We're drifting off to sleep later when I think of something and smile.

"Hudson?"

He hums to let me know he's listening.

"Your mom's going to be *so* happy."

Epilogue to the Epilogue
Scarlett

Just as Kendra predicted, Makayla and Ramona leave Elwood Hoyt at the end of spring, and the entire office breathes a sigh of relief. The first day without them, I treat myself to a little celebratory cookie during lunch. Without Kendra and her minions, the tight-knit group of first-years disbands fairly quickly.

Two weeks ago, I got a small package in the mail at work. I tore into it and shook the contents out onto my desk to reveal an oversized puka shell statement necklace decorated with gemstones (*yikes*) alongside a postcard that at first looked to be handwritten, but upon closer inspection came hot off the Vistaprint press.

Heyyyy! I'm loving Bali. Sent you a little something. When you get a chance, snap a photo of you wearing this necklace and post it to your socials alongside the hashtag—

Oh good lord. I threw the postcard away before I could finish reading it, but I saved the necklace for Annabelle. She'll love it.

Today is July 28th, a relatively unimportant Friday. It's going the way most summer Fridays have gone. Rather than staying in the office until 7:00 or 8:00 p.m., Hudson and I clock out at 6:00, our new normal.

He swings by my office to collect me, stopping in the doorway, watching me as I put the finishing touches on my last email of the day.

"It's 5:59," he taunts.

"I'm almost done! Don't distract me."

He doesn't say another word, but it doesn't matter. He's a walking distraction. I look over the top of my computer to see him fighting back a smile.

"One more second."

"I could go get the car…"

"*No!*"

I like when we leave together. Occasionally, when we're in the elevator alone, we can behave badly. We've had some full-on make-out sessions on our way to the ground floor. If there are cameras…I shudder to think of what the security guards have seen.

"There!"

I hit send and close my laptop with a triumphant slap. My work bag and phone, my jacket and notebook—everything gets snatched up as quickly as possible as I make my way to the door. I stop just a hair's breadth too close to Hudson, tip my head back, and meet his gaze. If we were at home, I'd kiss him. As it is, in the office, we have to abide by our rules (namely: no PDA). His attention slips down to my lips, and I can tell from the wicked gleam in his eyes that he's contemplating breaking our rules.

I press my hand to his chest, rise up onto my toes, and very nearly kiss him before I smile like a minx and push him out the door.

"Come on, come on. We're going to be late."

We're going to my parents' house for dinner, but this is no casual meal. This is not our standard Friday night.

Hudson is getting his promotion. Tonight, he will officially become a senior partner at Elwood Hoyt.

I only know because my dad let it slip the other day. "The board is finalizing the contract, don't get your hopes up" was the excuse he gave me at the time, but I got my hopes up *immediately.*

It's been incredibly difficult to keep the secret. I haven't been able to stop thinking about it, hounding my father, even pestering my mom for details. Her response: "Scarlett, how would I know if Hudson is getting a promotion? Your dad doesn't tell me any of that stuff. Now stop calling me at work."

I've had to suffer right along with Hudson, only *he* didn't know he was supposed to be an impatient mess like me. He's been living life as usual.

When my dad suggested we all come over for dinner on Friday and casually mentioned he'd invited Hudson's family and Lucy to join us, I knew it was finally happening. Last night, I was thinking about *the* moment—Hudson's dream coming true, fireworks, cannons, confetti—and I was feeling wistful and proud. I was supposed to be concentrating on the *Dateline* episode we were watching. Hudson made a comment about the plot, "I can't believe that's actually his son," and I replied in a lifeless tone, "That's crazy."

Then he reached for the remote and paused the show. "That's *not* his son. That's the chief of police. I knew you weren't paying attention." He furrowed his brows. "What's wrong?"

"Nothing." I pointed to the TV. "Rewind it a bit. I zoned out."

"No, you've been weird all day."

I laughed as my cheeks reddened. Then, alarmed at how easily I was starting to crack under pressure, I sat up and tried to get the remote from him. He held it aloft over his head. "It's nothing. *Hudson.* Give me the remote."

He didn't give it to me despite my stern tone and I could tell he wasn't going to drop the subject, so I did what I had to do. I seduced him. Thankfully I brought that little serving bowl of condoms with me when I moved in with him. It's come in handy a few times.

Now, we slow to a stop outside my parents' house. Cars line the street. I should have thought to have everyone park one block over.

"Is that my mom's car?" Hudson asks, leaning over to try to make out the vehicle parked in front of Barrett's.

"No," I say hurriedly. "That's my dad's loaner. He got a flat on the way to work."

I'm smart enough to think on my feet, but my acting skills are subpar at best. Practicing law is my only talent.

Hudson looks over at me, more suspicious than ever. "That's definitely my mom's car."

I frown and shake my head then throw in a long hum for good measure. "I really don't think so..."

"Scarlett...why is my mom here?"

I can't withstand his third-degree. I'm about to just turn and bail and make him chase after me up the path, but sensing my plan, he reaches for my arm and stills me. My smile is impossible to suppress.

"What is this?" he asks with a smile of his own.

I turn to him with pleading, puppy dog eyes. "Let's just go inside."

I don't want to ruin the surprise now, not when we're so close to the finish line.

He shakes his head, resolute as ever. *Stubborn man!* "Not until you tell me what I'm about to walk in on."

"Let's just go, okay? We're a few minutes late, and I'm sure everyone is hungry."

He relents and turns off the car. I grab the wine carrier filled with the bottles we picked up on the way over, but I shouldn't have bothered. Hudson loops around to my side and takes the wine from me before reaching down for my hand. "Promise me we aren't walking into something horrible."

I squeeze his hand. "I promise."

When we're halfway up the path, I catch movement in the living room window. Lucy.

Dammit.

Hudson sees her too. She and my mom are peeking out

from behind the drapes, and lo and behold, Renee is right there beside them. When they see us see them, they all duck in unison. The Three Stooges have nothing on them.

"*Scarlett...*" Hudson says with a playfully reproachful tone.

"I just thought we could have a fun family dinner!" I say, chock-full of innocence.

"But why the secrecy?"

We reach the stoop and the doorknob creaks and I realize we're seconds away from being ambushed, but it's too late to do anything. The door whips open to a cacophony of noise as Jack and Annabelle come barreling down the front hall, racing to get to us.

"Slow down!" Corinne chides half-heartedly.

"You're here!" my mother exclaims.

"Took you two long enough," Lucy teases.

Just before we're pulled into the chaos, I turn and lock eyes with Hudson and try to answer his questions with just a look. It's the best superpower couples have, this ability to silently say, *You can trust me. Tonight is going to be amazing. I promise.*

He winks in confirmation. *Message received.* Then Annabelle launches herself at me and Jack throws himself at Hudson.

"Luff hewr! Luff hewr! Luff hewr!" Jack shouts his favorite catchphrase. He says it every time he sees Hudson and me.

"Jack! He doesn't luff hewr, he *loves her*!" Annabelle corrects. She looks to Hudson for confirmation. "Right?"

Hudson smiles at me. "Right."

"How much?" Annabelle wants to know as she starts to tug me into the foyer. To her, it's quantifiable. "More than I love makeup?"

Hudson laughs. "Way more."

Annabelle's eyes go wide as saucers. "More than you love ice cream?"

"A lot more," he tells her.

Understanding the challenge, she goes big on the next round. "More than *all the stars and planets and the universe COMBINED*?!"

"*More*," he insists confidently.

This final answer blows her mind. She can't comprehend how it's even possible. "*Wow. That's amazing! Uncle Hudson, you have to marry her then!*"

Hudson catches my gaze as he leans down and lowers his voice. He's talking to her, but I still hear his reply.

"Don't worry..." He smiles. "I plan to."

Witty banter and slow-burn romance collide in the bestselling enemies-to-lovers romance.

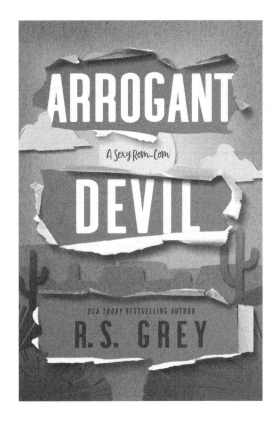

Sure, it could be the Texas heat messing with my head, but there's no way I'll survive the summer without silencing him with a kiss…

The "unputdownable" friends-to-lovers rom-com that'll have you kicking up your feet.

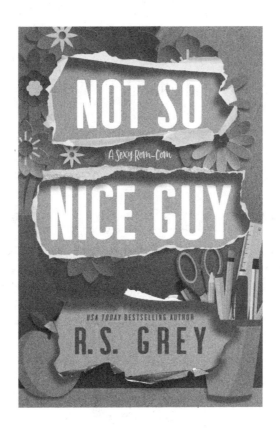

I want to assume he's playing a prank on me, just pushing my buttons like always—but when he lifts me onto the desk in my classroom and slides his hands up my skirt, he doesn't leave a lot of room for confusion…

Don't miss the exciting new books Entangled has to offer.

Follow us!

 @EntangledPublishing

 @Entangled_Publishing

 @EntangledPub

♥ Join the Entangled Insiders for early ♥ access to ARCs, exclusive content, and insider news! Scan the QR code to become part of the ultimate reader community.

an imprint of Entangled Publishing LLC